Music and Musicians

A Treasury of American Song by Olin Downes
and Elie Siegmeister

A Short History of Music by Alfred Einstein

Jean Sibelius by Karl Ekman

The Book of Modern Composers edited by David Ewen

Music for the Man Who Enjoys "Hamlet" by B. H. Haggin
Music on Records

Charles T. Griffes by Edward M. Maisel

Bohuslav Martinu by Milos Safranek

Dmitri Shostakovich by Victor Ilyich Seroff

Manuel de Falla and Spanish Music by J. B. Trend

Tchaikovsky by Herbert Weinstock

These are Borzoi Books, published in New York
by Alfred A. Knopf

Music and Musicians

A Treasury of American Song by Olin Downes
and Elie Siegmeister

A Short History of Music by Alfred Einstein

Jean Sibelius by Karl Ekman

The Book of Modern Composers edited by David Ewen

Music for the Man Who Enjoys 'Hamlet'
Music on Records by B. H. Haggin

Charles T. Griffes by Edward M. Maisel

Bohuslav Martinů by Miloš Šafránek

Dmitri Shostakovich by Victor Ilyich Seroff

Manuel de Falla and Spanish Music by J. B. Trend

Tchaikovsky by Herbert Weinstock

These are Borzoi Books, *published in New York*
by Alfred A. Knopf

The Musical Scene

THE
MUSICAL
SCENE

VIRGIL THOMSON

1945

ALFRED A KNOPF : *NEW YORK*

Manufactured in the United States of America
Published simultaneously in Canada by The Ryerson Press

FIRST EDITION

Contents

Contents

IV. OPERA

Contents

VII.   PROCESSED MUSIC

VIII.   GENERAL IDEAS

Introduction

THE FOLLOWING *selected essays and reviews, with one exception, appeared in the* New York Herald Tribune *between October 9, 1940 and July 23, 1944. They are not offered here as a complete picture of New York's musical life during that time but rather as a panoramic (here and there even stereoscopic) view of musical America as that has been visible to an American musician resident in New York. They have been arranged by subjects because they cover too short a period to give chronological order any specific value. They have been chosen in some cases because of what I imagine to be a general interest in the subjects covered, in others because I have wished to give a further circulation to ideas that I hope may be of use to other persons, whether professionals or laymen, whose relation to musical art is not wholly casual.*

I hope, further, that in spite of all the diversity of subjects and all the variation that exists in the thoroughness with which these have been treated, a clear attitude has been expressed toward the art and a clear view taken of its place in culture. That view is the result of much reflection on my part and of long practice as a writer of music. If it fails to appear at the end as either consistent or defensible, the book will have failed of its purpose. Certainly I do not feel adequate to summing it up here in a paragraph. But I hope it will communicate itself to the reader as a straightforward and eminently sensible attitude.

This does not mean that I hold my opinions to be all true. I do not. Nor do I consider them to be permanent. I am both submissive to facts and amenable to argument. And I consider my personal biases to be facts, not opinions. I will not even hold, therefore, that these do not carry some weight in the balance of my judgment. But if my opinions are not wholly unbiased, neither are they irresponsible. They are the opinions of a man from Missouri who is also a workman. For all the faults of judgment that may be found in them, I sincerely hope that they will not be considered as frivolously arrived at or too unfairly stated, my aim in this regard having been, as you may well suppose, to inform the reader rather than to protect anybody's career or to help perpetuate any given state of affairs.

Except for a reasonable correction of typographical accidents and grammatical slips, most of the pieces are printed as they originally appeared, though occasionally a more precise word or phrase has been substituted for a hastily chosen one.

I wish to express my thanks to Minna Lederman, editor of Modern Music, for her kind permission to include the article entitled "Chaplin Scores."

V. T.

Denville, New Jersey, 1945

Taste in Music

A TASTE *for* music, a taste for anything, is an ability to consume it with pleasure. Taste *in* music is preferential consumption, a greater liking for certain kinds of it than for others. A broad taste in music involves the ability to consume with pleasure many kinds of it.

Vast numbers of persons, many of them highly intelligent, derive no pleasure at all from organized sound. An even larger number can take it or leave it alone. They find it agreeable for the most part, stimulating to the sentiments and occasionally interesting to the mind. But music is not for them a passional experience, a transport, an auditory universe. Everybody, however, has some kind of taste *in* music, even persons with little or no taste *for* it. No subject, save perhaps the theory of money, is disputed about so constantly in contemporary life as the divers styles of musical expression, both popular and erudite, their nature and likability.

There are often striking contradictions between what musical people admire and what they like. Admiration, being a judgment, is submissive to reason. But liking is an inspiration, a datum exigent, unreasonable, and impossible by any act of the will to alter. It will frequently alter itself, however, without warning. And loyalty to things we once loved dearly brings tension into everybody's taste. Persons whose musical experience is limited may, indeed, be more loyal to old likings than persons who deal with music all the time. The latter tend to reject and to accept with vehemence; they are choosy. And their choosiness is quite independent of their judgment; it is personal and profoundly capricious. They can switch from Beethoven to boogie-woogie, from Bach to barbershop, with a facility that is possible only to those who take all music for their clothes closet. For practical living, man needs to be free in his thought and responsible in his actions. But in dealing with art, responsibility of thought, which makes for slowness of judgment, and freedom of action, which makes for flexibility of taste, constitute the mechanics of vigor.

The development of taste is not a major objective in musical education. What the young need is understanding, that whole paraphernalia of analysis and synthesis whereby a piece is broken up into its component details, mastered, restored to integrity, and possessed. Musical understanding depends not so much on the number of works one has learned in this fashion, provided examples from several schools have been included, as on the completeness with which the procedure has been carried out. Any student can be convinced by study that Mozart is a more accomplished workman than Grieg or Rachmaninoff. If he still likes Grieg and Rachmaninoff better, that is his privilege. Maturity is certain to alter, whatever they may be, his youthful predilections.

Persons unprepared by training to roam the world of music in freedom but who enjoy music and wish to increase that enjoyment are constantly searching for a key, a passport that will hasten their progress. There is none, really, except study. And how far it is profitable to spend time cultivating talent where there is no vocation every man must decide for himself. But if there is any door-opener to taste it is knowledge. One cannot know whether one likes, can use, a work unless one has some method beyond mere instinct for tasting it. The only known ways to taste a piece of music are to read it in score or to follow it in performance. And it is quite impossible to follow unfamiliar kinds of music without an analytical method, a set of aids to memory that enables one to discern the pattern of what is taking place.

But an ability to hear is not the whole of musical reception. A vote seems to be required, a yes or no as to whether one desires, for the present, further acquaintance. Now, the enjoyment of old musical acquaintance is such a pleasant thing for all and so quite sufficiently absorbing for the unskilled that nearly everybody leans toward a timid conservatism with regard to unfamiliar music. The too old, the too new, the in-any-way strange we resist simply because we do not know how to take them on. The lay public will try anything; but it will be disappointed, on first hearing, in anything it has no method for remembering. We like the idea of being musically progressive, because progress is one of our national ideals; but we do not always know how to conduct a progress.

Well, the way of that is long. It is nothing less, if one wishes to take part in America's musical growing-up, than learning to hear music correctly and learning to know one's mind. Persons who cannot follow music at all do well to admit the fact and let music alone. Persons who really hear it, whom *it* will not let alone, usually improve themselves by one means and another in their ability to hear patterns in sound; and with more and more music thus rendered available to them, they can choose at any moment their personal allegiances with a modicum of liberty. The tolerant but untrained, however, will always be a bit uncertain in their tastes. They will never know, for instance, whether they are entitled to vote publicly or not. They will consequently assume the privilege more proudly, more dogmatically, and more irresponsibly than musicians themselves are likely to do. And they will rarely know the difference between their tastes and their opinions.

It is the ignorantly formed and categorically expressed opinions of the amateur, in fact, that make the music world companionable. Professional musicians express, for the most part, responsible opinions; and these show a surprising tendency to approach, within twenty-five years, unanimity. There is not much difference of opinion any more, for instance, about either the nature or the value of Debussy's music, or of Puccini's, or of what Stravinsky wrote before 1914. But musicians' personal likings are eclectic; they imply no agreement of any kind. It is laymen who like to like together. Musicians' opinions influence nothing; they simply recognize, with a certain delay but correctly, the history of music. Lay opinion influences everything — even, at times, creation. And at all times it is the pronouncements of persons who know something about music but not much, and a bit more about what they like but still not too much, that end by creating those modes or fashions in consumption that make up the history of taste.

There is no doubt that lay opinion is in large part organized and directed by knowledgeable persons — by critics, college instructors, conductors, publishers' employees, and leaders of fashion. It is nevertheless not wholly under their control. The leaders of taste can no more create deliberately a mode in music than advertising campaigns can make popular a product that the public doesn't want. They can only manipulate a trend. And trends follow folk patterns. Nobody connected with a trend in music — whether composer, executant, manager, critic, consumer, or even resister — is a free agent with regard to it. That is why unsuccessful or unfashionable music, music that seems to ignore what the rest of the world is listening to, is sometimes the best music, the freest, the most original — though there is no rule about that either.

And so, thus caught up on the wheel of fatality, how can anybody really know anything about music, beyond its immediate practice or perception, least of all what he likes? Learning is a precious thing and knowing one's mind is even more so. But let none of us who think we belong to music fancy too highly our opinions about it, since in twenty-five years most of these will have either gone down the drain or become every man's private conviction. And please let none imagine, either, that his personal tastes are unique, indissoluble, and free. Those who think themselves most individual in their likings are most easily trapped by the appeal of chic, since chic is no more than the ability to accept trends in fashion with grace, to vary them ever so slightly, to follow a movement under the sincere illusion that one is being oneself. And those who imagine themselves most independent as judges make up the most predictable public in the world, that known to managements as the university trade, since intellectuals will always pay for the privilege of exercising their intellectual powers. Rarities of any kind, ancient or modern, are merely stones to whet their minds against. You can always sell to the world of learning acquaintance with that which it does not know.

In the long run, such freedom as anybody has is the reward of labor, much study, and inveterate wariness. And the pleasures of taste, at best, are transitory, since nobody, professional or layman, can be sure that what he finds beautiful this year may not be just another piece of music to him next. The best any of us can do about any piece, short of memorizing its actual sounds and storing it away intact against lean musical moments, is to consult his appetite about its immediate consumption, his appetite and his digestive experience. And after consumption to argue about the thing interminably with all his friends. *De gustibus disputandum est.*

The Musical Scene

COVERING
THE ORCHESTRAS

Age Without Honor

PHILHARMONIC–SYMPHONY ORCHESTRA, *John Barbirolli*, conductor.

Overture to Egmont	Beethoven
"Enigma" Variations	Elgar
Symphony No. 2, in D major	Sibelius

The Philharmonic-Symphony Society of New York opened its ninety-ninth season last evening in Carnegie Hall. There was little that could be called festive about the occasion. The menu was routine, the playing ditto.

Beethoven's Overture to *Egmont* is a classic hors d'œuvre. Nobody's digestion was ever spoiled by it and no late comer has ever lost much by missing it. It was preceded, as is the custom nowadays, by our national anthem, gulped down standing, like a cocktail. I seem to remember that in 1917 and 1918 a sonorous arrangement of *The Star Spangled Banner* by Walter Damrosch was current at these concerts. After so long a time I couldn't be sure whether that was the orchestration used last night. I rather think not. Last night's version seemed to have more weight than brilliance. It had the somber and spiritless sonority of the German military bands one hears in France these days. That somberness is due, I think, to an attempt to express authority through mere weighty blowing and sawing in the middle and lower ranges of the various orchestral instruments, rather than by the more classic method of placing every instrument in its most brilliant and grateful register in order to achieve the maximum of carrying-power and of richness. I may be wrong about the reasons for it, but I think I am right about the general effect, unless my seat was in an acoustical dead spot of the hall, which I do not think it was. The anthem, to me, sounded logy and coarse; it lacked the buoyancy and the sweep that are its finest musical qualities.

Elgar's "Enigma" Variations are an academic effort not at all lacking in musical charm. I call them academic because I think the composer's interest in the musical devices he was employing was greater than his effort toward a direct and forceful expression of anything in particular. Like most English composers, Elgar orchestrates accurately and competently. Now, when a man can do anything accurately and competently he is always on the lookout for occasions to do that thing. In the Continental tradition of music-writing orchestration is always incidental to expression, to construction, to rhetoric. Many of the greatest composers — Chopin and Schumann, for instance — never bothered to become skillful at it in any major way. Others, like Beethoven and Brahms, always kept its fanciness down to the strict minimum of what expression needs. I've an idea the Elgar Variations are mostly a pretext for orchestration, a pretty pretext and a graceful one, not without charm and a modicum of sincerity, but a pretext for fancywork all the same, for that massively frivolous patchwork in pastel shades of which one sees such quantities in any intellectual British suburban dwelling.

Twenty years' residence on the European continent has largely spared me Sibelius. Last night's Second Symphony was my first in quite some years. I found it vulgar, self-indulgent, and provincial beyond all description. I realize that there are sincere Sibelius-lovers in the world, though I must say I've never met one among educated professional musicians. I realize also that this work has a kind of popular power unusual in symphonic literature. Even Wagner scarcely goes over so big on the radio. That populace-pleasing power is not unlike the power of a Hollywood class-A picture. Sibelius is in no sense a naïf; he is merely provincial. Let me leave it at that for the present. Perhaps, if I have to hear much more of him, I'll sit down one day with the scores and really find out what is in them. Last night's experience of one was not much of a temptation, however, to read or sit through many more.

The concert as a whole, in fact, both as to program and as to playing, was anything but a memorable experience. The music itself was soggy, the playing dull and brutal. As a friend remarked who had never been to one of these concerts before, "I understand now why the Philharmonic is not a part of New York's intellectual life."

October 11, 1940

Sonorous Splendors

BOSTON SYMPHONY ORCHESTRA, *Serge Koussevitzky*, conductor.

A London Symphony   Vaughan Williams
Symphony No. 5, in C minor   Beethoven

Boston, October 11. — And so, in cerulean sunshine and through indescribable splendors of autumnal leafage, to Boston — the Hub of the Universe, the Home of the Bean and the Cod. The home, as well, of the Boston Symphony Orchestra, the finest by all-around criteria of our resident instrumental foundations.

The sixtieth season of its concerts opened this afternoon with Vaughan Williams's *London Symphony*. I remember hearing the work nearly twenty years ago in that same Symphony Hall, Pierre Monteux conducting. It is the same piece it was then, too, in spite of some cuts operated by the composer. The first two movements are long, episodic, disjointed. The third is short, delicate, neatly sequential, compact, efficacious, charming. The finale is rich and varied. Its musical material is of high quality, its instrumental organization ample and solid. Also it is not without expressive power. Perhaps one is accustomed to the lengthiness and the slow reflective atmosphere of the symphony by the time one gets to this movement. The improvement in melodic material that manifests itself as the work progresses helps, too. In any case, the last two of the symphony's four movements are anything but dull, which the first two are, and more than a little.

Making a program out of only that and Beethoven, out of one live Englishman and one dead German, classic and great though he be, is an obvious reference to current events and sympathies. The reference might have turned out in its effect to be not nearly so gracious as in its intention had those last two movements of the *London Symphony* not been in themselves so impressive, the finale so moving and deeply somber. It was written in 1913, I believe. It might have been written last month, so actual is its expressive content.

The Vaughan Williams symphony served also as a vehicle for a display of orchestral virtuosity on the part of Dr. Koussevitzky and his men such as few orchestras are capable of offering their subscribers. Not that the piece itself is of any great difficulty; it is only reasonably hard to play, I imagine. But the Boston organization is in such fine fettle after its Berkshire season that every passage, any passage, no matter what, serves as a pretext for those constant miracles of precision and of exact equilibrium that a first-class modern orchestra is capable of.

Musically considered, these refinements are more of a delight in themselves than a help of any kind to the work played. They rather tend, especially in the fine molding and rounding off of phrases, to interrupt the music's continuity, to give it an exaggerated emphasis all over that obliterates any real emphasis or meaning that the score may imply. Only the toughest of the classics and the most glittery of the moderns can satisfactorily resist that kind of polish in execution.

The Beethoven Fifth Symphony resists it quite satisfactorily indeed. Dr. Koussevitzky, be it said to his credit, doesn't try to get away with too much careful modeling, either. Rather he puts his effort into a rhythmic exactitude that adds to Beethoven's dynamism a kind of monumental weight that is appropriate and good. When he tries to achieve more of that weight by forcing the strings beyond their optimum sonority, the result is not so good. The sound that comes out is less loud and less weighty than that which would have come out if the point of maximum resonance had not been surpassed.

All instrumentalists know this; and conductors, of course, know it too when they are calm enough to remember it. But at the back of every conductor's mind is a desire to make his orchestra produce a louder noise than anyone else's orchestra can produce, a really majestic noise, a Niagara Falls of sound. At some time in the course of nearly every concert this desire overpowers him. You can tell when it is coming on by the way he goes into a brief convulsion at that point. The convulsion is useful to the conductor, because it prevents his hearing what the orchestra really sounds like while his fit is on. But if you watch carefully from the house you will usually find that the sound provoked out of a group of exacerbated musicians by any gesture of the convulsive type is less accurate in pitch and less sonorous in decibels than a more objectively conducted fortissimo.

It may seem graceless on my part to mention here a fault almost no conductor is free of and to imply by so doing that there is something particularly regrettable about Dr. Koussevitzky's sharing it. I do mean to imply exactly that, however, because somewhere, some time, some conductor must get around to doing some serious work on the orchestral fortissimo comparable to the work that has already produced from our orchestras such delights of delicacy. And I think it not unfair to suggest that perhaps our finest instrumental ensembles might be just the groups to profit most by such an effort, that maybe it is even their duty to do something about correcting the inefficiency that comes from being overstrenuous.

October 12, 1940

Velvet Paws

PHILADELPHIA ORCHESTRA, *Eugene Ormandy*, conductor; with the assistance of the WOMEN'S GLEE CLUB of the University of Pennsylvania, *Harl McDonald*, director.

CONCERTO FOR ORCHESTRA, IN D MAJOR HANDEL-ORMANDY
(First time here in this form)
SYMPHONY No. 1, IN E MINOR SIBELIUS
(In commemoration of the composer's 75th anniversary)
FOUR PART-SONGS for Women's Voices with two horns and harp BRAHMS
Edna Phillips, harp, *Mason Jones* and *Herbert Pierson*, horns
FESTE ROMANE RESPIGHI

THERE is a whispering campaign around New York which would pretend that the Philadelphia Orchestra has gone off too, and seriously. Do not believe it. The Philadelphia ensemble is as fine a group of orchestral players as exists anywhere, and the sounds that emerge from their instruments are in every way worthy of the superb musicians who play these instruments. Certainly last night's performance showed no evidence, to my ear, of carelessness, of indifference, or of sabotage.

Nowhere else is there such a string choir; one would like to stroke its tone, as if the suavity of it were a visual and a tactile thing, like pale pinky-brown velvet. If memory does not trick, that luxurious and justly celebrated string-tone is less forced, less hoarse and throaty than it was in the days of the all too Slavic ex-King Leopold, now of Hollywood.

There are conductors more highly paid than Mr. Ormandy, in all probability. There are certainly some more highly advertised. Very few musicians anywhere in the world, however, conduct an orchestra with such straightforwardness, such lively understanding, such dependable architectonics. No lackadaisical daisy he, and no Holy Roller, either. His every gesture is civilized, sane, effective. The resultant musical performance is in consequence civilized, sane, and effective beyond all comparison with that of his more showily temperamental colleagues.

Last night's program opened with Mr. Ormandy's own reorchestration of a Handel concerto. For once let us praise a man for tampering with the classics. The score is as brilliant and gay and Handelian as one could wish, a great deal more so than if the original text had been observed. I found it no end jolly.

I also sat through another Sibelius symphony, listening attentively. The melodic material was everywhere of inferior quality; the harmonic substructure was at its best unobtrusive, at its worst corny. The scoring seemed accurate and sure-fire.*

The formal structure, such as there was, was a smooth piecing together of oddments, not unlike what is known to the film world as "cutting." As in a well-cut film, occasions for compensating the essential jerkiness of the flow were exploited whenever they could be found; at those moments something took place not unlike the "plugging" of a theme song.

There is not space here, nor time tonight, to go into the Sibelius matter any further than this. Suffice it to say that for the present I stick to my opinion of last Friday, which was that I found his music "vulgar, self-indulgent and provincial." Respighi's brilliant but meretricious *Feste Romane* sounded last night like good clean musical fun in comparison.

October 16, 1940

* It has since come to my knowledge that Mr. Ormandy, like many another conductor, does not hesitate to alter a composer's scoring if he considers this to require improvement.

Three Orchestras

THE NEW YORK PHILHARMONIC, the Boston, and the Philadelphia Orchestras are justly celebrated organizations. Their personnel is tops. They are composed of expert instrumentalists, internationally trained, prepared to meet any emergency of technique or of style according to accepted formulas. These elements are as mutually replaceable and as anonymous as members of the Roman Catholic clergy. And the summum of their integrity, their consecration, and their efficacy is as beyond question.

The conductors of these orchestras, of all first-class orchestras everywhere, in fact, are, although in a pinch mutually replaceable, quite the opposite of anonymous. The modern world likes impersonal musicianship, but it will have none of impersonal conducting. The role of the orchestral conductor is therefore a dual role. He needs to be objective in rehearsal and dependable technically in performance, but he must project in the concert hall a personal and subjective interpretation of every work he conducts. If he lacks technical objectivity he is not a competent conductor, fails to draw the best from his players. If he lacks the power of personal projection, he does not hold his public. He should really be Bodanzky and Mary Garden at the same time.

Also, he must interpret an international repertory, because a resident symphony orchestra is a repertory theater. That repertory, all over the world, consists of the same fifty pieces. A small amount of playing-time a year — say five or ten per cent of it — is more flexible, consists of foreign novelties and compliments to local composers. The reasons for the standardization of symphony repertory are many, and all of them are not pretty ones. But the fact is that the standardized repertory is just another neutral background, like the standardized instrumental execution; it throws further into relief the glamour and the personality of the conductor.

Conductors' glamour and personality fall into three easily recognizable geographic types: the Slavic, the central European, and the Latin. There are excellent American conductors, but there is no such thing (not yet, at any rate) as American conducting. There is such a thing as American music, however; and most of

the unhappiness that exists about it in America is due to the fact
that there is no way of interpreting it in our high-powered concerts excepting a European way. An Arab or Chinese way would
be more advantageous, because that would be a frank translation,
comprehensible as such. But the most difficult thing in the world
is to translate an American book into British. Musically we are
Europe's child, just as we are linguistically Britain's; but we are
already another person, just as our language is already another
thing than England's English. It is the common grammar that deceives everybody. Still, the literary world is not so deceived as the
musical world is. We do not try to produce plays by Odets and
Saroyan and Erskine Caldwell with English actors or in an Anglo-
international manner. They would come out pretty funny if we
did. In fact, there is more to be said for playing Borodin here as
if it were by Roy Harris, which is one way of coming to understand it, after all, than there is for the present practice of playing
Roy Harris as if it were Borodin, which is a sure way of prevent-
ing anybody's ever understanding it.

However all that may be, the three European styles of conducting are what we have in our concert halls. Those styles, conven-
iently enough, are represented by the conductors of our three first
Northeastern orchestras. Dr. Koussevitzky holds the Slavic chair;
the Hungarian Mr. Ormandy is admirably central European, and
Mr. Barbirolli, for better or for worse, is unquestionably an Italian
conductor.

The characteristics of the Slavic style of playing are exaggerated
dynamism and facile emotivity. It seems to be made for Tchaikovsky and Tchaikovsky for it. There is a tendency among all
Slavs to overblow the brass and to encourage a thick and throaty,
an absorbent string-tone. That Slavic string-tone blends the highly
differentiated wind-instrument timbres unto itself in a muddy but
unified sonority that is a powerful carrying agent for the facile
and rather emotional substance of the Russian symphonists. Dr.
Koussevitzky, although he has a Slavic weakness for dynamic
exaggeration, is not Slavic-minded at all about string-tone; he is
pure Parisian, the purest Parisian we have on this coast.

The central European style of conducting is military, authoritative, and energetic. It is capable of a gentleness in soft passages
and of a nobility in loud ones that is incomparable. It is the musical language of the great Viennese masters from Haydn through
Schönberg, although it seems to have been made up both for and

out of Handel. Perhaps the Handelian is its most easily exportable form. Mr. Ormandy is an admirable exponent of this style. His authority is authoritative, his tenderness tender. He happens also to have inherited from his Slavic predecessor a superb choir of rich Tchaikovskian string-players. He has toned down their dynamic violence and toned up their lethargic throat-tones; but he has kept their rare and finely blended dark coloration, a bright dark thing like red copper. The instruments themselves are, I am told, all from the old Cremona fiddle-makers. At present the string sound that comes from them is like nothing else I have ever heard anywhere.

Koussevitzky is better at balancing a string-chord than anybody. He always was. When he first came to Paris, after the war, he could already do it, could do it with any pick-up orchestra. The French conductors themselves could not make such an exact equilibrium, a balance in which the most neutral viola part, the most secondary second-violin part, were as clearly perceptible as the top-line melody or the bass. His Boston string section is a lovely thing, thinner and more brilliant, as is the Parisian taste, than that of the Philadelphia band; and his chord-balances, just because of that thinner and higher-voiced sonority, are neater, more stable, more exact. The Philadelphia tone, however, in its present condition, remains a luxury product of unmatched quality, a unique experience for its delicacy and for its almost tactile sensuality.

Mr. Barbirolli is a Latin out of his natural water; perhaps, too, just a little over his head. By temperament a self-effacing accompanist, he is not at his best in a stellar role. He might be excellent at the opera. He is objective and clear-minded about music; he likes and produces from his band that centrifugal sonority that Latins love, a sonority that is not so much a blend of different sounds as a simultaneity of clearly differentiated ones. One has the feeling, all the same, that he might do better in rehearsal than in concert. He gives a reading rather than a performance. He deforms a composer's wish rather less than the more spectacular leaders do; but he rarely possesses a work and makes it his own. And I think he is bored by the necessity of being a personality. All of which gives him an air of being out beyond his depth. His honest but elementary little breast stroke is no match for the streamlined baton technique that both his public and his players are used to. So he gets frantic and conducts with his hair, always the first refuge of an Italian when he can't think of the right next move.

The Philharmonic does not have that tradition of great conductors under long tenure that the Philadelphia and the Boston have. The Philharmonic's best conductors, Mahler, Mengelberg, Walter, Furtwängler, Toscanini, have never stayed long enough to mold the orchestra into a thing at once expressive of its leaders and of the city and public it is supposed to honor; not, at least, in the way that the Philadelphia Orchestra seems to be at the same time Leopold Stokowski and Eugene Ormandy and also an appropriate symbol of that swanky and luxurious town. Nor in the way that the Boston seems, even after sixteen years of Koussevitzky, still to remember the martial elegance of Muck, the Gallic clear-headedness of Monteux, as well as to correspond in both programs and playing to that tradition of bourgeois dignity with intellectual open-mindedness that is Boston, the most characteristically Victorian and inveterately good-mannered of our intellectual centers.

I imagine the trouble with the Philharmonic is that nobody really cares. Nobody in New York could care, because New York is a musical market-place, a crossroads. We are not obliged to take our nourishment from any one source of supply, to trade with any one store. And so, whereas a really first-rate orchestra is a necessity to a proud provincial city, it maybe isn't worth bothering about here. We don't need to keep any conductor around all the time. We can let them come and go, because even the best among them need our metropolitan accolade far more than we need the steady presence of their rather terrifying tension.

And so New York takes on an Emil Paur and keeps him for years, a Josef Stransky, a Van Hoogstraten. Under such men the Philharmonic lies fallow, rests up, so to speak, for those terrific combats between the podium and the desks that mark the brief Metropolitan tenure of great conductors.

October 20, 1940

Music from Chicago
Points East and West

CHICAGO SYMPHONY ORCHESTRA, *Frederick Stock,* conductor.

OVERTURE TO EURYANTHE	WEBER
SYMPHONY No. 3, IN F MAJOR	BRAHMS
AMERICAN CREED	ROY HARRIS

(Written for and dedicated to the Chicago Symphony Orchestra;
first time in New York)

TILL EULENSPIEGEL   R. STRAUSS

FLOWERS on the stage and flowers in the musicians' buttonholes, two fiftieth seasons to celebrate, that of the Chicago Symphony Orchestra and that of our own Carnegie Hall, an exchange of visits between Chicago's orchestra and our own Philharmonic — what with all this and a new work by Roy Harris, last night was indeed a sufficiently festive occasion for flowers on the stage and flowers in the musicians' buttonholes.

The Chicago Symphony Orchestra sounds like a French orchestra. Its fiddle tone, thin as a wedge, espouses by resemblance that of oboe and trumpet, absorbs nothing, stands clear in the orchestral bouquet. All the instrumental sounds stand clear and separate. Their harmony is one of juxtaposition, not of absorptive domination. As in an eighteenth-century flower picture, all is distinct, nothing crushed.

Mr. Stock won his audience last night, as he has won audiences for thirty-five years, by playing them music very beautifully, not by wowing them.

I missed the *Euryanthe* Overture, save through a crack. The Brahms Third Symphony was a dream of loveliness and equilibrium. It is the best built, the most continuous of Brahms's symphonies; and it contains, on the whole, the best melodic material of the four. With no weakness of its structure to conceal and no gracelessness in its musical content to disturb the clarity of its message, it offered Mr. Stock occasion for one of those rare and blessed readings in which the music seems to play itself. Especially the end movements, the first and the last, floated on a Viennese lilt, pastoral, poetic, and effortlessly convincing. The passage in the finale was particularly happy where the wind plays sustained harmonic progressions which the violins caress with almost inaudible tendrils of sound, little wiggly figures that dart like silent goldfish around a rock.

Till Eulenspiegel was merry, though perhaps a trifle discontinuous. Its prankiness, however, was light and gay and nearer by far to the humor of its author than those weighty readings we sometimes hear that make it sound like the ponderous pleasantries of a machine-gun.

Mr. Harris's *American Creed* invites kidding, as all of his programistically prefaced works do. If we take his music as he offers it, however, we risk refusing a quite good thing. No composer in the world, not even in Italy or Germany, makes such shameless use of patriotic feelings to advertise his product. One would think, to read his prefaces, that he had been awarded by God, or at least by popular vote, a monopolistic privilege of expressing our nation's deepest ideals and highest aspirations. And when the piece so advertised turns out to be mostly not very clearly orchestrated schoolish counterpoint and a quite skimpy double fugue (neither of which has any American connotation whatsoever), one is tempted to put the whole thing down as insincere and a bad joke.

The truth, however, is other. Mr. Harris, though the bearer of no exceptional melodic gifts and the possessor of no really thorough musical schooling, has an unquenchable passion to know and to use all the procedures of musical composition. He has pondered over the medieval French melodic line and over the problem of continuous (non-repeating) melodic development, and he has come by this road to understand where the crucial problem lies in America's musical coming-of-age. That problem would seem to be how shall we absorb all of European musical culture rather than merely that current in Vienna between the years 1750 and 1850. Harris has learned by meditation and hard work that if we expect to produce music worthy to rank with that of the Viennese masters we must go through a selective evolution comparable to that which took place in Europe for at least three centuries before the miracle of Vienna occurred.

He knows that musical material, even folklore material, is as international as musical form and syntax, that localism is no more than one man's colorful accent. He knows this so well that he avoids, as though it were of the devil, any colorful accent whatsoever. He puts his musical effort on serious problems of material and of form. He does not always get anywhere in his music; but it is serious music, much more serious music than his blurbs would lead one to believe.

He is monotonous in his material and in his form. (All his pieces begin alike.) But every now and then something really happens. It happened last night in the closing pages of both movements of his *Creed*. It was unexpected, original (in spite of the Stravinsky allusion), and beautiful. And it had exactly as much to do with America as mountains or mosquitoes or childbirth have, none of which is anybody's property and none of which has any ethnic significance whatsoever.

November 21, 1940

Community Orchestra

PIONEER VALLEY SYMPHONY, *Harold Alexander Leslie,* conductor.

HEBRIDES OVERTURE   MENDELSSOHN
SYMPHONY No. 2 ("London"), IN D MAJOR   HAYDN
EVENING PRAYER and DREAM PANTOMIME from HANSEL AND GRETEL
                                                    HUMPERDINCK
SYMPHONY No. 5, IN E MINOR ("From the New World")   DVOŘÁK

PIONEER VALLEY is a name employed locally to designate that portion of the Connecticut River valley that lies above Northampton and below the Vermont border. It is agriculturally and industrially prosperous. Tobacco, apples, and the manufacture of precision tools are the sources of its livelihood and the economic bases of its culture. It is the seat of at least three (that I know of) residential secondary schools of national repute. Through its proximity to Smith College at Northampton and to the University of Vermont at Burlington its residents are in constant touch with the major intellectual tradition. It has no submerged proletariat and no millionaire residential colony. The valley comes as near to being an integrated community, both socially and intellectually, as any district I know of in this part of the United States, excepting perhaps certain communities in New York State and in Pennsylvania that are wholly organized about a religious faith.

Three years ago Pioneer Valley caught the symphony-orchestra bug. An ambitious young violinist from Greenfield, the valley's metropolis, organized in the fall of 1939 a Young People's Symphony. Finding that there was more interest in concerted musical practice than this organization could satisfy, he got together the following season an adult group also. Managerial problems were handled during the first season by the Kiwanis Club of Greenfield. This last season the Pioneer Valley Symphony Association has managed itself. Its year's budget was $2,500. All but $500 of this has been met by the sale of tickets.

The orchestra consists of seventy-five to eighty musicians. They rehearse in Greenfield, coming from considerable distances weekly for that purpose. Those for whom the trip would constitute a financial strain receive mileage. The personnel is drawn from all walks of life. The organizer and conductor, Mr. Harold Leslie, is a Greenfield boy, a graduate of the New England Conservatory and a pupil of Dr. Koussevitzky. Five public concerts have been given this season, three in Greenfield, one in Northfield, and one in Brattleboro.

I heard the concert in Northfield last Saturday night. The program was distinguished, the playing admirable. Mr. Leslie is obviously a conductor of talent and a musician of sound knowledge. He makes no show of temperament, but his conducting gestures are obeyed. He achieves correct orchestral balances and a nice homogeneity of tone. He read all the works with complete clarity and with real musical comprehension. Rarely have I heard an amateur orchestral concert so glowing with musical life. It was even played in tune. His orchestra, his audience, and himself were all as clearly representative of the New England musical tradition as anything could be.

That tradition has always been a sound one. New England is the only region of the United States where music has been for a hundred and fifty years integrated and incorporated with the whole intellectual tradition, where music has been taught and practiced as a form of communication and not as a special activity. As a result, New England and a few communities farther west that are its cultural progeny have provided most of the backbone for whatever musical tradition we have that is transmissible as a part of our whole intellectual tradition.

It is not accident that has given to the Boston Symphony its unique role in American musical life of the last forty years. It is

not accident that enabled Dr. Archibald Davison and the Harvard
Glee Club to reform choral style and repertory in the United
States during the 1920's. It is not accident that Boston has turned
out so many well-schooled composers, from Lowell Mason to
Walter Piston. Nor is it quite by accident that the upper middle
region of the Connecticut River valley should go about following
the national fad for symphonic exercise in such a sound and sensible manner as it has.

Whether the expansion of orchestral interest that has caused
the founding of some 30,000 symphony orchestras in the United
States during the depression decade will survive this new decade
so inauspiciously inaugurated with wars and rumors of wars I
could not prophesy. But I am quite certain that any community
feeling an urge toward such exercise would do well to observe
the results, artistic and social, achieved in two years by the Pioneer
Valley Symphony Association. I grant you, of course, that few
communities have such natural advantages to start with in the
form of cultural and social unity plus complete access to the best
in intellectual and musical tradition.

April 29, 1941

It's About Time

NBC SYMPHONY ORCHESTRA, *Arturo Toscanini,* conductor, with
Earl Wild, pianist, and *Benny Goodman,* clarinetist, as soloists.

MEMORIES OF MY CHILDHOOD	C. M. LOEFFLER
CHORIC DANCE NO. 2	PAUL CRESTON
(First Performance)	
A LINCOLN LEGEND	MORTON GOULD
(First Performance)	
A RHAPSODY IN BLUE	GEORGE GERSHWIN
Soloists, Messrs. *Wild* and *Goodman*	

MR. TOSCANINI has played four American pieces in a row. He did
it yesterday afternoon at a concert given before an invited audience in Studio 8-H, Radio City, the program being broadcast as
the season's first of the NBC Symphony Orchestra. Whether this
conductor, in his whole American career, which covers well over

thirty years, has formerly played that much American music all together I am not sure. But undeniably his previous encouragement of local art has been microscopic. Well, it's never too late to mend. And yesterday's gesture, which one hopes is the beginning of some fuller amends, was gratefully received by a large hand-picked audience.

It was handsomely carried out, too, with all the attention to detail and careful effort to understand the spirit of musical works that are characteristic of Mr. Toscanini's conducting. If the renditions were not the most beautiful one could imagine, that is probably due to the fact that the NBC orchestra is not the finest instrumental group in the world. It plays with attention, as all radio orchestras do; and some of the soloists are first-class. But the ensemble is far from homogeneous, and nowhere is there much extra beauty of tone. Also there were not yesterday enough strings to balance the brass and percussion, so that the tuttis all sounded clattery. Nevertheless, the renditions, if not especially lovely, were at all times spirited, neat, and snappy.

Loeffler's *Memories of My Childhood* is old-fashioned impressionism of the Franco-Bostonian school. It is full of trick orchestration, and its contrapuntal texture is respectable. It is literate music-writing, but it doesn't get off the ground. It meanders gracefully without ever taking flight.

Morton Gould's *Lincoln Legend* takes the air a little better, but it is always having to make emergency landings in swampy places. After sitting on some vaguely Middle Western landscape for a time, it gets off to quite a promising joyride with *John Brown's Body* and *The Old Grey Mare*; but a lack of something necessary constantly pulls it back to earth. It next does some desultory hedge-hopping and then finally bogs down not far from where it started. It, too, is full of trick orchestration, though less objectionably than other works I have heard by this composer.

Paul Creston's Choric Dance No. 2 sounds to me like a fine piece. The material is interesting, the development of it imaginative, the rhythm far from banal, and the sentiment sustained. His instrumentation is sonorous, well calculated, and appropriate. The work has atmosphere, too, and personality. It sounds like a choric dance. It does not sound like somebody's memories of his musical education.

Gershwin's *Rhapsody in Blue* is a modern classic. It has stood tough treatment from lots of people, and it is still a beautiful and gay work. It got tough treatment yesterday, from Mr. Goodman's opening lick to Mr. Toscanini's final wallop. Goodman established a tone of high virtuosity. Mr. Wild, the piano soloist, carried this on and added an affetuoso radio manner that alternated brilliant and violent execution of the hotcha passages with a studied and rather boring rubato in the lyrical ones that made one wish he would stop fooling around and let the show get on. Mr. Toscanini didn't have a chance to do much to the piece till the song-like theme with horn accompaniment came in.

Mistaking this for Tchaikovsky (it does sound rather like *Romeo and Juliet*), he leaned on it heavily and then began building up a Warner Brothers finale. It all came off like a ton of bricks. It was the *Rhapsody in Blue* all right, as what rendition isn't? But it was as far from George's own way of playing the piece as one could imagine. George played it straight, kept the rhythm going, even in the passages of free recitation, which he treated as comments on the more animated parts, not as interruptions of them. He didn't moon around, and he didn't get brutal.

I don't expect every artist to do every piece just as the author used to. If a work is any good, it can stand lots of mishandling and lots of reinterpreting. But I was a little sorry yesterday to hear this gay, sweet, rhapsodical number treated to a routine glamorizing that rubbed all the bloom off it and left its surface as shining and as glittery as a nickel-plated Apollo Belvedere.

November 2, 1942

Boston's Pops

EVERY city has some kind of summer concert series offering a mixed repertory of music old and new from which the lighter veins of composition are not excluded. New York takes its Philharmonic concerts at the Lewisohn Stadium without much admixture of popular tunes. The Goldman Band provides us our dosage necessary of military marches, of selections from operetta, of Viennese waltzes, of popular overtures and suites no longer considered respectable to hear at two-dollar concerts or even at the Stadium.

Boston's particular version of all this is its famous Pop Concerts. These take place in Symphony Hall with the full Boston

Symphony Orchestra playing (renamed for ten weeks each year
"The Boston Pops Orchestra") and Arthur Fiedler leading. (I
should like to add his name to those of Smallens and Barlow as
excellent and thoroughly experienced American conductors.) For
the Pops season all the seats are removed from the main floor and
the surface of this made level so that it can be filled with tables.
Food and drink is offered reasonably. The balcony seats are sold
to non-consuming listeners for seventy-five, fifty, and twenty-five
cents.

This set-up seems normal enough, though no other American
city has ever been able to reproduce it. What the Boston customers get is all the pleasures of a Continental café plus a concert of
the Boston Symphony Orchestra. There are no outdoor noises or
bugs. The air-conditioning is mild. Smoking is permitted. The
service is silent and satisfactory. The repertory is uninhibited.
The house is packed with music-lovers of all ages, and there are
lots of young men with their girls. This is the fifty-sixth season of
the series and Mr. Fiedler's twelfth as conductor.

The charm of these evenings is partly due to food and tobacco
and democratic assembly and partly, of course, to the music.
Really it is due to the contiguity of all these. But the music itself
has a charm quite rare and unexpected these days that is due to
the application of the Boston Symphony's excellent musicianship
to a whole range of musical repertory that seldom gets properly
played at all. The standard symphonies are always getting themselves well played. The Sousa marches and the more popular
overtures occasionally get themselves rendered well enough. But
there is a whole section of the musical library that seems destined
either to constantly inadequate execution or to complete neglect.
I mean pieces like Handel's Largo, the waltzes of Strauss and
Waldteufel, Schubert's *Serenade*, Saint-Saëns's *The Animal's Carnival*, Chabrier's *España*, Tchaikovsky's *Marche Slave* and *1812*,
and many another work perennially loved by all.

This repertory, known to the music-publishing trades as "popular classics and semi-classics," is the bridge between simple song
and the high art realms of music. It is what enables everybody
to understand Beethoven and Mozart. It is the door through which
young people enter into the magic domain of musical comprehension. It is infinitely touching to hear it played with loving care by
such a band and listened to with lively ears by such an alert audience as Boston's.

A week ago I wandered into Symphony Hall and after some difficulty (for the house was sold out, as usual) obtained entry. The orchestra was playing the waltz scene from *Faust*. I have known the piece, as everyone else has, since I was a baby. For thirty years I haven't cared much for it. I only realized the other night that it has been at least that long since I have heard it well played. Even at the opera houses they rarely use enough strings. And besides, one isn't always willing to sit through *Faust* just to hear the Prelude and the Waltz and the final Trio. At the Pops it was perfect. So was Tchaikovsky's *Nutcracker Suite* that followed. Hearing this light but charming music from the back of the hall played with all the tonal beauty and dynamic perspective that it was intended to have, I was carried back in fancy to the brilliance of the great opera houses of thirty and more years ago. And I remembered Igor Stravinsky's description of what he had hoped to do in his ballet scores, *Le Baiser de la Fée* and *Jeu de Cartes*. "I wanted," he said, "to evoke the memory of the brilliance and the charm of the ballet spectacles of our former Imperial Opera."

Also on the program was a selection of favorite melodies from Victor Herbert. The audience was visibly transported to remembrance of light-opera days. There was also a piece about a mosquito that had to be repeated. And a set of variations on *Yankee Doodle* by Mr. Morton Gould. The latter purported to be a swing version, but only one chorus really got off the ground. That was this citizen's opinion. The rest of the audience enjoyed the piece enough to demand its repetition. But even this crochety spoil-sport is glad to have heard the work. Mr. Fiedler, in the course of putting some of every kind of music on every program, plays a great deal of serious music by living composers. He even commissions new works from time to time. Walter Piston's ballet *The Incredible Flutist* was the result of such a commission; it was given its first and, to my knowledge, only choreographic rendition at those concerts.

Koussevitzky rehearses the orchestra three times for each of his programs, and he prepares twenty-four programs during his season of thirty weeks. Fiedler has two rehearsals for every seven programs, and he plays about sixty-five concerts (with very little repeating in them) during the Pops season of ten weeks. That means that familiar symphonies and such, as at our own Stadium concerts, rarely get rehearsed at all. New pieces and revivals (I

noticed Weber's *Abu Hassan* Overture on the bill for last week)
get read through. This seems to be sufficient, even for most of
the gramophone recordings. For the Pops Orchestra, before a
ruling of the American Federation of Musicians forbade further
recordings by members of the Boston Symphony Orchestra, has
long been a favorite with record-buyers.

The Boston Pops are really a lovely success story. They have
no budget troubles. They have no audience troubles. They have
no program troubles. They just play everything and play it beautifully, and everybody loves them and comes every night to hear
them and to eat sandwiches with beer or to sip cool punches and
juleps in the friendly ambiance of good old Symphony Hall.

June 8, 1941

Band Music

INELUCTABLE is the charm of the military band. Frequently incorrect, however, is the military denomination. One uses it, lacking
a proper term, for ensembles like that which plays of a summer
evening in Central and Prospect Parks under the leadership of
Messrs. Goldman and son. From a military band, strictly speaking,
one expects a possibility of ambulation not easily concordant with
the use of the tubular chimes and of the Italian harp, though no
doubt our new motorized armies, did they not consider the noises
of engine and of caterpillar tread appropriate and sufficient music
for their parades, might solve the problem of the portative harp
and chime as neatly and as elegantly as the cavalry long ago
solved that of the kettledrum. More classical, of course, is the
practice whereby really military outfits exercising in the field
leave behind them in barracks all instruments of unwarlike appearance and symbolism, though they hesitate not to employ
these indoors for celebration of the peaceable and sedentary concert rite.

Wholly peaceable and sedentary of a summer night is our mu-
nicipality's pride, the Goldman Band. Equally peaceable is the
crowd, both sedentary and deambulant, that assists at these
musical ceremonies on the Mall. The opening concert of the sea-

son last Wednesday night was almost too peaceable for my taste. I should have liked more music in the military style and less duplication of symphonic repertory. It is scarcely worth while going out to the Mall to hear Tchaikovsky's *Romeo and Juliet* or the Sibelius *Finlandia*, both of which are plugged all winter at indoor concerts and on the radio and both of which sound infinitely better, if we must have them in the summer, played with strings by the Philharmonic at the Lewisohn Stadium.

The question of repertory for band concerts is a vexing one. It is not that the general public won't take high-class music. If that were true there would be no problem. The truth is that New York's proletarian public, which is both musical and highly literate, will take any amount of symphonic repertory or of anything else. It seems to me the duty of all musical organizations to play for this avid and absorptive public all of that organization's best and most characteristic literature. We do not put up with string quartets playing transcriptions of piano music nor with organists who insist on playing Wagner. Why military bands should fill up nine tenths of their programs with versions of symphonic stuff I do not know.

I know, of course, that the library of original band music is not large. It consists chiefly of marches, though these constitute in themselves a unique repertory. There are also a certain number of "characteristic" or "genre" pieces by bandmasters, most of which are too cute for current tastes. There is also the further and much larger field of what we call "popular" music. Such music must naturally be performed in "arrangements"; but since it is never played anywhere except in arrangements, it is legitimate to consider all arrangements of it as equally appropriate to the instruments for which they are made. Such compositions frequently contain, indeed, writing for wind ensemble that is in every way idiomatic, sonorous, and satisfactory.

I am not protesting against the *use* of *arrangements*, in so far as that term means free versions of familiar melodies. I protest against the *abuse* of *transcriptions*, by which I mean the translation to other instrumental media of works that are both satisfactory and easily available in their correct form. The fad for orchestral transcriptions of organ music and other eighteenth-century matter is so far a harmless one; it serves chiefly to prove the classical culture of conductors and of modernist composers. It does not yet occupy the major part of our orchestral programs. Band programs are nowadays almost wholly occupied with transcriptions of orchestral music. To their detriment, I think.

One can forgive band leaders for playing the *Lucia di Lammermoor* sextet and the Overture to *William Tell*. The snobbery that has eliminated these admirable works and others like them from the programs of our two-dollar concerts has left us no place to hear them save on the Mall. I fear rather that any extension of symphonic snobbery to these frankly popular circumstances may end by eliminating from our lives altogether the repertory of popular "classics" and "semi-classics" that gave to band concerts formerly such charm and such power of sentimental appeal.

Among popular "classics," or among the "semi-classics," if you prefer, that it is pleasant to hear at band concerts I place all selections from the works of Richard Wagner. Not that these works are unavailable at the opera. It is rather that many familiar passages from them, having long ago extracted themselves like nut meats from their theatrical context, lead today as independent an existence as that of any Italian overture or air. They are constantly being played (slightly transformed) at orchestral as well as at band concerts. I find the band versions rather more satisfactory, on the whole. The absence of violins removes that juicy-fruit quality that is so monotonous in the orchestral versions. This is less bothersome in the theater than at a concert because there are usually fewer strings and because the placement of the brass instruments throws these last into still further relief. In the versions for military band everything takes on what seems to me ideal Wagnerian proportions. The brass becomes a true *harmonie*, or village band, and all the woodwind and percussive sonorities simply outgrowths and accents of this, like a daisy's petals. The out-of-doors gives to the music's substance, too, a healthiness that is far from unbecoming. It ceases to demand from us the routine emotional responses that it seems to need for survival in the concert hall. It stands on its own feet for once as perfectly good music in theatrical vein, and not devoid of a certain Teutonic dignity.

Everything, however, is trimming and filling at a band concert, except the military marches. These are the historical reason for its existence, and they comprise the only repertory that is unique to it. That repertory, which is neither small nor monotonous, contains almost the whole memorable work of a great and characteristically American master, the late John Philip Sousa. It comprises as well many fine pieces from the pen of Mr. Edwin Franko Goldman, our band's elder leader. It was nice to hear young Goldman's excellent transcription of Stravinsky's *Fire Bird* Lullaby and Finale. It was nice to hear Henry Cowell's original piece for band, called *Shoonthree.* It was charming indeed to hear two movements of Haydn's Trumpet Concerto executed with neatness and delicacy on the cornet by Mr. Leonard B. Smith. One sat through the Wagner with toleration of its open-air qualities and through the Tchaikovsky and the Bach and the Sibelius with what was already getting to be patience. What one really brought home from the evening was exactly what one had gone for, two marches by Goldman *père.*

Everything else, excepting Mr. Cowell's piece, can be heard to better advantage at the Stadium and during the season's course certainly will be. I find it a little excessive to have to sit through so much frankly non-essential repertory in order to hear two short works from the band's essential repertory. I do not consider that the replaying of all that classical truck shows a raising of the Goldman Band's cultural standard. Quite the contrary. It shows submission to the plugging procedures of the Appreciation Racket. The cultural result is the same as what happens to cooking when farmers stop eating what they grow because somebody on the air has told them nationally advertised canned goods are superior to the home-grown pea.

June 22, 1941

Landscape With Music

THE HOLLYWOOD BOWL is more agreeable to the eye than to the ear. Its seating space is like a fan laid against a Spanish hillside. Its slow rise in elevation from band shell to top seats is considerable, but this is continued in such a gentle slope by the concave mountain behind that the scalloped top of the land seems rather to finish off the architect's design than to enclose it. The natural advantages of the site become thus more gracefully protective than imposing; and the whole scene takes on, right in the middle of a suburb, an effect at once of openness and of isolation. That intimacy with the empyrean which Nature and the designer have offered here would be even more inspiring if it were not for cool evenings and heavy dews that turn the mind toward sweaters and perhaps a flannel belly-band.

"Symphonies Under the Stars" is the grandiose, if somewhat supersibilant, title of the concerts held in this spacious locale throughout July and August and into September. The Philharmonic Orchestra of Los Angeles constitutes the executant musical body. Guest conductors ranging from Erno Rapee through Bruno Walter and Sir Thomas Beecham lead it. Artists as solid in popular favor and as diversified in musical allegiance as Artur Rubinstein, Oscar Levant, and Gracie Allen add star quality. Programs range from the folksy to the standard symphonic type, Sunday representing the lowest common denominator of musical initiation and Thursday (servants' night out) being reserved for conductors and repertory of the intellectual, or classic, tradition. The acoustics of the place are not very good, and the orchestra did not impress me in one hearing as being quite up to Eastern or to Middle Western standards of musical refinement. But the shell of the Bowl is charming, and its public is amiable; moreover, programs are comprehensive and the visiting artists distinguished. What it seems chiefly to lack for full perfection is first-class musical sounds.

At the opening concert of the season last Sunday the program was frankly popular and, in honor of the Fourth of July, wholly of American authorship. MacDowell, Victor Herbert, Gershwin, Cadman, Sousa, and Handy (by *The St. Louis Blues*) were the standard composers represented. Ferde Grofé, Louis Alter, Morton Gould, Rodgers and Hart, and Meredith Willson — a light-theater and radio group — made up the younger contingent. There were, in addition, a medley of service songs (sung by a male chorus of ten or twelve voices plus a young lady from the night clubs, named Ginny Simms) and a work of anonymous origin entitled "Concerto for Index Finger" (of which hand was not stated), executed on a toy pianoforte by the ever delightful Gracie Allen, Mr. Whiteman conducting.

Mr. Grofé conducted his own *March for Americans* (What could the title mean? Is it orthopedic or merely exclusive?) and a movement from his *Grand Canyon Suite*. Mr. Grofé's musical intention is of a mild order, and his conducting last Sunday was not noticeably effective. Captain Willson led two movements from his symphony, *The Missions of California*, and later Sousa's *The*

Stars and Stripes Forever. His own pieces, which were harmonious and faintly funereal, like the religious music in films, were neatly conducted. And his *Stars and Stripes* was a rousingly straightforward performance in the best military style I have heard employed during this war in any symphonic rendition of that superb work.

The rest of the evening belonged to Mr. Whiteman, except for what was taken of it by Miss Simms for the rendering (with crooning cadenzas) of William C. Handy's masterpiece, *The St. Louis Blues.* Miss Simms is apparently not aware that the inhabitants of that city pronounce its final "s" and that the omission of the auxiliary verb "have" in "would not gone" is both traditional and correct. Mr. Whiteman accompanied her admirably.

He did more, however, than accompany a soloist for Gershwin's *Rhapsody in Blue.* He gave the work shape and ease, in spite of Mr. Ray Turner's rather poundy piano-playing. Spontaneity is the charm of that piece, and spontaneity is about the last quality one ever encounters nowadays in its performance. It has become tense and violent and assertive. Mr. Whiteman brought it back, so far as he could with uncooperative pianism, to its original mood of meditation and (as the title says) rhapsody.

It is, of course, permissible to make any interpretation one likes of any piece. Nobody is ever patently right about music. But many musical renditions are patently wrong. Leopold Stokowski and George Balanchine, for example, were clearly in error when they fancied Bach's *Matthäuspassion* to be an appropriate accompaniment for pantomime. I believe it to be incorrect and ineffective, when conducting the *Rhapsody in Blue,* to concentrate on climax-building at the expense of spontaneous lyricism. Efforts to make *William Tell* music out of it and Holy Grail music are equally, in my opinion, doomed to failure.

As an example of what I consider a misreading of both the composer's thought and the work's expressive possibilities, I quote from the *Hollywood Bowl Magazine,* official annotated program book of the "Symphonies Under the Stars":

"Gershwin's 'Rhapsody in Blue' comes in striking contrast to the Willson music from the idyllic valleys of California. There is a passionate cry for deliverance from the cement-and-steel canyons of New York City in this deeply emotional, nervously actuated rhapsody. The bells echoed in the Gershwin opus are those of the Elevated and the Underground, are workshift bells all of which

Gershwin's New Yorkers, for whom this rhapsody is written, try to forget.

"It is almost as if Gershwin were voicing all the frustrations and longings of the men and women of twentieth-century New York, in one frantically sustained almost deliriously self-forgetting heart cry for release from reality."

It is not George Gershwin's writing, it seems to me, that should be called "frantically sustained almost deliriously self-forgetting," but rather that of Mr. Bruno David Ussher, author of the program notes. Mr. Whiteman, for whose musical organization the piece actually was written, has a sounder idea both of its feeling content and of how to sustain its continuity without getting frantic than any other conductor I have ever heard lead it.

July 11, 1943

Music at the Golden Gate

SAN FRANCISCO is better off for music during the summer than most other American cities. At the moment there is fare, and plenty of it, for all appetites. The proper bars are full of sweet swing, the improper ones of hotter stuff. There are, as musical shows, something with Ethel Waters, called *Laugh Time,* and the Ballet Theater, both playing indoors. There are popular opera and orchestral concerts playing (though not every day, absolutely free, nevertheless) outdoors at the Sigmund Stern Grove. There are military bands around, also. Two major string quartets are operating in the Bay region. The London and the Budapest Quartets divide their work between, respectively, Berkeley (at the University of California) and San Francisco and Oakland (at Mills College), each giving eight or more concerts. There are solo recitals, too, with modernistic programs. And there are weekly concerts of hot music at the C. I. O. Hot Jazz Hall.

The outdoor concerts, so far as I have heard them, are, just as in Los Angeles, more notable for the beauty of their locale (all grass and trees and family picnics and no gravel or concrete anywhere) than for any especial distinction of execution or of repertory. The Budapest Quartet, however, is in fine form. The London's work is even more elegant, with John Pennington, William

Primrose and C. Warwick Evans at their old places, and Laurent Halleux replacing the late Thomas Petrie as second violin. At a concert of French music given the other evening in the art museum, Virginia Morley and Livingston Gearhart revealed themselves to be not only a top-flight team of duo-pianists but musicians who understand what modern music is about. They played two great works that one rarely hears, Stravinsky's Concerto for two pianos alone and Debussy's three-movement rhapsody, *En Blanc et Noir*. It was equally a pleasure to hear serious music written for two pianos and to hear two pianists playing any music as if that were a serious occupation and not a form of badminton.

The Hot Jazz Concerts are a result of some lectures delivered last spring by Rudi Blesh at the San Francisco Museum of Art. These were illustrated by records from Mr. Blesh's own collection, as well as by non-processed executions. For the latter there was brought here from Louisiana no less an artist than Willie "Bunk" Johnson, considered by many the finest of all trumpet-players. Johnson was an original member of the earliest hot group known, the Original Superior Band, organized in 1891 in New Orleans. For many years its leader, he is celebrated in the histories of hot music not only for his integrity as an artist but for his mastery of that imperious trumpet tone chiefly familiar to laymen nowadays through the work of his pupil Louis Armstrong.

At the closing of the lecture series many lovers of the hot wished to keep Mr. Johnson around, but the local musicians' union, which, it would seem, is not favorable to the hot style, has made it difficult for him to work. Negroes and whites are not allowed to play together, for one thing, and the informal participation in public music-making of visiting artists is forbidden, for another. There is, moreover, some kind of general ruling against jam sessions. Mr. Harry Bridges, regional director of the C. I. O. and long a patron of cultural activities (the San Francisco Symphony Orchestra is playing for his membership next week), came to the rescue of hot art by arranging a place for it in his own union clubrooms. As a result, Bunk Johnson's Hot Seven play every Sunday afternoon all afternoon in an auditorium now known as the C. I. O. Hot Jazz Hall under the management of the Hot Jazz Society of San Francisco. Persons not members of this society can join at the door if properly introduced. Last Sunday there were perhaps five hundred people, a youngish but not adolescent audience consisting of well-dressed working people, professors, a goodly number of service men, both enlisted and commissioned, and one pretty young lady in a welder's uniform, complete with metal hat. Dancing was permitted in the back of the hall, and drinks were available in an adjoining bar.

The music was executed in the style known as New Orleans. The bass, a tuba, played straightforwardly and right on the beat. The drums indulged in no fancy work. Neither did the banjo. Piano, clarinet, trumpet, and trombone improvised with the greatest freedom but also with an astonishing sobriety. Nobody tried to show how fast he could play or how high. At no point was there any attempt to swing the beat or to fake a fury. Neither did any soloist try to conceal the tune. Variations were developed musically out of it and never left its expression for mere flambuoyancy, though Billy Singleton, who played piano as guest in several numbers, did plenty of expert work in thirds and chromatic octaves. Bob Barton, a youngster, played trombone with a fine dirty tone. Ellis Horne, the clarinet, is an accomplished mature artist and no show-off.

"Bunk" Johnson himself is an artist of delicate imagination, meditative in style rather than flashy, and master of the darkest trumpet tone I have ever heard. He is also the greatest master of "blue," or off-pitch, notes it has been my pleasure to encounter. The degrees of his deviation from normal pitch are infinite, and the taste with which he exploits this variety merits no less a word than impeccable. His timbres, his intonations, and his melodic invention are at all times expressive, at all times reasonable, and at all times completely interesting. His work takes on, in consequence, and so does that of those working with him, depth, ease and lucidity. Nothing could be less sentimental or speak more sincerely from the heart, less jittery or move around more freely. Certainly no music was ever less confused.

The basic rhythm of his band is so solid and so plain that its effect on players and public alike is the opposite of that nervous exasperation that is frequently a result of jazz performance. It stills, rather, the nerves and allows the mind free play in that purely auditory perception of feeling that is the alpha and the omega of music. I suspect Mr. Bridges is right. This sort of music is as cultural an activity as any and more so than most. Certainly it is more rarely to be encountered at a high degree of purity than the symphonic stuff. Both kinds of music, of course, are deplorably commercialized these days. Its purity, nevertheless, a non-commercial quality, is wherein any music's cultural value lies.

August 8, 1943

The Philharmonic Centenary

LETTERS have been arriving numerously of late protesting against the meager plans announced by the Philharmonic-Symphony Orchestra for the celebration of its hundredth anniversary next year. Why these protests should be sent to me rather than to the directors of the Philharmonic I do not know, unless perhaps it is thought that the directors of that body are impervious to suggestion and complaint, and my correspondents hope to seduce me into waging through the press a campaign doomed apparently to failure otherwise.

The centennial festivities, as announced in the press of Saturday, March 15, consist in relieving the monotony of Mr. Barbirolli's tenure, which runs for one more year, in very much the same way as has been done this year, by a parade of guest conductors. These would be Stokowski, Walter, Mitropoulos, Rodzinski, Goossens, Fritz Busch, and possibly Toscanini and Koussevitzky. The Old Man had not yet replied to the invitation; and Mr. Petrillo, president of the National Federation of Musicians, had not yet given formal consent for the Philharmonic musicians to play under the good Doctor, who is not a member of the union, though unofficial advices from union headquarters seemed to indicate that such consent would be granted without difficulty.

The chief complaints against the inadequacy of this program are two: it honors no conductor of American birth or training, and it commissions no new compositions, American or other.

I must say that if I had been making out the list I should have put in Alexander Smallens and Howard Barlow, both American-trained and both interesting conductors; and I should have preferred Pierre Monteux and Thomas Beecham among the available European-trained to either Goossens or Busch. Under no circumstances, however, should I have made out any such list at all. A string of guest conductors, though obviously the first thing the Philharmonic management would think of, is the last thing the

Philharmonic musicians need. These have been so thoroughly guest-conducted for twenty years now that they have become temperamental, erratic, and difficult as only first-class musicians can become when subjected to every known variety of browbeating and wheedling. The best birthday present the Philharmonic could offer itself and us would be a good permanent full-time conductor, somebody worthy of the job and capable of assuming all its musical responsibilities. It's no use saying such conductors don't exist. I know three out of work and at least three more who could be stepped up most deservingly from provincial posts.

As for the commissioning of musical works, both Boston and Chicago seem to have picked pretty good musical values, plus doing themselves honor, in so celebrating their fiftieth anniversaries. I hadn't really expected anything like that of the Philharmonic; but I am disappointed, all the same, at its not having been done. I hadn't expected it because I am a little cynical about that institution.

As I pointed out earlier in the season, it doesn't play a very important part in New York's intellectual life; nor has it since the days of Gustav Mahler. It was, to say the least, quiescent under Stransky from 1911 to 1922. From 1922 on, under Mengelberg and Toscanini, each of whom ranked as a regular conductor of the Philharmonic for about ten years, but who really worked here only part of the time each season, there were some brilliant performances of classic works. The whole weight of these men's prestige was thrown against living music. Guest conductors performed certain new scores on tolerance; Boston, Philadelphia, and Cleveland brought most of them for us to hear; local societies were organized for the exposition and dissemination of others. The Philharmonic office in the 1930's made no concealment of its position. The maestro did not "like" modern music; he was under no obligation to conduct any of it at the Philharmonic. Mr. Barbirolli has played more new music than Toscanini, but little of it has been significant or striking in any way. He has been the center of much controversy, virtually none of it concerned with the æsthetics of musical composition.

Thus it has come about that the Philharmonic-Symphony Orchestra, both personnel and management, though pretty much up to the minute on conducting, has worked for thirty years on the sidelines of creative music — that is, of music as she is really writ. The personnel is not entirely on the outside, because the boys do

play other music other places; and they all get brought up to date
a bit summers at the Stadium, where the repertory is livelier. Yes,
and Arthur Judson has other managerial irons in the fire than the
Philharmonic, quite a few. But still the fact is that the current
Philharmonic tradition, the tradition in force ever since its merg-
ing with the National Symphony in 1921, is one of fine instrumen-
talism and fancy conducting, not of intimate collaboration with
the creators of music. And that is why I permit myself a certain
cynicism in reply when people write or ask me why new works are
not being commissioned to fête the hundredth year. The old
Philharmonic is a tricky bird. Give her a good master and she'll
lay you golden eggs. But don't expect those golden eggs to hatch
live goslings. Above all, don't expect an organization that has for
thirty years either ignored the existence of the more vigorous
movements in contemporary music or snubbed them ostentatiously to suddenly start giving money away for their encouragement.

Not that a sudden change is inconceivable, provided some
more fundamental change were to take place in the organization's
musical policy. But this year, at least, the Philharmonic has shown,
indeed, very little sign of having a musical policy. Each concert
has seemed more or less fortuitous. Mr. Barbirolli, who is supposed to be the conductor, has been replaced by guests for nearly
one third of the concerts. A great deal of contemporary music has
been played, for a change, but selected, it would seem, from a
grab-bag. Two world-famous violinists have both played the same
concerto in the same season. I have found little logic in the pro-
gram-making, whether the works played were ancient or modern.
This applies equally to those of the conductor and to those of his
guests.

It is classical to celebrate a feast by giving way for one day to
one's besetting weakness. But, ladies and gentlemen who direct
the destinies of the Philharmonic, do you really think another
whole year of it is without serious risk? Your conductor has already accepted for this season what amounts to the status of a
guest. He has accepted for next year to be one among eight. That
means that for two years the musicians will have had no conductor, no unified command, hence no real discipline. For twenty
years they haven't had much, I admit; but once a year Mengelberg
or the Old Man turned up and told them what was what. Barbirolli was all right, too, I suppose, as long as he conducted, or was

allowed to conduct, his own orchestra. But do you really think the temperamental Philharmonic, if left for a whole year without any conductor of its own at all, won't blow sky-high one day when some equally temperamental guest says "Boo" to it?

Musical composition has gone on for some years now with small blessings from the Philharmonic; and though I could wish things were otherwise, it would be against nature to expect much more right now. But I do think, birthdays aside, that that venerable institution is tempting Providence to go on playing around with guest conductors when what she really needs is a lord and master who will take some of the jumpiness out of her and put her to work on a five-year plan of some kind, building something in America's musical life that would be worthy of her history and of the city that loves her and supports her and complains about her.

What would such a plan be? Nothing less than the building of an audience for American music and the building of an American repertory for that audience. Nothing is easier. Half the countries in Europe have accomplished a similar thing deliberately. The technique of it is known. Nothing would be a worthier job for our Philharmonic; and, of course, it could be fantastically a success. Everybody is ready. Local audience, radio executives, national public, composers even. And the naming of an American conductor, which would be necessary, because Europeans have only the vaguest conception of what American music is about, would not present the difficulty it does when we envisage, as we do now, that problem as one of naming an American to conduct a repertory ninety-five per cent European.

I'm afraid I'm dreaming about the present I should like to give the Philharmonic, one first-class, full-time American conductor complete with five-year plan and full authority to execute it. But I may as well return to my cynicism. I cannot offer such a present. And there is about as much chance of the Philharmonic offering it to itself as there is of Toscanini conducting Schönberg's *Fünf Orchesterstücke* at an NBC broadcast.

March 23, 1941

Being Odious

PHILHARMONIC–SYMPHONY ORCHESTRA, *Bruno Walter*, conductor, with *Joseph Szigeti*, violinist.

THE DREAM PEDLAR	WHITHORNE
(First performance by this orchestra)	
SYMPHONY NO. 3, IN E FLAT ("Rhenish")	SCHUMANN
VIOLIN CONCERTO IN D MAJOR (K. 218)	MOZART
SYMPHONIC POEM, VLTAVA (THE MOLDAU)	SMETANA

THE WHOLE evening invited comparisons. Mr. Whithorne's *Dream Pedlar* invited comparison with all the pieces of similar title and texture that one has ever heard, and man and boy one has heard a lot. Writing whimsey for a hundred musicians used to be considered a proper activity for composers who were both gentlemen and scholars. Arnold Bax enjoyed a certain reputation at this in the post-war decade. Mr. Whithorne does it with skill. His music is neatly calculated and rather better knit than most.

Schumann's "Rhenish" Symphony invited dual comparison with his own non-symphonic works and with the works of the other Romantic symphonists. On both counts it comes off unfavorably. It has not the technical freedom of his pianoforte and chamber writing, and it lacks the orchestral amplitude we enjoy in the symphonic writing of many a lesser personality like Berlioz or Brahms or even Tchaikovsky. All the same, it is fine music, noble and manly and full of real tunes. It was especially a pleasure to hear it in Mr. Walter's poetic and exuberant rendition.

The Mozart Violin Concerto invited comparison with Mozart's concertos for other instruments. It is less fine music than almost any of his pianoforte concertos, for example, though the last movement is first-class. The Smetana *Moldau* reminded one of pop concerts and a whole repertory of pleasantly patriotic pieces seldom heard any more, even at pop concerts. It has a fine big tune, too.

Mr. Szigeti invites comparison with other violinistic great. His tone is not so majestic as Kreisler's, and his intonation is less impeccable than that of Heifetz. His Mozart is more interesting than that of either, though it was not at its best last night. His E-string squeaked a bit. The lower ones, especially the third and fourth, were warm and pungent, however. If he exaggerated Mozart's dynamism, as if the concerto were something in the gypsy style, he did bite into the rhythmic texture of it deeper than those artists do who take such care for keeping Mozart round and gentle and, as the swing boys would say, "sweet." The Szigeti Mozart last night, though a little out of hand, was definitely on the "hot" side. For one who vigorously objects to sweets with his meat (and Mozart is certainly meat) that was a pleasure too. It didn't come off right, but Szigeti is on a good track.

Mr. Walter invites comparison, naturally, with the others who have conducted the Philharmonic-Symphony Orchestra this season. There is a German verb, *musizieren,* which means *to make music.* It applies more clearly to Mr. Walter than to either Rodzinski or Mitropoulos. These others have their excellences and their special abilities, but they don't make as good music as Mr. Walter does.

Mr. Walter has no special trick of excellence. He is excellent all over. He is not the greatest conductor in the world, though he is a very great one. His Mozart, for instance, though justly famous for its sensible tempos and its general lack of fussiness and folderol, I consider less fine than that of Sir Thomas Beecham. His Debussy is certainly less magical than that of either Monteux or Furtwängler. And Dr. Koussevitzky can no doubt beat him at Mussorgsky, though Walter need yield to none on German music. Take him all round, he is as fine a leader as we have heard with any orchestra this year; and the Philharmonic itself sounds better than it ever has in my memory. *Walter musiziert.* And that is a pleasure for those who like music with their concerts.

January 31, 1941

Diminishing Artistic Returns

BOSTON SYMPHONY ORCHESTRA, Serge Koussevitzky, conductor.

SYMPHONIE FANTASTIQUE	BERLIOZ
MATHIS DER MALER	HINDEMITH

THERE is a point in the perfection of artistic skills beyond which further progress is without artistic value. The surface becomes so shiny that nothing else can be perceived. The Boston Symphony

Orchestra has been dangerously close to that point for several years now; and if last night's concert in Carnegie Hall is typical of the orchestra's present work, one may well judge that the point of optimum precision has now been passed.

Matters of musical understanding, of stylistic penetration, and of interpretative warmth all aside — for these constitute the inner substance of music — its outer substance, sound, is wholly a matter of precision. Precisions of attack, of pitch, of color, of phrasing, of force, of blending constitute the musical amenities. Ultimate perfection in any of them is unattainable, but a reasonable degree of accuracy makes it possible for the meaning of music to be transmitted. Overmeticulousness about any of them will more often than not defeat this end.

One has heard string quartets play so carefully for beauty of tone that all the attacks became tenuous and the rhythm got lost. One has observed them so preoccupied about simultaneity of attack that the repeated split second in which the players look at one another before beginning each phrase ends by destroying the music's line. One has heard all the amenities sacrificed for a relentless rhythm or a climactic effect; and on the whole this procedure is probably less injurious to musical communication than the more delicate violences.

Some of the precisions observed by the Boston Symphony Orchestra last night were good for the music and some were not. In both the Berlioz *Symphonie Fantastique* and the Hindemith *Mathis der Maler* the instrumental colors, the mixtures and shades of sound, were more delicately differentiated and more expressively exact than this listener has ever heard them before. But their exactitude was achieved at the price of such watchfulness that both pieces seemed lacking in coherence and in continuity. In both of them, for example, Mr. Koussevitzky took such long breaths between phrases that one forgot there was supposed to be any sequence among these.

This wide spacing of phrases, plus the use of tempos rather slower than the standard French ones, dragged the Berlioz work out a good ten minutes longer than it is accustomed to last. (Forty-six minutes is the average timing of it; fifty minutes is a long version. Koussevitzky took an hour.) The first three movements seemed interminable. I did not time the Hindemith work, but it seemed slow, gasping, and overemphatic. All this was the result of too much care about phrase attacks and instrumental blending.

The attacks and the blending were incredibly precise. But the beautiful and spicy sounds we heard were less a performance *of* music by Berlioz and Hindemith than they were a performance *by* the Boston Symphony Orchestra.

February 10, 1944

The Personality of Three Orchestras

ORCHESTRAS are not wholly the product of their conductors. Their conductors train them and put them through their paces in public. But the conductor is one personality, and the orchestra is another (in private life a hundred others). A good orchestral concert is really more a duet than a domination.

Our three great Eastern ensembles, for instance — the Philadelphia, the Boston, and the New York Philharmonic — are as different from one another as the cities that created them and that forged them slowly into the image of each city's intellectual ideals. Conductors from outside have been had in to aid this formation, and a few of these have left traces of their own taste on that of the cities they have worked for. But chiefly their function has been to care for a precious musical organism, to watch over it, to perfect it in the observance of the musical amenities, and to allow it to mature according to its own nature and in accordance with its community's particular temperament. The conductor is never a static participant in such a process. He matures, too, in harmony with the community if he stays a reasonable length of time, is nourished and formed by local ideals, becomes a part of the thing to which he has contributed his special abilities.

Serge Koussevitzky and Eugene Ormandy are cases in point of my thesis. They have been ripened and refined by their association with the Boston and the Philadelphia orchestras in a way that was not predictable at all during their previous careers. It was obvious always that both would go far, but it was not indicated to prophecy that Koussevitzky, the temperamental Slav, would become a master of orchestral understatement or that Ormandy, the boyish and straightforward central European, would become a sort of specialist of delicately equilibrated orchestral sensuality. These developments, I am sure, are as legitimately creditable to environmental influence as to any previously manifested characteristics. Contact with orchestras of powerful temperament and specific orientation, as well as responsibility to cities of ancient and irreducible character — Boston, the intellectually elegant and urbane; Philadelphia, where everything, even intellectual achievement and moral pride, turns into a luxury, into a sort of sensuous awareness of social differences — contact, conflict, and collaboration between their strong European and the even stronger local traditions has given to these conductors their quality of being both the creature and the guiding hand of their own orchestras.

It is surprising (and most pleasant) to observe how two orchestras as accomplished as these can differ so completely in the kind of sounds they make. Boston makes thin sounds, like the Paris orchestras, thin and utterly precise, like golden wire and bright enamel. Nothing ever happens that isn't clear. No matter what the piece, no matter how inspired or how mistaken the conductor's understanding of it, the Boston execution is always transparent. So perfectly turned out is any of its executions that, whether becoming to the work or not, it has a way of separating itself from it. It neither conceals the work nor presents it; it walks down the street beside it, rather, very much as a piece of consummate dressmaking will sometimes do with the lady who thinks she is wearing it.

The Philadelphia sonorities are less transparent, and the tonal balance is less stable. Because the sounds that make it up are all rounder and deeper and more human. They breathe; they seem almost to have sentience. They have a tactile quality, too, like a skin you might touch; yet they are never heavy nor hot. They are warm and moist and alive compared to Boston's Swiss-watch-like mechanism. As a price of this vibrancy, however, the Philadelphia Orchestra is not always easy to conduct. It is probably the most sensitive orchestra in the world. The leader can get a fortissimo out of it by lifting a finger, and he can upset the whole balance of it by any nervousness. Boston is tougher, more independent. No matter how the conductor feels or what mistakes he may make, the orchestra always plays correctly, saves its own face and his. Philadelphia is less objective, less rigidly mannered. But at its best it gives a more touching performance, achieves a more intimate contact with its audience. Boston, for all its glacial perfection, has no intimacy at all. No matter where one sits, the music seems very far away.

Our Philharmonic is a horse of another color and one that has had far too many riders. It has been whipped and spurred for forty years by guest conductors and by famous virtuosos with small sense of responsibility about the orchestra's future or about its relation to our community's culture. It has become erratic, temperamental, undependable, and in every way difficult to handle. The sound of it has of late years been more like an industrial blast than like a musical communication. By moments there has been lovely work, but such moments have had an air of being accidental, the result of one day's well-being in the life of a neurotic. When the Philharmonic has been good it has sometimes been very good, but when it has been bad it has as often gone clean out of bounds.

Mr. Rodzinski has undertaken to heal its neuroses. At least we presume that is what he has undertaken. Because improvement is noticeable already in tonal transparency, and a faint blush seems to be appearing on the surface of the string sounds. Rhythmic co-ordination, too, though far from normal, is definitely ameliorated. It is to be hoped sincerely that progress will continue. But let no one imagine that forty years of ill-treatment are going to be wiped out in a season. The Philharmonic will have to be retrained from the ground up, schooled for dependability, and accustomed to being able to count on its conductor. Under a steady and responsible hand it should in time develop into a team worthy of its magnificent personnel and of its nation-wide public. What specific virtues it may eventually develop are unpredictable. At present its faults, like those of any spoiled child or horse, are more easily definable than its qualities. But it would be surprising if an orchestra so carefully selected, functioning in a city so sophisticated musically as New York, did not, once convalescence from old ills is firmly established, manifest characteristics of specific originality.

October 17, 1943

CHIEFLY CONDUCTORS

Conducting Reviewed

EXCEPT for the regular visits of the Boston and the Philadelphia orchestras, New York has heard no outside symphonic ensembles this season. But we have heard conductors from everywhere. We have heard none of these (excepting Koussevitzky and Ormandy and possibly Barbirolli) under ideal conditions. By this I mean that they have mostly been heard conducting orchestras they had not selected or trained, orchestras that are not their orchestras. Under such circumstances the finer details of execution, if not absent altogether, are always lacking in the spontaneity that is a product of long association between the musicians and their leader. On the other hand, the leaders (and the musicians too) have all been heard under identical conditions, so that comparisons of musicianship and of style are more fairly based than usual. The Philharmonic and the City Symphony have been running what it is legitimate to consider as a kind of competition which, if it did not exhibit everybody at his best or anybody completely, did show them all playing the same game with the same equipment.

There is no question, I think, that with standard Philharmonic equipment Mr. Koussevitzky has produced the best all-around result of the year. His work and that of the orchestra sounded assured, sensible, eloquent, correct. No air of improvisation and no unexpected technical emergencies marred its musicality or interrupted its flow. It was calm and powerful and efficient and well bred. Its most impressive quality was its dependability. One knew from the beginning it was going to be all right, and it was. Buying a ticket to one of his concerts was like buying a ticket to a concert by Toscanini or buying a record by Beecham, a wholly calculable investment.

Everybody else who has led the Philharmonic this season has been, by comparison, a blind date. The great Stokowski, ordinarily a conductor of high technical finish, did some good work and some very bad. Rodzinski, of Cleveland, a most efficient workman on the whole, did brilliant renditions of Hindemith and of Berlioz; but having spent more time rehearsing one of these than was proportionately allowable, he gave an unprepared reading of Mendelssohn's *Midsummer Night's Dream* that was higglety-pigglety. Busch's work was neither musically nor technically quite up to big-time standards; and the same is true, I understand (I unfortunately missed his concerts), of Goossens's. Damrosch was variable in his readings, but he got the loveliest sound out of the Philharmonic I have ever heard anybody get. Mr. Barbirolli, the Philharmonic's titular conductor, was conducting his own orchestra and so not fairly admissible to the guest competition. His work was very much as it always is, competent but a little rough; and his musical conceptions were lacking in nobility.

The Mitropoulos concerts were wholly dependable technically. Musically they varied a good deal. Some of them were nervous and violent, others calm almost to the point of platitude. He played more of the important new music than any of the other leaders did, played it clearly and efficiently and for the most part convincingly. Of them all, his case remains the least decisive. He is a great workman, certainly. He is an interesting musician, certainly. The exact nature of his musical culture and personality remains, however, vague. He seems to be oversensitive, overweaning, overbrutal, overintelligent, underconfident, and wholly without ease. He is clearly a musician of class, nevertheless, and a coming man of some sort in the musical world.

The contrary from every point of view is Bruno Walter. Musically he is most dependable, though his effective range of repertory is small, being limited chiefly to the German romantics. His specialty is the late German romantics, Bruckner and Mahler, though his Schumann is equally fine and his Beethoven has juice. At one time he enjoyed considerable prestige for his conducting of Mozart, though his readings in this repertory have never been able to stand competition with Beecham's. Nevertheless, in the narrow field of his specialization Walter is a rich musical mind, a conductor whose work has breadth and depth and a certain grand sincerity. He is also a technician of high quality. Unfortunately, he is undependable technically. His concerts, even the best of them, are marred by a sloppiness of beat and a general indifference to shipshapeness of execution that tend to alienate those elements of the public that are not wholly absorbed by the music he is playing. At his best he is one of the great living interpreters of music. When not at his best, he is still an authentic musician and worth hearing. But the concentration of thought and energy that underlies his best work seems not always to be wholly at his command.

The City Symphony has worked under a great variety of leaders this year, and I have not been able to hear them all. The great ones, of course, have been Beecham and Reiner. The former is a flood, a volcano, an earthquake, and as unpredictable as any of these. The latter is as calculable as the stars and about as distant. It is too bad we didn't hear them both with the Philharmonic instead of several of the lesser musicians whom we did. But it was an invaluable privilege, of course, for the Mayor's boys to play under them. It is invaluable also to have two orchestras in New York completing each other's repertory and playing to somewhat different musical publics. The City Symphony has produced a great deal of new music and has been honored by the appearance of hitherto little-known soloists and conductors. Among the latter, all of whom I have not heard, Mr. Henri Pensis impressed me as being extraordinarily dependable both technically and musically, an artist of high intelligence and power. I fancy he, too, is some kind of coming man and that we shall be hearing more and more of him.

At orchestral concerts of less than heroic pretensions it is not fair to match conductors, because on these occasions the music itself is more the subject of everybody's interest than the executant style. But in a seasonal review of conducting one does remember, all the same, the excellent work of Stiedry and Szell at the New Friends of Music, the liveliness of Saidenberg with his Little Symphony and of Farbman with his so-called "Symphonietta," the thoroughly intelligent programing of new music by Miss Petrides at the concerts of her "Orchestrette Classique," and the elegant renditions of classic small scores by Adolf Busch and by the French flutist René Le Roy. All these one is thankful for, all these and Alfred Wallenstein, too, who plays reams of fine music, new and old, over the radio and plays it admirably.

The season's finest orchestral playing, as a whole, has been done by the Boston Symphony. The most satisfactory renditions I have heard of modern pieces were Mitropoulos's readings of Aaron Copland's *Statements* and of Hindemith's Symphony No. 1

with the Philharmonic. The most revelatory of an older work I should say was Beecham's rendering of Haydn's Ninety-ninth at a concert of the Philadelphia Orchestra, though his playing of the Berlioz "Chasse Royale" from *The Trojans in Carthage* at a concert of the City Symphony will run his Haydn a close second for vigor and finesse and sheer musical grandeur.

The best single conducting job I heard at the Metropolitan Opera this winter was Beecham's *Faust*. The best dramatic conducting I have heard outside the Met was Smallens's *Porgy and Bess*, though Fritz Busch's *Macbeth* at the New Opera Company merits a memento. For these and all similar blessings may we ever remain duly thankful.

April 19, 1942

Pipe-Organ Obsession

PHILADELPHIA ORCHESTRA, *Leopold Stokowski*, conductor.

OVERTURE TO LEONORE, No. 3	BEETHOVEN
VARIATIONS ON A THEME BY HAYDN	BRAHMS
SIEGFRIED'S DEATH, from GÖTTERDÄMMERUNG	WAGNER
SYMPHONY No. 6	SHOSTAKOVICH

(First time in New York)

IT becomes increasingly clear to this listener that Leopold Stokowski's concept of orchestral music is derived from organ-playing. He cares nothing for the spontaneous collaboration that is the joy of ensemble players, the kind of perfect concord that swingsters call being "in the groove" and that French instrumentalists refer to as "the little blue flame." He treats his men as if they were 110 stops of a concert organ, each complete with swell-box, all voiced for solo use and mutually adjusted for producing balanced chords of any timbre at any degree of loudness or softness.

His latest seating arrangement is an adaptation to orchestral uses of pipe-organ antiphony. He long ago did away with the classical symphonic antiphony of first violins on one side against seconds on the other, through both of which pierce succeeding layers of supporting woodwind, brass, and percussion. He has his musicians arranged now with all the strings massed at back center as if these were a single homogeneous body of foundation tone, like Great Organ diapasons, with woodwinds out in front, like a Choir Organ or *positif*, and with the brasses at the right and left downstage corners, like the heavy solo reeds of a French organ, the horns playing antiphonally on one side against the trumpets and trombones on the other.

This massive acoustico-architectural layout established, he proceeds to play on the whole thing with his bare fingers as if it were a solo instrument. Nothing is left to the musicians' personal taste or feeling. He even went so far last night as to mold Mr. Kincaid's flute passages by hand, an insulting procedure toward an artist of Mr. Kincaid's stature, but a necessary procedure for producing the kind of one-man musical performance that Mr. Stokowski has in mind.

He carries his pipe-organ obsession to the extent of imitating organ rhythm, even. Now the organ, a mechanical wind instrument, knows no lilt or swing. It executes an even scale and an evenly progressive crescendo or diminuendo. It can play *sforzando* and *fortepiano*, but its accent knows no beat. Its rhythm is entirely quantitative, a question of long and short note-values, never of beat-stresses varied within the measure.

To have made Brahms's Haydn Variations, with their Viennese lilt and only occasional passage of non-accentual music that sets off by contrast their otherwise steadily swinging rhythm, into something that sounded like nothing so much as a skillful organ transcription of these same Variations is a triumph of will-power as well as of conductorial skill. The thoroughness and clarity of the technical procedures by which this deformation was operated make any questioning of its æsthetic value seem like quibbling, since, as always with Stokowski, the means employed, no matter what æsthetic end is achieved by them, are a contribution to orchestral technique.

It is just as well that he chose for his technical exhibition last night music that could take it. Beethoven's *Leonora* No. 3, Brahms's Haydn Variations, and Siegfried's Death Music from *Die Götterdämmerung* are all fool-proof and virtuoso-proof. No matter how you play them, they sound.

Shostakovich's Sixth Symphony, like all the later works of that gifted and facile composer, is pretty hard to conceal, too. It is clear, obvious, effective, old-fashioned. It is not, perhaps, as successfully pulled off as his First and Fifth. Its allegiance seems to be divided between a romanticized, and hence attenuated, neo-classicism and a full-blooded Muscovite orientalism à la Borodin. Each movement begins with a gesture of goodwill toward the lately reputable International Style and goes off as quickly as possible into the atmospheric market-place-and-landscape painting that Russians have always loved so enthusiastically. It is a pleasant piece and not without a certain concentration at moments. If it were signed by an American composer, say Harl McDonald or Walter Piston, it would be classifiable as good salable academicism.

December 4, 1940

Impeccable Musical Tailoring

BOSTON SYMPHONY ORCHESTRA, *Serge Koussevitzky*, conductor, with *Alexander Borovsky*, pianist.

SYMPHONY IN D MAJOR, "Haffner" (K. 385)	MOZART
CONCERTO GROSSO for chamber orchestra	BOHUSLAV MARTINŮ
(First time in New York; piano parts played by	
J. M. Sanromá and *Bernard Zighera*)·	
PIANO CONCERTO NO. 1, IN B-FLAT MINOR	TCHAIKOVSKY
Mr. Borovsky	
OVERTURE, "1812"	TCHAIKOVSKY

ONE has known New York men who always had their suits made in Boston and elderly ladies from various parts of the Eastern seaboard who would never go anywhere else for a hat. Certainly we do not produce here or import at present from any other provincial center such perfect musical tailoring as that which the Boston Symphony Orchestra exhibits for us in Carnegie Hall ten times a season and which was again displayed yesterday afternoon.

The reasons for this superiority are many, not the least of them being more ample rehearsal time per program than most other orchestras can afford. Another is Mr. Koussevitzky's long period of incumbency as conductor and drill-master of the outfit. A third is, no doubt, Boston itself, a city whose intellectual tradition is both robust and elegant. Boston is, indeed, in no small degree responsible for what Koussevitzky is today. Always a brilliant and a powerful leader, he has grown mellower there and stronger. Boston has refined his crudities of style and deepened his musical culture. It has steadied a man once flashy and erratic and made of him a true musical master.

It is easy to disagree with anybody's musical interpretations, but rarely can one disagree with an artist on such clear grounds as one can with the good Doctor. This is where musical tailoring and the Boston manner become valuable beyond their mere intrinsic charm. Toscanini's musical workmanship is always of a high order. But it is opaque; one can't easily hear pieces through it. Koussevitzky's is clarity itself, the presentation of it to the audience authoritative but gentlemanly. No matter how wrong one may think him about any given musical rendition, there always seems to be room for his conception and for one's own in the same concert hall.

There is some free mental space, also, between the way he thinks a piece should be played and the Boston Orchestra's rendition. This is due, curiously enough, to the exactitude with which the orchestra renders his conception plus an observance on both his and its part of all the musical amenities. Forceful expression is never expected (at least, the oversteppings in this respect are rare) to justify vulgar tone from the brass, messy fiddle-playing, incorrect phrasing, or false tonal equilibrium. This care for what I call the musical amenities makes the Boston Orchestra very easy to listen to, even when one doesn't care much for the work one is hearing; and it makes it impossible to get angry with its leader for not being invariably of the same mind as oneself about interpretative matters.

Yesterday the Mozart was not at all my kind of Mozart; but it was lovely, all the same. It was streamlined, grave, distant. The minuet, as usual, was fast. The finale was a marvel of delicate precision in the string work. The Tchaikovsky B-flat minor (or "Juke-Box") Piano Concerto was balanced and lucid, and the orchestra actually sounded as if it were accompanying a pianoforte instead of spanking it. Mr. Borovsky, the soloist, played well enough, at least without *schmalz,* though his two hands did not always sound together. The *1812* Overture was ripsnorting and good fun. The brass was triumphantly sonorous at the end without sounding coarse. Bravos followed.

The novelty was Bohuslav Martinů's Concerto Grosso for

chamber orchestra, a fine and vigorous work by a fine and vigorous composer. Mr. Martinů is a worthy heir to the tradition that produced Dvořák and Smetana. His music is Czechish in melodic character, internationalist and neo-classic in technique. His instrumentation is fresh in sound, the usage he makes of a piano being most original and successful. The superbly rhythmic and resonant piano-playing of Messrs. Sanromá and Zighera was, I am sure, responsible in no small way for the fine effect of it all. From the spontaneous burst of applause which followed the last chord it seemed probable that Mr. Martinů may have fathered a sturdy little repertory piece. In any case he is the author of a most agreeable one.

January 11, 1942

Britain Wins

NEW YORK CITY SYMPHONY ORCHESTRA, *Sir Thomas Beecham,* conductor; concert in series presented by Mayor LaGuardia and the New York City WPA Music Project.

THE FAITHFUL SHEPHERD, suite for orchestra   HANDEL-BEECHAM
SYMPHONY NO. 31, IN D MAJOR ("Paris")   MOZART
SYMPHONY NO. 7, IN C MAJOR   SIBELIUS
FRANCESCA DA RIMINI, FANTASY AFTER DANTE   TCHAIKOVSKY

THE CONCERT that Beecham conducted last night with the New York City Symphony Orchestra proved several interesting things. It proved first of all the dictum that there are no bad orchestras, only bad conductors. No orchestra has played better this season in New York City, by any imaginable standards, than Mayor La Guardia's WPA boys played for Sir Thomas. The program was a difficult one, too, and all of it new to the ensemble. It proved also that Beecham is an A-1 man of music as well as an A-1 man of the orchestra. Such lyric grace in the interpretation of Handel and such majestic proportions in the reading of Mozart are not available, to my knowledge, in the work of any other living conductor. His excellence in the eighteenth-century repertory, indeed, is known and everywhere recognized. That he should be equally convincing in Sibelius and Tchaikovsky is news to these parts.

He won his audience with the first phrases of the Handel. It is a fine piece, in every way gracious and lovely; and the Beecham orchestration of it is neat, tasteful, and far from timid.

The Mozart "Paris" Symphony, No. 31, in D major, is a noble work. Particularly noticeable in the execution of it, as in that of the Handel, were the silken sonority of the strings and their precision. Also the utterly convincing nature of the tempos. I have long wondered why Beecham's Mozart tempos were always so satisfactory. I think this is due to his preoccupation with the Grand Line of his interpretations. Whenever an artist has a reasoned conception of any musical work as a unit unrolling itself in time, rather than as a series of more or less interesting moments, the tempos naturally fall into place. It also becomes possible to refine and elaborate the detail to quite a high degree when that, too, is all in its place as a part of the Grand Line.

Pleasing indeed were the breadth and sustained continuity of the Mozart slow movement. Conductors are likely to keep these movements low in dynamics and to get moony over them. Either that or to go kittenish and break their continuity into fragments. The current conception of a Mozart andante is that of a slice of thin sugary ham, spiced up by a minuet, between two slabs of some more sustaining musical fare. Beecham played last night's slow movement as if it were the second act of a three-act opera, the one upon which the whole work turns.

A Sibelius expert informed me he had never heard the Seventh Symphony played so well. I have never heard Tchaikovsky's *Francesca da Rimini* played so well. It was eloquent and sweeping and tender. Its pianissimos and its loud work were both superior to what we currently hear from even the best orchestras. Nothing was overstated; nothing was unclear or at any time tonally vulgar.

I was not converted into a Sibelius-lover by rehearing after many years the Seventh Symphony. Beside Tchaikovsky, from whom its whole æsthetic and most of its technique are derived, it sounded pretty amateurish. I do not believe for a moment that its gray and dirty-brown orchestral coloring is a depiction of either the Finnish soul or the Finnish landscape. The Finns I have known have all been brighter and more striking in character, and the countryside of that athletic people has always been depicted to us through art and photography as blazing with clear color and with sunshine. I think Sibelius just orchestrates badly.

However that may be, we have reason to be proud of our New
York City Symphony Orchestra. And though Sibelius may be a
more gifted composer than I think he is, two certainties remain
after last night's triumphal success. One is that nobody has to take
seriously any longer the excuses of the Philharmonic for not playing any better than it currently does. Because if the WPA can
play like that, the Philharmonic can too. The other certainty is that
in sending us Sir Thomas Beecham as a musical ambassador,
Britain has certainly delivered the goods.

April 7, 1941

More Beecham

NEW YORK CITY SYMPHONY ORCHESTRA, *Sir Thomas Beecham,*
conductor, presented by Mayor LaGuardia and the New York City
WPA Music Project.

Symphony No. 102, in B-flat major	Haydn
Symphony No. 36, in C major ("Linz")	Mozart
Paris, Impressions of a Great City	Delius
Symphonic Variations	Dvořák

The second Beecham concert of the New York City Symphony
was a triumph like the first. The house was full and loved it.
Sir Thomas was in form and looked as if he were loving it. The
orchestra played as if they loved both him and music.

Beecham alone of the great conductors, as Nikisch did before
him, collaborates with an orchestra rather than conquers it. As a
result his orchestra always sounds like an ensemble of skilled musicians rather than like a Panzer division on the march. This particular attitude toward music-making places him at once as the
survivor of a vanished epoch and the hope of the next. He is the
obvious rallying-point for all those musicians, young and old, who
have had enough of musical Cæsarism.

Not that he is lacking in authority or discipline. He has more
of both than most. But these are imposed and accepted, as such
things can only be imposed and accepted in the Republic of Art,
by the exercise of friendliness and human consideration. As a re-

sult of this courteous and pleasant manner, he achieves a spontaneity of collaboration that is in every musical way superior to the
machine finish that makes the work of less humanely tempered
men sound dead and horrid.

Noticeable in both his concerts this-season has been the consistent musicality of his fortissimos. He can make the WPA boys play
as softly and as loud as the musicians do in any other orchestra.
But one is never conscious of any forcing of the sonority. Koussevitzky often forces his strings beyond the point of maximum resonance. Mitropoulos makes all the instruments sound powerful but
husky. Walter is not infrequently sloppy, inexcusably sloppy about
his tuttis. Toscanini seems not to care what kind of noise comes
out of his musicians' efforts, provided there is a certain equilibrium
of one kind of sound against another and provided the whole
machine is kept rolling. Stokowski, of course, sacrifices everything
to the production of an organlike sostenuto dominated by overplayed brasses. Beecham, on the other hand, lets the strings domi-
nate the ensemble, keeps them in command of tonal coloration,
as is undoubtedly the correct tradition of orchestral execution, as
it is of orchestral writing; and yet he seems to have no difficulty
about building or sustaining majestic fortissimos in which the
strings sound full and easy and unforced.

In contrast to the subtlety and flexibility of his string work at
all dynamic levels, he keeps his woodwinds cool and neatly precise, in the French taste. His brasses, too, are kept quietly rich,
never allowed to scream. And he has a nice sense of dosage, spicy
but not obtrusive, in dealing with the percussion section.

Last week I commented on the excellence of his musical interpretations both of eighteenth-century and of nineteenth-century
repertory. This was again manifest last night in the brilliance and
wit of his Haydn, in the majesty and mystery of his Mozart. (A
Bostonian composer of my acquaintance was not entirely happy
about the leisurely pace of both minuets.) The Delius piece last
night was made to sound like the almost first-class impressionism
it is. And the Dvořák came off as the Czechish charm-number that
composer would write so prettily and so infallibly.

All this I mention simply for the record. I should like to impress on my readers that Beecham's interpretative excellence is
the achievement of no mere gifted musical amateur. It is the expression not only of a sound musical culture but of a skilled
orchestral technique as well. Sir Thomas makes music sound con-

vincing because he is convinced of how it should sound. He succeeds finally, however, not only by being able to imagine the result, but by being able to convince a hundred musicians that nothing is needed for its achievement beyond intelligent goodwill and the exercise of their instrumental skill within that range of sonorities traditionally considered legitimate and beautiful.

April 14, 1941

Showy Conducting

PHILHARMONIC–SYMPHONY ORCHESTRA, *Dmitri Mitropoulos,* guest conductor.

OVERTURE TO LEONORE, No. 2	BEETHOVEN
SYMPHONY No. 4, IN B-FLAT MAJOR	BEETHOVEN
SINFONIA DOMESTICA	R. STRAUSS

IT was a big show, everybody showing off but Beethoven. Mr. Mitropoulos was showing how well he could make unpopular Beethoven sound and how popular he could make unpopular Strauss. Strauss was showing what he could do with a large orchestra and the most humdrum of subjects. The Philharmonic musicians were showing Mr. Mitropoulos and the audience how elaborately well they can play, if asked. The audience itself was definitely on the brilliant side.

Beethoven's Overture to *Leonore,* No. 2, was conducted by Mr. Mitropoulos with a firm mastery of what he wanted. What he mostly wanted was spectacular contrasts in the Verdi manner of *ppppp* versus *fffff.* The pauses were exaggerated, too. The effect on this listener was about what it would be if Orson Welles were to apply his invasion-from-Mars technique to the recounting of a bedtime story as familiar as "Little Red Riding Hood" or "The Three Bears." The contrary applies to the interpretation of the same composer's Fourth Symphony, an ungrateful work for the most part, which was turned into, especially at the end, quite exciting entertainment.

Strauss's *Sinfonia Domestica* is second only to his *Alpine Symphony* in unpopularity. It is very long and very elaborate, and it rather too closely resembles its subject. Twenty-five or thirty years ago there used to be found occasionally in business offices a framed motto that read: "Life is just one damn thing after another." Mr. Strauss's musical picture of an average day in his own family is rather like that. It goes on and on without anything happening musically that is in any way memorable.

Mr. Mitropoulos's conducting of it was in every way sensational. He gave it continuity; and he pulled out of his men the most sensational sonorities in order to give it, if possible, vividness. He worked very hard and succeeded beyond all imaginable success. Everybody was so worked up by the end of it that the crying of "Hurrah!" and "Bravo!" was only natural, to let off one's steam. My neighbor remarked as the conductor took many bows: "My! He must be tired."

We were all tired, I think. We all felt we had been through a work-out of some kind. We had been put through our paces as audience very much as the Philharmonic had been put through its technical gamut.

It is not possible to chalk up a complete score for any conductor on one concert. Mr. Mitropoulos is obviously a great orchestral technician. His musical taste, as expressed in last night's program, seems neither fresh nor particularly sound. Admitted that he made a dull Strauss work interesting to listen to and a dullish Beethoven symphony vaguely exciting. He didn't make either of them sound like better or worse music than they are. He merely lifted them out of their usual semi-oblivion and used them as what the theatrical world calls "vehicles." It was interesting to hear what he could do *with* the Strauss, less interesting to hear what he did *to* the Beethoven.

The program was like certain parties one has been to. The right names were there, but all the wrong people. Nevertheless, a really good time was had. Mr. Mitropoulos conducts the wrong pieces magnificently, shows them a whale of a time. This listener had a whale of a time, too. Maybe that is the right way to conduct second-class works. It will be interesting to hear what he does *with* or *to* Mozart, Schubert, Debussy.

December 20, 1940

The Maestro

NBC SYMPHONY ORCHESTRA, *Arturo Toscanini,* conductor.

OVERTURE TO THE MAGIC FLUTE	MOZART
SYMPHONY NO. 104, D MAJOR	HAYDN
SYMPHONY NO. 8, F MAJOR	BEETHOVEN

ARTURO TOSCANINI conducted his first concert of the winter yesterday afternoon in the NBC's Studio 8-H. The program was classical, and the Maestro was in good form. If the orchestra didn't sound in any choir — strings, woods, or brasses — quite as beautiful tonally as one might have wished, that is probably no fault of his. It is doubtful whether real symphonic mellowness is obtainable in that hall, anyway, which is too wide and too shallow to have an acoustic focus. Everything sounds a little raucous there except the brass instruments, and they sometimes hardly sound at all.

There is no other living conductor so unfailingly attentive as Toscanini to the music he conducts. His mind never wanders, never runs ahead of the measure or lags behind it. I fancy the quality of his own attention is in no small way responsible for the absorption with which audiences listen to him. And I think it is responsible, too, for the equalized surface tension, that solid, expensive, luxury-product feel that is one of the most striking characteristics of his performance. Whether he goes deep into the substance of a work or, in one man's opinion, misses its sense completely, he always builds its architecture soundly and fits in the detail so smoothly that the piece comes out all streamlined, like a plywood bomber or a racing yacht.

It is not merely that his tempos are all a shade fast, like those of many another elderly musician (Saint-Saëns used to play the piano so fast the ear could scarcely follow). There is an element in his beat, too, that tends to make the music go round and round. He marks the meter so clearly that every down-beat takes on a slight stress — not a pulsation or lilt, as in Viennese waltzes, but a tiny, tiny dry accent, like the click of a well-running machine. This mechanical purring both gives to his readings a great rhythmic clarity and assures the listener that all is under control. It is

also, nevertheless, a little bit lulling. One gets hypnotized by the
smooth-working mechanics of the execution and forgets to listen
to the music as a human communication.

I do not think that any down-beat accentuation was presup-
posed by the classical symphonists — by Haydn, Mozart or Beethoven. When they wanted stresses they always wrote them in,
even on a down-beat. I think they made their meters clear through
the contours and quantities of their musical drawing and that
their accentuation patterns derive their great expressive (and
surprise) value from their complete independence of the basic
meter. If I am right about this, if Toscanini's addition of regular
measure stresses, however small these may be, to an already indicated pattern of irregular, non-metrical stresses in classical symphonies is uncanonical, it is also a fault.

It confounds accent with meter, instead of setting meter against
accent. It simplifies orchestral conducting and rather oversimpli-
fies the exposition of a piece. It smooths down the detail and trivi-
alizes it, sacrifices personal expression to grandeur of architectural effect. This is the characteristic procedure of the best Italian
opera conductors, and it is electrifying in the theater. I do not believe, however, that it gives as vivid a rendering of classical Viennese symphonies as a clear dissociation in every measure of meter
versus accent does.

November 1, 1943

Absolute Theater

PHILHARMONIC–SYMPHONY ORCHESTRA, *Arturo Toscanini*
conducting; fifth program of the Beethoven Festival yesterday afternoon with *Ania Dorfmann,* pianist; *Mishel Piastro,* violinist, and *Joseph
Schuster,* cellist, as soloists in the following program of BEETHOVEN's
music.

OVERTURE TO FIDELIO, IN E MAJOR, OP. 72
CONCERTO FOR PIANO, VIOLIN, CELLO, AND ORCHESTRA IN C MAJOR, OP. 72
SYMPHONY IN A MAJOR, No. 7, OP. 92

YESTERDAY afternoon's Toscanini concert at Carnegie Hall, the
fifth of his Beethoven series, revived (temporarily, I imagine)
two rarely heard works, the *Fidelio* Overture and the Triple Con-

certo for violin, cello and piano. It also reinvigorated (rather un-
duly, I thought) the well-known Seventh Symphony. And it gave
further opportunity for studying the approach of the most celebrated conductor in the world to the music of the greatest of all
symphonic composers. A Beethoven cycle is always profoundly
satisfactory, no matter who conducts it. A Toscanini concert is
always stimulating to an audience, no matter what the program
is. That public enthusiasm about the present series should run
high is not surprising. That I am unable to share it wholeheart-
edly is a matter of sincere regret to me.

The Triple Concerto is a work that Beethoven experts have
never much admired. Its tunes are long and lovely; but, being a
little too long and lovely, they proved difficult for him to develop.
Their working out is a shade laborious. Also the concerted solo
instruments do not produce a sound which opposes itself advan-
tageously to that of the orchestra. They sound poor, like a hotel
trio, rather than rich, as a single instrument does, or as a group
can that is chosen for its intrinsic harmoniousness, when contrasted
to the more massive but less brilliant sound of an orchestral tutti.
The artists did their best yesterday to produce an ensemble, but
all three sounded better separately than together. Miss Dorfmann
and Mr. Schuster played with fine tone, fine rhythm, and full
authority. Mr. Piastro's work was less stable, his tone shifting
between one of great sweetness and one of a certain acidity, the
latter quality being due, I think, to an occasional fault of pitch.

The Seventh Symphony was not so much the full Seventh
Symphony as a highly dramatized outline or syllabus of the
Seventh Symphony. Its main melodic material, its harmonic
progress, and especially the dynamic pattern, the chiaroscuro of
it, were wholly clear. Unfortunately many of the rapid string
passages were not audible in detail. This skimping of the fast
work was probably unavoidable at the given speed, but it is not
usually considered the best musical style to play non-theatrical
works at a speed at which their detail cannot be executed satisfactorily by the group performing them.

The first movement was the only one that seemed comfortable
in its tempo, and that got into some trouble about rhythm along
in the middle. It got into trouble at the same place it nearly always gets into trouble, namely, about half-way through, where
more care is required than was expended yesterday if the six-eight
time is to be prevented from turning itself into two-four. The sec-

ond movement came out as a barcarolle, the third and fourth rather in tarantella vein. In none of them was there any sense of mystery to make the Beethoven fury seem interiorly dramatic rather than merely of the stage.

At all times the effect, save for surface roughnesses, was certainly that desired by the conductor. No conductor I know of seems to have in his inner ear so clear an auditory image of a piece as Toscanini does. His psychological power over his executant musicians and over his audience is due, no doubt, to the preciseness with which he knows what he wants out of both. The musical value of what he wants varies, as it does with any conductor, from work to work and even from concert to concert. What varies surprisingly little is the efficacy of his personal domination of both orchestra and public. And what is most surprising of all is that his personal assertion, unlike that of his more romantic or poetic rivals, is very little a thing of personalized emotion. It is a kind of Latin clarity about the main lines of tonal architecture, especially the dynamic ones, and a ruthless insistence that the piece be accepted in terms of these. Music is never at ease under his whip, and it rarely sings. But its shape and progress are always wholly clear. And if his mastery of emphasis does not always convince one of his full comprehension of a composer's meaning, the theater-like build-up of the whole thing is both terrifyingly effective and wholly worthy of the applause it so automatically provokes.

May 2, 1942

The Toscanini Case

ARTURO TOSCANINI's musical personality is a unique one in the modern world. One has to go back to Mendelssohn to find its parallel. A reactionary in spirit, he has none the less revolutionized orchestral conducting by his radical simplification of its procedures. Almost wholly devoted to the playing of familiar classics, he has at the same time transformed these into an auditive image of twentieth-century America with such unconscious completeness that musicians and laymen all over the world have acclaimed his achievement without, I think, very much bothering to analyze it.

They were satisfied that it should be, for the most part, musically
acceptable and at all times exciting.

Excitement is of the essence in Toscanini's concept of musical
performance. But his is not the kind of excitement that has been
the specialty of the more emotional conductors of the last fifty
years. Theirs was a personal projection, a transformation through
each conductor's own mind of what the conductor considered to
be the composer's meaning. At its best this supposed a marriage
of historical and literary with musical culture. It was derived
from the conducting style of Richard Wagner; and its chief trans-
mitters to us have been the line that is von Bülow, Nikisch, and
Beecham. For musicians of this tradition every piece is a different
piece, every author and epoch another case for stylistic differentiation and for special understanding. When they miss, they miss;
but when they pull it off, they evoke for us a series of new worlds,
each of these verifiable by our whole knowledge of the past, as
well as by our instinctive sense of musical meaning. Theirs is the
humane cultural tradition. And if their interpretations have sometimes been accompanied by no small amount of personal idiosyn-
crasy and a febrile display of nerves, that, too, is a traditional con-
comitant of the sort of trancelike intensity that is necessary for the
projection of any concept that is a product equally of learning and
of inspiration.

Toscanini's conducting style, like that of Mendelssohn (if
Wagner is to be believed about the latter), is very little dependent on literary culture and historical knowledge. It is disembodied
music and disembodied theater. It opens few vistas to the understanding of men and epochs; it produces a temporary, but intense,
condition of purely auditory excitement. The Maestro is a man
of music, nothing else. Being also a man of (in his formative
years) predominantly theatrical experience, he reads all music
in terms of its possible audience effect. The absence of poetical
allusions and of historical references in his interpretations is significant, I think, of a certain disdain for the general culture of his
individual listeners. In any case, whatever he may have inherited
of nineteenth-century respect for individualistic culture was sacrificed many years ago to an emphasizing of those musical aspects
that have a direct effect on everybody. It is extraordinary how
little musicians discuss among themselves Toscanini's rightness or
wrongness about matters of speed and rhythm and the tonal
amenities. Like any other musician, he is frequently apt about

these and as frequently in error. What seems to be more important than all that is his unvarying ability to put over a piece. Like
Mendelssohn, he quite shamelessly whips up the tempo and sacrifices clarity and ignores a basic rhythm, just making the music,
like his baton, go round and round, if he finds his audience's attention tending to waver. No piece has to mean anything specific;
every piece has to provoke from its hearers a spontaneous vote of
acceptance. This is what I call the "wow technique."

Now, what are we accepting when we applaud a Toscanini
rendition? Not personal poetry, certainly; nor any historical evocation; nor a literal and academic reading of a classic score. I think
it is his power of abstraction we are acclaiming, the abstraction
of a piece's essential outline. If he has reduced conducting motions
to their essential outline, too, that is not mere elegance on his part,
nor ostentation either; it is a systematic throwing away of all refinements that might interfere with his schematic rendition. His
whole accent is on the structure of a piece. Its thematic materials
are the building blocks with which that structure is erected. Expression and ornamentation are details to be kept in place. Unity,
coherence, and emphasis are the qualities that must be brought
out.

Both theatrical experience and bad eyesight are probably responsible for the Toscanini style. When one cannot depend on
reading a score in public, one must memorize everything. And
when one memorizes everything, one acquires a great awareness
of music's run-through. One runs it through in the mind constantly;
and one finds in that way a streamlined rendering that is wholly
independent of detail and even of specific significance, a disembodied version that is all shape and no texture. Later, in rehearsal,
one returns to the texture; and one takes care that it serve always
as neutral surfacing for the shape. But shape is what any piece is
always about that one has memorized through the eye and the
inner ear. Playing a piece for shape and run-through gives (if the
piece has any shape at all) the most exciting effect that can ever
be produced. It is the same procedure as that of directing a melodrama on the stage, character and dialogue being kept at all times
subsidiary to the effects of pure theater, to the building up in the
audience of a state of intense anxiety that is relieved only at the
end of the last act.

The radical simplification of interpretative problems that all
this entails has changed orchestral conducting from a matter of

culture and of its personal projection into something more like engineering. Young conductors don't bother much any more to feel music or to make their musicians feel it. They analyze it, concentrate in rehearsal on the essentials of its rhetoric, and let the expressive details fall where they may, counting on each man's skill and everybody's instinctive musicianship to take care of these eventually. Poetry and nobility of expression are left for the last, to be put in as with an eyedropper or laid on like icing, if there is time. All this is good, because it makes music less esoteric. It is crude because it makes understanding an incidental matter; but it is a useful procedure and one wholly characteristic of our land and century. About its auditory result I am less enthusiastic than many. I find Toscanini's work, for the most part, spiritually unenlightening, except when he plays Italian music. But that is only a personal experience; many musicians find otherwise. And those of us who like more differentiation, more poetry, and more thought in our music, who find his much advertised fidelity to the notes of musical scores to be grossly exaggerated, his equally advertised "perfection" to be more so, and both of these aims, even when achieved, to be of secondary importance, even we must admit, nevertheless, the reality of Toscanini's musicianship and achievements. For good or for ill, and most probably for good, orchestral conducting will never be the same again.

I say most probably for good, because it is noticeable already that lesser conductors analyze music better than they used to and that this simple extraction of a work's formal essence tends to facilitate rather than to obfuscate differentiations of style and expression in the conducting of men whose musical experience is more limited but whose general culture is more ample than Toscanini's. Many of his contemporaries and most of his famous predecessors have had more interesting minds. Almost none has been so gifted a natural musician and so strictly professional a showman. He has simplified the technique of the art by eliminating all the hangovers of Late Romantic emotionalism and by standardizing a basic technique of musical rendition that is applicable to any piece in the world, whether one understands its spirit or not. This may be treason to culture, or it may be merely a radical purging of culture's own fifth column. I fancy it includes a bit of both. In any case, I believe that the introduction of a new cultural understanding into orchestral rendition, as one observes this in the work of Smallens, for instance, and in that of most of the other good American conductors, is as directly traceable to Toscanini's having previously eliminated practically all cultural understanding from it as the means of their doing so have been facilitated by his radical simplifications of conducting procedure.

Toscanini's influence lies, so far, chiefly in America. Europe has its Furtwänglers and its Beechams and its great French conductors like Monteux and Münch. And it has no need of exchanging their interpretations or their working methods for anything so oversimplified as Toscanini's. The Romantic tradition has already transformed itself there into a modern tradition that is as rich and as complex and as generally satisfactory to the mind as the tradition of Wagner and Nikisch was. That tradition is too complex for us. We admire the work of the great European conductors, but we do not quite understand how it is done. A century of importing them has not revealed their secrets to our local boys. We watched Toscanini work for ten years at the Philharmonic; and now there are 30,000 symphony orchestras in the United States, practically all of them led by the local boys. He is the founding father of American conducting. Whether we like or not the way he interprets music (and I don't much, though many do), his place in our musical history is certainly an important one.

In any European sense, he is not a complete musician, as the late Karl Muck was, and perhaps not even a great technician, as Reiner is, for example. He is too completely self-taught to be wholly responsible to any Great Tradition. But he is a thoroughgoing professional, although self-taught; and he has shown our musicians how to be thoroughgoing professionals too, although self-taught. The value of this contribution to our musical life cannot be overestimated. Any influence Toscanini might possibly have on European musical life would be anti-cultural. His ruthless clearing away here, however, of Romantic weeds and unsuccessful implantations has made a space where conductors are already being grown locally. And a steady supply of good American conductors to the local market is the thing above all else needful right now to the public understanding and the autochthonous development of American musical composition.

May 17, 1942

COMPOSITIONS AND COMPOSERS

Bach Goes to Church

CANTATA SINGERS, *Arthur Mendel,* conductor; complete performance of JOHANN SEBASTIAN BACH's CHRISTMAS ORATORIO yesterday evening in two sessions at All Souls Church, Eightieth Street and Lexington Avenue, for the benefit of the Myra Hess Fund for British Musicians. Soloists: *Rose Dirman,* soprano; *Jean Bryan,* contralto; *Donald Dame,* tenor; *Seymour Matthen,* bass. Harpsichordist, *Ralph Kirkpatrick;* organist, *Heinz Arnold.*

THE CLOSER the performing conditions for Sebastian Bach's concerted music are approximated to those of early eighteenth-century provincial Germany the more that music sounds like twentieth-century American swing. The exactitude with which a minimum time unit is kept unaltered at all times, the persistence of this unit as one of exactly measured length rather than of pulsation, the omnipresence of the harpsichord's ping, like a brush on a cymbal, the constant employment of wiggly counterpoint and staccato bass, all make it a matter of preference between anachronisms whether one puts it that Bach has gone to town or that some of the more scholarly jitterbugs of the town have wandered into a church.

Last night's performance of the *Christmas Oratorio* was full of swing and gusto. The soloists, particularly the ladies, Miss Rose Dirman and Miss Jean Bryan, both of them possessors of lovely voices, sang their arias to the accompaniment of solo woodwinds as neatly and enthusiastically as if they were playing instrumental duets with Benny Goodman. The gentlemen sang the magnificently dramatic recitatives with clarity and dispatch. The chorus came in on the big numbers as if these were the gayest of contrapuntal merry-go-rounds, which indeed they are; the high trumpets played out of tune, as they must have in Leipzig at Bach's own Thomaskirche; and the inexorable rhythm of Mr. Ralph Kirkpatrick's harpsichord continuo sustained the whole with a vigor and a brightness rarely encountered these days.

It was Mr. Mendel's intention to reproduce as closely as possible the sonorities of what may be called the world premieres of the work, for the six Cantatas that it comprises were never executed under Bach in any one day, as these took place under the composer's direction more than two hundred years ago. Instrumentally the revival was highly credible, except that the Thomaskirche organ, still playable, is more frankly bright in sound than any modern instrument. The chorus of thirty-two voices, a number somewhat larger than Bach had available, sang with good rhythm and surprisingly clear German diction. But the fuzzy, fluty quality of Anglo-Saxon vocalization bears little resemblance to the harsh and sonorous brilliance of a Continental chorus. And when we remember that in Bach's choir, according to Albert Schweitzer, the treble parts were all sung by boys, whose voices are more penetrating, even, than those of women, it is terrifying to imagine the piercing noises that must have filled that stone-pillared and stone-walled auditorium with rejoicing.

Even without the resonance that must have been literally an earful for St. Thomas's congregation, the final chorus with three high trumpets tooting for dear life in the neighborhood of high D was as jolly a bit of Christmas cheer as has come your reviewer's way this Nativity. God rest you merry, gentlemen! Let nothing you dismay!

December 31, 1940

New Star Reveals Old

NEW YORK CITY SYMPHONY ORCHESTRA, *Reginald Stewart*, conductor; concert yesterday at 5:30 in Carnegie Hall, with *Luigi Silva*, cellist, as soloist.

ROMEO AND JULIET	TCHAIKOVSKY
CONCERTO IN D MAJOR FOR CELLO AND ORCHESTRA	BOCCHERINI
(First American performance in its original form)	
SYMPHONY No. 7, IN A MAJOR	BEETHOVEN

LUIGI BOCCHERINI was the greatest composer of all time for the violoncello. Not even old Sebastian Bach nor the French masters of the viola da gamba and the bastarda wrote so skillfully, so idiomatically, so brilliantly as he for the played-between-the-legs bowed instruments. He was also a symphonist of renown and a great composer by almost any standard of estimate.

It has been customary, when executing his cello concertos and his symphonies in modern orchestral circumstances, to amplify the orchestrations, to thicken them unmercifully, with the result that only the music's characteristic melodic and harmonic outlines remain, but none of those instrumental dispositions that are so brilliantly, so satisfyingly thin in his scores. Mr. Luigi Silva has had the wit and the sound musical sense to present the musical world with something that, if it is not completely Boccherini, is far nearer to its original than what we usually get.

He found the original score in the Library of Congress. From this he made an edition, now distributed by the New York Public Library, that is completely faithful to the original in all the string parts, the original being scored for cello solo and string orchestra. To these he has added, for performance in large halls, discreet reinforcements of the tuttis by two flutes, two oboes, two horns, and two bassoons, a normal symphonic ensemble of Boccherini's epoch. It is thus possible either to execute the concerto as chamber music, exactly according to the author's specifications, or to execute it in Carnegie Hall, as was done yesterday, with, I should say, less falsification than a literal reinforcing of the string parts by a too large number of players would have produced.

Yesterday's effect was one of delicacy and grandeur. The con-

certo is in every way lovely as music. Its execution, moreover, was
the only execution that this announcer has ever heard of a concerto for cello and orchestra in which the solo instrument seemed
to be properly balanced against its orchestral complement. Not
for nothing did Boccherini so carefully write no other cello parts
and virtually none even for the violas when the soloist plays. He
is accompanied by violins only, for the most part, these written
softly and divisi. The solo part lies high, as was Boccherini's taste;
and Mr. Silva's cadenzas (he played his own) carry the tessitura
to practically Himalayan heights by means of harmonics. The third
of these cadenzas, an imitation of hunting-horn harmonies, was
accompanied by two real horns in the most charming way imaginable.

November 3, 1941

The Gluck Case

THE JUILLIARD SCHOOL used to give modern operas. They did but
they don't any more, as the ditty hath it. Their latest production
was Gluck's *Iphigenia in Tauris,* a work that sometimes passes in
the modern world for the most classic of musical classics, but that
in its own day was considered a triumph of novelty and of fashion.
I have no quarrel with a pedagogical policy that eschews today's
modernism in favor of that of a century and a half back. I am all
for bringing up young on the ancient models of things, even though
this may imply glorification of the Agamemnon family. The young
take more things in their stride than we do maybe, anyway, including what Mr. John Peale Bishop, I think it was, once rhymed
so prettily as "Iphigenia's incestuous desires." The purpose of this
article is not to correct anybody's morals but to offer a warning
to whom it may concern that Gluck's operas are not quite such
model matter for musical imitation as their historical prestige
might suggest.

That prestige is as much a result of publicity as it is of intrinsic
musical excellence, though the latter, as anyone knows, is not
wholly wanting. Gluck had a gift from his prodigious early years
of making himself a center of controversy and of intellectual excitement. He perfected this gift in Italy, where he learned, as

well, a great deal about sheer theater and became a skilled harmonist and orchestrator. Counterpoint he never mastered, but he got to be extremely expert at musical prosody.* Arriving in Paris with this far from negligible equipment for dramatic composition, he proceeded to make himself a protagonist and eventually the victor in one of those Parisian wars about æsthetics that have always been characteristic of French intellectual life.

The Gluck-Piccinni quarrel was really a revival, or continuation, of the famous *querelle des bouffons,* which had been going on for half a century. Everybody from Rameau to Jean-Jacques Rousseau had taken part in it. Its chief point of controversy was the respective virtues of the French and Italian operatic styles. The former prized correct declamation above melodic charm and admitted symphonic interludes as desirable to full musical expression. The latter prized tunefulness and easy theatrical effect and refused to consider music as wholly subservient to literature. The French side called the Italian school irresponsible and frivolous; the Italian defenders (Jean-Jacques among them) found the French opera static, pompous, and dull.

Piccinni was a charming composer, in many ways a more gifted and skillful musician than Gluck; and he was fabulously successful at the Opéra. Gluck's backers were mostly literary people. What they wanted was a composer who could placate the melody-fanciers without sacrificing correct declamation or obscuring the literary content of a dramatic poem. Gluck was exactly what they needed, an Italian-trained composer with a healthy German respect for the French language. And so they turned him on to the business of staging a contemporary literary movement by pretending merely to revive the past.

This latter game is old French strategy. Racine had taught manners, language, and moral conduct to the bourgeoisie and court of Louis XIV by pretending merely to retell the plots of Seneca and Euripides. The authors of the Enlightenment were busy preparing (quite consciously) a political revolution; but to conceal the novelty of their reflections about society, economics,

---

* Debussy, in his famous *Lettre ouverte à Monsieur le Chevalier W. Gluck* (*Monsieur Croche, antidilettante;* Paris, 1921), accuses the Austrian composer of incorrect French prosody. Textually, he says: " *Entre nous, vous prosodiez fort mal; du moins, vous faites de la langue française une langue d'accentuation quand elle est au contraire une langue nuancée.*"

and law they pretended that they were merely studying ancient Greece and Rome. When Greco-Roman analogies were weak or insufficient they brought the prestige of the natural sciences into play and based their argument on a wholly fictitious figment known as the "natural man." Gluck took advantage of this argument in his famous preface to *Alceste* to pretend that his music was superior to that of all other composers because, whereas theirs was merely music and perishable, like all that follows æsthetic fashion, his could never die, being a true depiction of "nature" itself. (By "nature" he meant, as any man of the eighteenth century did, what the nineteenth called "human nature" and what our own is likely to term "psychology.") I have heard Salvador Dali defend his painting with the similar argument that it was superior to mere "art" because it was an exact picture of his own dreams (dreams being the only "reality" surrealism admits).

All this is purest sales-talk. Dali is an intellectually fashionable painter, as Gluck was an intellectually fashionable composer. The more they try to explain this fact away, the more it becomes clear that their relation to a literary movement is fuller justification for the fame of their work than either their original power or their intrinsic skill, though in neither case is the latter element wholly negligible. For all his talk of "reforming" the opera, Gluck did nothing of the kind. Dr. Paul Henry Láng, of Columbia University, likes to maintain that he had no influence on any subsequent operatic composition. Berlioz certainly admired and studied the orchestral writing in Gluck, because he quotes liberally from it in his *Treatise on Instrumentation*. Wagner used him as a battle cry for his own career, which he also called a "reform," and rewrote some of the scores. All this has accomplished exactly what Gluck's own polemics accomplished: namely, to keep him famous, while the operas are given more and more seldom. The revival of interest in pre-Revolutionary French opera that has accompanied our own searchings among seventeenth- and eighteenth-century composers for reference points in defense of modernism has occasionally foundered on Gluck, for the simple reason that Lully and Rameau, its real masters, are not easily singable by modern voices. And so managers and conductors are likely to make a great point of reviving Gluck and pretending that it is pre-Romantic opera.

This is not true. The literary content of Gluck's librettos is the

purest Classic Revivalism; and the Classic Revival, like the subsequent Medieval Revival, is one of the more sentimental and ob-
scurantist aspects of the Romantic movement. Particularly is this
true in music, where there were not even any ancient texts to revive. Gluck's choral passages are straight Protestant hymnody of
the school popularized in America by Lowell Mason. His arias
are watered Handel. His characters are artificial without being
even symbolic. His recitative, the second-best element of his musical composition (after the instrumentation, which is tops, in
spite of his abuse of string tremolando) is definitely inferior to
that of Rameau, on which it is modeled. Because of his contrapuntal deficiency, his music is lacking in animation and in interior
life. His melodies follow the harmony rather than generate it. The
whole is lacking in surprise. Every number is predictable after
four bars.

The most nearly individual note in his music is one derived
from its literary and fashionable associations. That is a sort of
sugary pastoral flavor that permeates his whole concept of classical antiquity. Everybody on the stage walks around as blithely as
if he were about to become an ancestor, or a founding father of
some future republic. The Agamemnons, even, that bloody and
incestuous clan, express themselves musically with all the placidity
of a prosperous agricultural family. They complain about hard
times, of course, as is the habit of such families; but they are really
mostly busy impressing everybody with how noble they are in
their suffering.

Many people find Gluck's music enchanting. Some of these
like it because they like sugar from any period. Others like it
because they think they get a glimpse through it of pre-Revolutionary operatic style. To these latter I suggest that they beg,
bully, and bargain with the producing agencies till they get a
chance to hear the operas of Rameau and of Handel. Once acquainted with these, I doubt if they will ever take Gluck's classical antiquity seriously again, just as there is no possibility of really
liking his camouflaged Romanticism with anything like the warmth
we feel toward the full-blooded article in Mozart and in Beethoven.

As a career-boy, he made his fortune and got knighted by the
Pope. He was a second-class composer, nevertheless. As a succes-
sor to the great of his century he was distinctly an anticlimax.
As much so as the well-known line from Iphigenia's first aria in

Tauris (a companion piece to our own "for God, for country, and for Yale"):

> "J'ai vu se tourner contre moi
> les dieux, ma patrie et mon père."
>
> *March* 8, 1942

The Seasons in Brooklyn

BROOKLYN SYMPHONY ORCHESTRA, *Carl Bamberger,* conductor; last concert of the season last night at the Brooklyn Academy of Music with the BROOKLYN INSTITUTE CHORUS and the NEW CHORAL GROUP OF MANHATTAN as the assisting choruses in JOSEF HAYDN's oratorio THE SEASONS. Soloists: *Harriet Henders,* soprano; *Edward Kane,* tenor; *Alois Poranski,* baritone.

RARELY have I passed a pleasanter summer. I refer to the second section of Haydn's *The Seasons,* which I heard last night at the Brooklyn Academy of Music. Spring was cheerful and autumn lusty, winter lugubrious and grand. But it was the long, lazy summer that I loved most of all.

Musical literature contains no finer collection of landscape painting than Haydn's homage to the year. There is virtually one of everything. A sunrise, a frog, a quail, a storm, a harvest, a vintage, complete with love and waltzing, a communal spinning-song, every kind of weather known to the temperate regions, and finally a hymn of praise to God and truth and the reviving earth. There are people, too, nice, plain, farm people, giving the measure of man at all times to this Romantic landscape with figures.

No two pieces of it are alike. The musico-pictorial invention is constant and enormous. The accuracy of the pictures and the economy of musical notes with which they are drawn are surprising and impressive. Debussy himself was no more reticent or more powerfully suggestive. Both he and Mendelssohn were less humane.

Grand indeed is the drinking-waltz entitled "Joyful, joyful the liquor flows." The winter spinning scene is the most interesting piece of its species I have ever heard. The prelude to winter is an atmospheric piece of the most effective kind. Its title: "The Thick

Fogs at the Approach of Winter," might be by Erik Satie. "The Farmer's Joyful Feeling about the Rich Harvest," another instrumental interlude, is everything its title says. The storm is as grand as Beethoven's, the sunrise as noble as Prokofiev's. But nowhere that I know is there so full and melodious an outpouring as the long summer aria for soprano, "O, how pleasing to the senses." Neither Bach nor Mozart ever uttered so steady a flow of rich song.

The chorus sang handsomely under Mr. Carl Bamberger's direction. The orchestra and soloists were a little rough. All that made no difference. The reading of the work was lucid and utterly persuasive. It so happens I had never heard it before or read it. That is why I am a bit lyrical about it now. It seems to me to represent Haydn at his most imaginative and ingenious, the oratorio (or cantata) formula at its least stuffy and most gracious, and the art of musical landscape painting at its most complete. I am deeply grateful to the Brooklyn Symphony Orchestra and its assisting choral groups for this revelation of a neglected masterpiece. Please, may we hear it more often?

March 19, 1942

Haydn, Beethoven, and Mozart

LATELY I have been reading and rereading the Haydn piano sonatas. Like all of Haydn's music they represent a gold mine of melody and of instrumental imagination. There is scarcely one that does not contain some passage familiar to us all, familiar, I may add, more often than not because of Beethoven's unacknowledged quotation of it in sonata or symphony. They also represent, as do equally the piano sonatas of Mozart and of Beethoven, the counterpart to the symphonies of these masters. If one wants to understand the latter, one must study the former; and vice versa.

What strikes me most about Haydn is that of the three great Viennese masters he is by far the most melodious. His thematic invention is the most varied of them all and his thematic development the most tuneful. His whole musical concept is lyrical. For this reason he is at his best in the non-lyrical movements. The first movement and the minuet are commonly his richest. The development of his first-movement themes through a cycle of sonata-form

modulations gives symmetry and weight to what might be merely
graceful if no such formal layout were employed. Similarly, the
minuet's quality of dance music enforces a certain objectivity
upon his process of composition that adds to Haydn's abundance
of personal fancy the welcome solidity of a straightforward and
easily understood human significance. The rondo, Haydn's most
frequently observed last-movement scheme, gives too much play
to his musical imagination, obliges him too little to expression.
The same is true of his slow movements, which are melodious and
full of incidental invention, but which do not say much.

The truth is that Haydn wrote music like an old bachelor
(which, for all practical purposes, he was). A self-contained and
self-sufficient lyricism is its dominant characteristic, an avuncular
generosity its chief means of contact with the listener. Of
humane objectivity it has virtually none save in the jolly and waltz-
like dance movements, where he remembers his peasant upbringing. The encounter of his native lyrical abundance with sonata-
form formalities, however, as that takes place in his first
movements, produces a kind of three-dimensional grandeur that is
acceptable in terms of its sheer musical magnificence, without regard to what its expressive intention may be. In this respect
Haydn's instrumental music looks backward to that of Domenico
Scarlatti and the Bach family, just as his oratorios resemble
strongly those of Handel. His technical procedures are those of
Romanticism; but his thought is neither expansive, like Beethoven's, nor dramatic, like that of Mozart. It is a lyrical fountain
forever overflowing and constantly inundating everybody with
melody.

Beethoven really was an old bachelor. But he never liked it.
All his music is cataclysmic, as if he were constantly trying to
break out of his solitude. His first movements state the problem
squarely. His slow movements are less interesting, because they
try unsuccessfully to avoid it; they tread water. His minuets and
scherzos reopen the problem and announce the hope of a solution.
The finales, almost always the finest and certainly the most characteristic movements in Beethoven, are the solution that the whole
piece has been working up to. That solution is usually of a religious nature. It represents redemption, the victory of soul over
flesh. It varies from calm serenity to active triumph, but joy is its
thesis. In the Ninth Symphony a German ode on that subject is
inserted to clinch the matter. The bonds of solitude are broken

because they are imagined as being broken. That breaking is of a purely mystical nature, a temporary identification of the self with God or with all humanity. The form of the musical expression is free and infinitely varied. The finales show Beethoven at his most personal and most masterful. They are grand, terribly serious, and, for the most part, inspiring.

Solitude was unknown to Mozart. Except for a short time in Paris, just after his mother died there, he was probably never in all his life alone for so much as half a day. His music, likewise, is full of dramatic animation. His themes are like people, his developments a working out of their contrasting natures. His first movements, in spite of the beauty of their material, are little more than a first act or prelude to the drama of the rest. The slow movements are always the crux of the matter, the freest, grandest, and most fanciful part of any Mozart sonata or symphony. They are impossible to interpret unless one considers them as theater, as a dramatization of real characters, a conflict among other people's emotions. The minuet which follows (in the quartets it more commonly precedes) is pure ballet. It has nothing to do with Haydn's peasant gambols. It is slow and stately and complex. It, too, shows a conflict of sentiments, as if the dramatic struggles of the preceding movement were here resolved, or at least appeased, through observance of the social amenities. It is a tense and static little affair.

The finales are not dramatic at all. They are mostly fast and always furious. Nothing in music, excepting maybe five or six of the Bach organ fugues, have that kind of power and insistence, as of an element unchained. They do not have to be played at breakneck speed. Those for piano solo definitely profit by moderation in this regard. But rhythmic tension they must have and dynamic contrast. They are the moral of the piece. They show, as Mozart was always trying to show in his operas, how marvelously vigorous life can be when people make up their minds to put their petty differences on the shelf and to collaborate in full good will at being human beings together. Their whole effect can be spoiled unless the preceding movement, whether that is an adagio or the more usual minuet, is presented at a contrasting tempo. Any speed that suggests the scherzo in rendering a Mozart minuet not only falsifies the significance of the minuet itself but steals, as well, the fire of the movement that follows.

December 21, 1941

Mozart's Leftism

PERSONS of humanitarian, libertarian, and politically liberal orientation have for a century used Beethoven as their musical standard-bearer. I employ the word *use* deliberately. Because it is hard to find much in Beethoven's life or music — beyond the legend of his having torn up the dedication of his "Heroic" Symphony to Napoleon when that defender of the French Revolution allowed himself to be crowned Emperor — to justify the adoration in which he has always been held by political liberals.

Wagner, yes. Wagner was full of political theory; and he got himself exiled from Germany (losing a good opera job at Dresden in so doing) for participating in the unsuccessful revolutionary uprising of 1848 beside his friend, the philosopher of anarchy, Mikhail Bakunin. If he had not gone pseudo-Christian and jingo at the end of his life, he would probably be venerated by members of the Third and Fourth Internationals in the same way that Beethoven is worshipped (rather than really listened to) by adherents of the Second.

Mozart, both his life and his works inform us, was more continuously occupied than either of these other composers with what we nowadays call "leftism" (not to be confused with "left wing," Communist Party euphemism meaning the Communist Party).

Mozart was not, like Wagner, a political revolutionary. Nor was he, like Beethoven, an old fraud who just talked about human rights and dignity but who was really an irascible, intolerant, and scheming careerist, who allowed himself the liberty, when he felt like it, of being unjust toward the poor, lickspittle toward the rich, dishonest in business, unjust and unforgiving toward the members of his own family.

As a touring child prodigy Mozart was pampered by royalty, though he worked hard all the time. But after the age of twelve he was mostly pushed around by the great, beginning with Hieronymus Colloredo, Archbishop of Salzburg, going on through Grimm and Madame d'Epinay in Paris, and ending with the Emperor Francis I of Austria. He took it like a little man, too. Few musical lives bear witness to a more complete integrity of character in sickness and in health, in riches and in poverty, such little riches as he knew.

Mozart was not embittered by illness and adversity; he was tempered by them. Furthermore, he was acquainted with French libertarian ideas, having been fully exposed to these in Paris, where he spent his twenty-third year. But he was never at any time a revolter. He was an absorber and a builder. He never tried to throw out of the window his Catholic faith or his allegiance to his Emperor, in spite of much unpleasant treatment from both Church and State. He merely added to them his belief in human rights and the practice of Masonic fellowship as he had learned these in Paris and in Vienna.

The three great theater-pieces of his maturity, *Die Zauberflöte*, *Le Nozze di Figaro*, and *Don Giovanni*, are all of them celebrations of this faith and fellowship, of what we should call liberalism or "leftism" and what the eighteenth century called Enlightenment.

Die Zauberflöte, in spite of its obscure libretto, is the easiest of these to grasp. Mozart, like practically all other self-respecting men in those days, like the French King and his own Emperor, even, like our own George Washington and Benjamin Franklin, was a Freemason. Freemasonry was not the anti-Catholic secret society it became in nineteenth-century America, and it was far from being the conspiracy of job-holding that it developed into under France's Third Republic. It was more like Rotary than like anything else we know. Something between that, perhaps, and organized Marxism. It softened the manners and broadened the viewpoint of all classes in society. Even in Austria, the most retarded country in Europe politically, its fellowship was practiced without interference or suppression.

On account of changes that were operated upon the libretto of *Die Zauberflöte* during its composition and mounting, the fairy-story allegory it tells has always been considered obscure. Obscure it is in its details, if you like, in its mixing up of Zoroaster with Egypt and Japan. But surely its main moral, that married happiness and dignity are to be won only by renouncing pride and snobbery and by conducting oneself as an ethical being, is clear. And certainly its textual references to liberty, equality, and fraternity are unmistakable.

If this were Mozart's only work with ideas of the kind in it, we could discount its humanitarian content as we discount the stilted verses of *Idomeneo*. But it is not. *Figaro,* to Beaumarchais's satirical play, was revolutionary in its egalitarianism; and *Don Giovanni* is the most humane and tolerant piece about sacred and profane love that anybody has ever written.

In Lorenzo da Ponte, who made the libretti for *Figaro* and *Don Giovanni,* Mozart had a collaborator ideal to his taste. They worked together so closely that the libretti seem almost to have been made to fit the music, the music to come spontaneously out of the libretti. With a da Ponte text he was able to do completely what he was able later to do only partially with Schikaneder's fairy tale *Die Zauberflöte* — namely, to transform the whole thing into an expression of his own ideas.

The reason why the "meaning" of the two more naturalistic works is less easy to grasp than that of the fairy tale is that the humanitarianism of the fairy tale is its only easily comprehensible element. In the others practically everything is stated directly *but* the composer's attitude toward his characters.

Beaumarchais's play is straight social satire, a poking fun at the nobility for not being noble enough. It is closer to pamphlet journalism than it is to humane letters. It is what we might call a snappy and sophisticated little number. Mozart and da Ponte changed all the accents, made everybody human, gave to all the characters, to masters and servants alike, the human dignity of their faults and of their virtues. They produced out of a piece of propaganda that was scarcely literature one of the most touching pictures of eighteenth-century life that exists.

Don Giovanni is a tragicomedy about sacred and profane love. Its dramatic tone is of the most daring. It begins with a dirty comic song, goes on to a murder, a series of seductions, a sort of detective-story pursuit of the murderer in which one of the previously seduced ladies plays always a high comedy role; a party, a ballet, a supper scene with music on the stage, a supernatural punishment of the villain, and a good-humored finale in which everybody reappears but the villain.

The villain is charming; the ladies are charming; everybody in the play is charming. Everybody has passion and character; everybody acts according to his passion and his character. Nobody is seriously blamed (except by the other characters) for being what he is or for acting the way he acts. The play implies a complete fatalism about love and about revenge. *Don Giovanni* gets away with everything, Donna Elvira with nothing. Donna Anna never

succeeds in avenging her father's unjust murder. Punishment of
this is left to supernatural agencies. Love is not punished at all.
Its sacred (or at least its honorable) manifestations and its profane (or libertine) practice are shown as equally successful and
satisfactory. The only unsatisfied person in the play is Donna
Elvira, who is not at all displeased with herself for having sinned.
She is merely chagrined at having been abandoned.

Mozart is kind to these people and pokes fun at every one of
them. The balance between sympathy and observation is so neat
as to be almost miraculous. *Don Giovanni* is one of the funniest
shows in the world and one of the most terrifying. It is all about
love, and it kids love to a fare-ye-well. It is the world's greatest
opera and the world's greatest parody of opera. It is a moral entertainment so movingly human that the morality gets lost before
the play is scarcely started.

Why do I call it leftist? I don't. I say the nearest thing we know
to eighteenth-century Enlightenment is called today liberalism
or leftism. But there is not a liberal or leftist alive who could have
conceived, much less written, that opera. It is the work of a Christian man who knew all about the new doctrinaire ideas and respected them, who practiced many of the new precepts proudly,
and who belonged to a humanitarian secret society; but who had
also suffered as few men suffer in this world. He saw life clearly,
profoundly, amusingly, and partook of it kindly. He expressed no
bitterness, offered no panacea to its ills. His life was the most un-
speakable slavery; he wrote as a free man. He was not a liberal;
he was liberated. And his acquaintance, through doctrine and
practice, with all the most advanced ideas of his day in politics, in
ethics, in music, was not for nothing in the achievement of that
liberation.

December 15, 1940

The Berlioz Case

THERE are lots of books in print about the life and works of Hector
Berlioz. Several of these, perhaps the best of them, are by the
composer himself. All of them are preoccupied with the problem
of matching up the "greatness" of his music with the nature and

extent of its prestige or popularity. Some maintain that for all its
world-wide dissemination and all its undeniable expertness, it is
somehow or other not "great" really. Others hold that for all its
undeniable "greatness" and its world-wide acceptance in orchestral repertory, certain of the larger works are unjustifiably neglected.

Leaving aside for a moment the hazy concept of "greatness"
and looking at the ascertainable facts, it is not possible to deny
that a considerable body of Berlioz's work has enjoyed success
both within and without the composer's native land for more than
a century. Even during his lifetime Berlioz was recognized as an
original master. His *Fantastic Symphony,* the *Roman Carnival*
and *Benvenuto Cellini* overtures are still played all over the world.
The first of these has even been made into a successful ballet, like
the "*Pathétique*" of Tchaikovsky and the Fourth of Brahms
Harold in Italy, though less popular than these, holds its place in
repertory as one of the rare works of real distinction ever written
for solo viola with orchestra. At least three of the big choral works
— the Requiem Mass, the Te Deum, and a sort of opera-oratorio,
The Damnation of Faust — are given as frequently as the availabil-
ity of the unusually large musical forces required for their execution permits. They have probably been heard in the musical centers as frequently during the last century as Beethoven's *Missa
Solemnis,* Verdi's Requiem, Bach's Mass in B minor, or Haydn's
oratorios.

There are certain works of Berlioz that are heard less often, just
as Beethoven's *Mount of Olives,* Mozart's Requiem and his Mass
in C minor (both unfinished), César Franck's *Beatitudes,* Mahler's
Ninth Symphony, and Boito's *Mephistopheles* are. None of these
works is more difficult to perform than the previously named ones,
but all are a little less grateful to conduct and less satisfying to
the musical public, on account of certain musical weaknesses or,
in the case of the Mozart works, their unfinished state. Among the
grandes machines, as the French call them, of Berlioz that do not
achieve frequent performance in their entirety are his two operas,
The Capture of Troy and *The Trojans at Carthage,* his *Symphonie
Funèbre et Triomphale* (written for outdoor performance to celebrate the tenth anniversary of the 1830 Revolution), the oratorio *L'Enfance du Christ,* and the "dramatic symphony" *Romeo
and Juliet,* which Mr. Toscanini has chosen to revive for the opening of the Philharmonic's second century of concert seasons.

The last work turns out to be one of those that deserve in every generation a complete rehearing but that are more remarkable for the quality of certain already well-known excerpts than for any stylistic or spiritual integrity of the whole. The quality of these easily extractable sections, which are three, — Romeo at the Capulet's ball, the Garden and Love scenes, and the Queen Mab scherzo — is unique. There is nothing exactly comparable to this kind of Berlioz elsewhere in music. For vigor, delicacy, dramatic power, tenderness, melodic freshness, and orchestral sophistication they are "great" music, if that term means anything at all. Other sections of the work are suffused with an original and most distinguished species of musical poesy. Still others, especially the finale, are routine bombast. It is of no demerit to Berlioz that he did not sustain his highest level of creative power throughout a long work for chorus, soloists, and orchestra. No composer ever did. It is rather to his credit that he sustained it in this work through three whole numbers of a certain length. And it is lucky for us that all three are instrumental pieces (the off-stage chorus in the Garden Scene can be omitted without grave falsification of the effect) and can thus be heard more frequently than would be possible if they required the mobilization of choral troops.

The undisputed facts about Berlioz's music are still these. It has always been admired and played, even when expensive to execute. Certain works are less frequently performed than others. The musical world, which has usually been in agreement about this master's best qualities no less than about his particular weaknesses, has always granted him world primacy in the art of instrumentation and profound originality of dramatic expression, as well as a highly personal, an inimitable approach to the procedures of musical composition. The razor edge, moreover, of his mind has never been denied. He was terrifyingly articulate both as a composer and as a critic. Also, his *Treatise on Instrumentation* is considered as fundamental a contribution to musical knowledge as Rameau's and Fux's works on harmony or Sebastian Bach's *Art of Fugue*. If world-wide admiration, both lay and professional, and a profound influence on the technique of his art do not define "greatness" in a composer, then I give up.

That Berlioz's musical production is uneven in quality is of no importance. So is everybody else's. That a just balance between expression and virtuosity is less regularly achieved in them than in the works of his classical-minded predecessors is not surprising.

He was, after all, a Romantic; and the aim of all the Romantics was to produce a new kind of intensity by upsetting the classical ideal of a just balance between expression and virtuosity. They all overstepped the classic bounds of taste. Liszt's music is over-rhetorical. Wagner's is full of Germanic jingo and shameless in its exploitation of his own and his audience's erotic instincts. Schumann's is boisterous, Mendelssohn's stuffy, Brahms's timid and overrespectful of the past. Even Verdi, the purest of them all, made sometimes such pure theater that all sane sense of plot and character disappears. Only Chopin, in the whole nineteenth century, wrote music regularly, habitually according to an æsthetic that would not have shocked Mozart or Handel.

In any age, moreover, the work of the most original creators is the least even of all in quality. Perhaps "greatness" is a quality that precludes originality. In that case, respect for it is merely a worship of power and of the status quo and should be discouraged. One of the surest marks of high quality in art is the existence side by side of undeniable and universally acceptable beauty with elements that never cease to surprise. If this latter quality is absent the work is no longer alive. If it is too constantly present the work gets put away on a shelf eventually for reference use only. The music of Hector Berlioz is neither dead nor buried. Much of it is as alive and beautiful as anybody's. *Romeo and Juliet* contains three pieces that rank with the *Fantastic Symphony* and with his celebrated overtures. Even the whole work is worth reconsidering from time to time. Its revival after sixty years has done honor to the Philharmonic and to Mr. Toscanini and given pleasure to a musical public that paid as high as eleven dollars a seat to hear its opening performance.

The Damnation of Faust, which Dr. Rodzinski has promised us for next month, is an even grander work. The only real trouble about Berlioz's music is that there isn't enough of it that is written for orchestra alone. What there is is fine. But the bulk of his work requires massive concentrations that are not easy to assemble, such as full orchestra and four hundred choristers plus twenty-eight trumpets and trombones and fourteen kettledrums, as in one section of the Requiem. This effort is very much worth making from time to time. But every time it is made one finds that his really grand pieces of music are exactly the ones that everybody has always known to be grand, usually orchestral interludes that are quite playable as excerpts. I do not think Berlioz suffers from neglect. Nearly everything is played in the current concerts that is possible. And the big "machines" that constitute the bulk of his production are given, one or another of them, about as frequently as those of any other composer are. In Paris they are given more often than here, of course. But they are, after all, French music. And the musical culture of New York has always embraced the Germano-Slavic and the Italian, just as that of London has, more readily than the products of the Gallic mind.

October 11, 1942

Theater and Religion

ARTURO TOSCANINI, conducting the NBC SYMPHONY ORCHES–TRA, assisted by *Zinka Milanov*, soprano; *Bruna Castagna,* contralto; *Jussi Bjoerling*, tenor; *Nicola Moscona*, bass, and the *Westminster Choir, Dr. John Finley Williamson*, director, Saturday night at Carnegie Hall in a concert for the Alma Gluck Zimbalist Memorial of the Roosevelt Hospital Development Fund, with the following program of GIUSEPPE VERDI'S music.

TE DEUM, for two four-part choirs and orchestra
REQUIEM, composed in memory of Alessandro Manzoni, for four solo voices, chorus, and orchestra

MANAGERS refer to him as The Maestro. Orchestral players call him The Old Man in much the same spirit of reverence and healthy fear with which persons resident on the banks of the Mississippi never use any other name for that mighty stream than simply The River. This department had anticipated employing the polite but noncommittal form, Mr. Toscanini. After last Saturday night's rendition of the Verdi Te Deum and Requiem, we feel more like shouting to the city simply: "The Old Man is back!"

No better piece could he have chosen than the Verdi Requiem to make us appreciate his qualities as a master of musical theater. Gaudy, surprising, sumptuous, melodramatic and grand is Verdi's homage to Italy's poet and his own dear friend, Manzoni. No religious musical work of the last century is more sincerely or more completely what it is. Theatrical religion or religious theater? Let him answer who could tell us the same of nineteenth-century Neapolitan church architecture. Nowhere as in Naples does the eye find such constant verification of what the ear tells us when we listen to Palestrina, to Bach, to Mozart — namely, that to the sincerely religious there is no difference between sacred and secular style.

Verdi, though not a particularly pious man, was a sincere Catholic; he was also a sincere man of the theater and a sincere Italian. His Requiem is as sincere a piece of theatrical Italian Catholicism as has ever been written. Sincere Protestants often find it shocking. Sincere non-believers are likely to find it comic. But so might any one find the Dies Iræ itself who had no stomach for horror.

The only sound æsthetic standard I know of that covers all works and epochs is that anything is all right if it is enough so. That is to say that extremism in art, when it really is extreme, and middle-of-the-road normality, when it is really clear and comprehensible to all men, carry in their very extremism and universality the hallmarks of their authenticity. The Verdi Requiem has never raised any eyebrows in Naples (with which city, the seat of Verdi's greatest operatic successes, I like to identify it spiritually) or even in Milan (where it was first performed, in 1874). The question of its acceptance into the musical tradition of Protestant America is still, on account of its extreme theatricality, undecided.

As music that is not only very beautiful in itself, but that is also really "enough so," I give it my vote. I have not always been of that mind; I have long considered it an oddity of which the intrinsic worth scarcely justified the difficulties of a proper execution. After Saturday's performance I have no reserves.

The Maestro conducted it as if it were no more complicated than the "Miserere" from Il Trovatore and no less splendidly compelling than Otello or La Traviata. The Westminster Choir, handsomely gowned in white satin and violet velvet of ecclesiastical cut, sang perfectly. But perfectly. The soloists, Zinka Milanov, Bruna Castagna, Jussi Bjoerling, and Nicola Moscona, sang like stars from some celestial opera house. The two ladies merit each a mark of 99 per cent for their rendition of the impossible Agnus Dei passage in parallel octaves unaccompanied. The kettledrummer, whose name I do not know, merits mention in heaven for his two-stick, unison explosions in the Dies Iræ and for the evenness of his Verdian *ppppp* rolls elsewhere.

Worthy of mention, too, is the implied homage to a regretted

musician in the choice of this particular program by Mr. Toscanini
to raise money for the Alma Gluck Zimbalist Memorial of the
Roosevelt Hospital Development Fund. Just as the great expatri-
ate Italian could have chosen no work more advantageous for
himself to conduct, I can think of no more appropriate piece of
music with which to honor the memory of a much-loved opera
singer than Verdi's sincerely and superbly operatic Requiem.

November 25, 1940

The "Brahms Line"

JOHANNES BRAHMS was not during his lifetime a popular composer. Even today his works are little known and less loved by the
concert-going publics of France, Italy, Spain, Mexico, and the
South American republics. In the German-speaking countries, in
Scandinavia, in Holland, in England, and in the United States a
certain kind of musician has long borne his music great love. But
neither the Latin nor the Slavic musical civilization has so far absorbed it at all. Its popularity among us has been growing steadily
of late until today it ranks in popular favor with the music of
Tchaikovsky and of Sibelius. This season the Brahms symphonic
works have far outnumbered in performance the works of Beethoven, of Mozart, and of Schubert. The emergence of Brahms as
a popular symphonist concords (in time, at least) with the noticeable confluence of two musical currents; and the result of that
confluence is certain to be worth watching. These currents are the
growing conservatism of the "advanced" musical world, the world
of modernism in style and structure, and the deeply inveterate
conservatism of the non-professional music public.

A devotion to Brahms has always been, at least in our century, the mark of a quite definite musical conservatism. Even in
his own day, which is not far past, this was mostly so, too. His
whole musical program was traditionalist. He aimed to reinvig-
orate the classic style rather than to transform it or to add to it.
In this he was the direct (and bitter) opponent of Richard Wagner. Wagner considered the works of his predecessors and of his
contemporaries as equally grist for his mill, and he considered the
business of his mill to be the turning out of a new kind of music

for new kinds of social usage. He called this "the music of the future." Brahms considered his role to be that of a preserver of the classic tradition against the destructive tendencies of Romanticism. He modeled his contrapuntal style on the practices of Bach and of Mozart; his formal layouts in the long works he copied directly out of works by Mozart and Beethoven. His only voluntary concession to Romanticism was in the direction of chromatic harmony, and that was fairly hesitant.

Brahms was not by instinct a popular figure. He rather despised the non-professional public, and he had more gift for tiny-craft in music-writing than for sustained eloquence. He was nevertheless obliged, even though an opponent of Wagnerian demagogy, to do something about sustained eloquence, because no German could have success as a serious composer who did not obviously continue in the line of Beethoven. Brahms worked at this line assiduously, and finally, in his forties, produced a symphony. Later he produced three more. It was hard work for him, because his musical imagination was more lyrical than heroic and his instrumental style more at home with the scrupulosities of chamber music than in the broader symphonic manner. Neither was he any such master of the orchestra as his more radical contemporaries, Wagner, Berlioz, and Liszt.

He succeeded by sheer determination, and by the constant imitation of classic models, in pulling off these works most creditably and in building up for himself in Germany, in England, and even in America a devoted public of musicians who considered him to be the direct heir of Bach and Beethoven. The justice of that opinion is not a matter for present dispute, but its existence has long been an undeniable fact. A curious recent development in the Brahms controversy is that instead of having to wait for acceptance by the whole intellectual music world (which would include, of necessity, the Latins and the Slavs), the Brahms music has now achieved popular acceptance here without benefit of clergy.

In this it has separated itself from the work of those composers who have reached the masses with all canonical benediction. Beethoven and Wagner and Bach and Mozart our public has been taught to love. And if the modernists have sometimes regretted their haste in throwing the weight of their prestige on the side of Richard Wagner in his (and his widow's) campaign to popularize his operas, the fact remains that all over the world they did it. Brahms they nearly always resisted, as they mostly resisted Tchaikovsky and Sibelius. In all three cases the general public in Scandinavia, in England, and in the United States has stepped in and offered its accolade spontaneously.

This fact might well take some of the wind out of Brahms's academic admirers, leave them defending a lost cause that is no longer lost and yet still not wholly won academically, if it were not for the fact that new support has suddenly come to them from an intellectual source, from the heart of modernism itself. Ever since about 1914 modern music has been decreasingly revolutionary in its aims and increasingly conservative in its procedures. The so-called "neo-classicism" of Stravinsky and Hindemith and other accepted leaders of the modernist movement, though by no means without value historically and even intrinsically, is none the less a position of defense rather than of attack. Its stabilizing tendencies are proved by the fact that it has enabled a great number of modernist composers to accept teaching posts in academic institutions, its cultural aim being frankly the incorporation of modern stylistic procedures into what is left, if any, of the classic tradition.

The joke of it all on the neo-classic modernists is that their program turns out to be exactly that of Johannes Brahms. Modern music has, in the words of a recent correspondent, writing of the Hindemith First Symphony, "executed a masterly retreat to the heavily fortified Brahms Line." Examine ten, almost any ten, modern symphonies and you will see, I think, that this is true. If my correspondent is right (and I think he is), it turns out that at the same time that our general public is taking to Brahms as a frankly popular symphonist like Tchaikovsky and Sibelius, the modernist intellectuals discover themselves to be following in exactly his pattern of basic traditionalism with contemporary surfacing. They also find themselves faced, as Brahms did, with the necessity of climbing down from their power of ivory tinycraft and doing something about symphonic eloquence. If they don't, the symphony public won't respect them; and if the symphony public doesn't respect them, they are likely to lose their teaching jobs.

It is sad to see official modernism turn out to be, after all, doubly conformist and wholly conservative. Maybe after the war there will be musical advance from the Brahms Line again. But for the present both the general public and most of the intellectual musicians are immured behind its surprisingly solid bastions.

And if it is not pleasant to see modernist composers timidly pulling their punches and, what is worse, striking in many cases below the public's belt, it is salutary to observe that same public rising spontaneously to the work of a man who, though not a grandly original master, was a musical workman of high integrity and unquestioned nobility of thought.

April 26, 1942

Acquaintance with Wagner

About once a year your reviewer ventures to dip an ear again into the Wagnerian stream. He thinks he ought to find out whether anything about it has changed since the last time or if anything has possibly changed in him that might provoke a reversal of judgment about it all and a return of the passionate absorption with which he used to plunge himself into that vast current of sound. This season's expedition took him to hear *Die Walküre* last Tuesday evening at the Metropolitan Opera House. So far as he could tell, nothing has altered since last he heard the work.

The tunes are the same tunes as before, some excellent and some not so excellent. The symphonic development of the leitmotives continues to vary in interest according to the musical value of the leitmotives themselves. Those that contain chromatic progressions, arpeggios, or skips of a major sixth still become monotonous on repetition, while those based on narrower skips and diatonic movement continue to support expansion without apparent strain. Wagner never learned the elementary rules of thumb that aided Bach and Handel and Haydn and Mozart and even Schubert to estimate the strength of melodic materials. His rhythmic patterns are frequently monotonous, too; and he has a weakness for step-wise modulating sequences.

The instrumentation remains rich in sound and highly personal. And if it often creates its theatrical excitement by the use of mere hubbub, that excitement is still a dependable effect and the instrumental dispositions involved are acoustically sound. It has long seemed to me that Wagner's original contributions to musical art are chiefly of an orchestral nature. Indeed, orchestration is the one element of musical composition in which Wagner had sound training, exception being made for the rules of German declamation, which he derived for himself by studying the works of Mozart and Weber and Meyerbeer. His music-writing is more varied in quality than is that of any other composer of equal celebrity, even Berlioz; but no matter what the quality, it always sounds well. It is always instrumentally interesting and infallibly sumptuous.

Sometimes the musical quality runs high, too. There are unforgettable moments of invention in any of Wagner's operas, though the percentage of memorable pages out of his whole production will probably be inferior to that in Verdi and certainly far less than what one can find in Mozart. And their excellence is not due wholly to orchestral orotundity; he wrote often charmingly for the voice, as well. He wrote rather more effectively, however, it seems to me, for the higher voices than for the lower. His tenor and soprano roles are more pleasing and more expressive than his alto, baritone, or bass writing. His Ortruds and his Frickas are always a slight bore; and King Marke, Wotan, Hunding, Fafner, even for habitual Wagnerians, are proverbially great big ones. He had little feeling for the heavier vocal timbres, and there is no real liberty in his handling of them.

Well, all that is all that. Wagner was a gifted and original composer, though an unusually uneven one. And his lack of early musical instruction is probably the cause of his major faults, though I doubt if ignorance could be held responsible for any of his virtues. He was not, as a matter of fact, an ignorant man; he was merely an autodidact, lacking, like most autodidacts, more in æsthetic judgment than in culture. He read voluminously and understood what he read; he reflected in a penetrating way about æsthetic matters, and he mastered easily any musical technique he felt he needed. His troublesomeness on the musical scene has always been due less to the force of his musical genius (which was recognized from the beginning) than to the fact that neither instinct nor training had prepared him to criticize his own work with the objectivity that the quality of genius in it demanded. As a result, every score is a sea beach full of jewelry and jetsam. Fishing around for priceless bits is a rewarding occupation for young musicians, just as bathing in the sound of it is always agreeable to any musical ear. But musicians are likely to find nowadays that the treasure has been pretty well combed and that continued examination of the remnants yields little they hadn't known was there before.

What continues to fascinate me is not Wagner's music but Wagner the man. A scoundrel and a charmer he must have been such as one rarely meets. Perfidious in friendship, ungrateful in love, irresponsible in politics, utterly without principle in his professional life, and in business, of course, a pure confidence-man, he represents completely the nineteenth-century ideal of toughness. He was everything the bourgeois feared, hoped for, and longed to worship in the artist. The brilliancy of his mind, the modernity of his culture, the ruthlessness of his ambition, and the shining armor of his conceit, even the senile erotomania of his later years, all went into a legend that satisfied the longings of many a solid citizen, as they had long made him an attractive figure to aristocrats and intellectuals.

To know him was considered a privilege by the greatest figures of Europe, though many of these found the privilege costly. His conversation was stimulating on every subject; his wit was incisive and cruel; his polemical writing was expansive, unprincipled, and aimed usually below the belt. He was the most inspiring orchestral conductor and the most penetrating music critic of his century. His intellectual courage and the plain guts with which he stood off professional rivalries, social intrigues, political persecution, and financial disaster are none the less breathtaking for the fact that his very character invited outrageous fortune.

All this remains; it is available in many books. The music remains, too; and it is available at virtually every opera house in the world. It would not bring out the crowds or incite conductors and vocalists to the serious efforts it does if it did not have, in spite of its obvious inequalities, strength beneath its fustian still. To deny that strength were folly. To submit to it is unquestionably a pleasure. But what your reviewer would like most of all is to have known the superb and fantastic Wagner himself.

February 21, 1943

Dissent from Wagner

A RECENT article of this column wherein it was suggested that the music of Richard Wagner was perhaps less interesting intrinsically than the personality of the man behind it has brought a certain amount of correspondence to the music desk, much of it, surprisingly, complimentary. The widow of a famous music critic wrote: "Your 'Acquaintance with Wagner' seems to me the last and best word on the gentleman. I read it with the greatest interest and shall keep it for future reading." A Bostonian composer mentioned Wagner's "overbearing confusion" and called him "to me the least satisfactory of the larger musical phenomena."

Many persons, of course, consider Wagner the *most* satisfactory of the larger musical phenomena. But that he *is* one of the larger musical phenomena is not disputed. What has long been argued about is the nature of the phenomenon and its value to civilization. Its value to individual persons is a private matter, and the voting or ticket-buying power of those persons is a statistical fact. Neither private pleasures, however, nor public devotions prove anything in art. Unless there is unanimous acceptance of a man's work, which is rare, it is the people who don't like it that have the last word in its evaluation.

There is no sounder proof of Shakespeare's central position in English literature, or of Dante's in Italian, than the fact that nobody objects to it. Such a position in music is occupied, through common consent, by a triumvirate — Bach, Beethoven, and Mozart. Wagner's pretensions to universal authority are inadmissible from the very fact that the music world is not unanimous about admitting them. Mozart is a great composer, a clear value to humanity, because no responsible musician denies that he is. But Wagner is not an absolute value from the very fact that Rossini denied it and Nietzsche denied it and Brahms denied it and, in our own time, Debussy and Stravinsky have denied it. This does not mean that, with the exception of Rossini, all these composers (including Nietzsche) have not stolen a trick or two from Wagner or accepted him as a major influence on their style. They have. But the fact that they have accepted his work with reservations is what proves my thesis.

Similar reservations are current about the music of Berlioz, of Gluck, of Weber, of Verdi, of Mahler, Strauss, Hindemith, Milhaud, and Aaron Copland, not to speak of the symphonists that descend from Brahms — the line of Tchaikovsky and Franck and Sibelius and Shostakovich and Roy Harris. These men represent musical values of a high order, but the values they represent are not satisfactory to all. They are therefore minor masters. J. S. Bach and Handel and Haydn and Mozart and Beethoven and Schubert and Chopin are major masters. So, very probably, are Schumann and Debussy. Richard Wagner is not. He could not be with so many musicians against him.

It is not the purpose of this essay to prove that liking Wagner's music is a low taste. Its purpose is to demonstrate that Wagner's music is a taste like any other, wholly legitimate but in no way sacred. The great masters are a bore to many people; they actively annoy almost none. But the minor masters annoy a great many people in a great many ways. There are excellent musicians who simply cannot stand the Berlioz bravura; others find it invigorating. There are those who are ravished by the sweetness of Grieg, carried away by the emphases of Verdi, or deeply shaken by the Tchaikovskian eloquence. To others all this is superficial. A Wagnerian bath is the cleansing flood for their souls. Still others find refreshment in the acidities of Stravinsky or in the dry champagne of Scarlatti and of Couperin.

All tastes are legitimate, and it is not necessary to account for them unless one finds it amusing to do so. Distastes are equally legitimate, including a distaste for music itself. If one has a distaste for the great masters of music, or a complete indifference to them, one is not a musician; that is all. But if one is a musician and if one has serious reservations about the music of any given composer, those reservations are grounds for suspicion that such music is not wholly straightforward. If the reservations are shared by other musicians, even a few, over a reasonable space of time, then that music has failed to convince the world of its purity.

It is the thesis of this reviewer that the music of Richard Wagner is an achievement somewhat less remarkable than that of the undisputed major masters of our tradition. The argument for this thesis is the simple syllogism that the canonization of a major master in any art requires a virtually unanimous vote of the initiates and that Wagner has never got anything approaching such a vote. He hoped, and many of his friends believed, that he would get it eventually, that the hesitant of spirit would come round. In the decade succeeding his death they seemed to be about to. The peak of his music's prestige within the profession occurred around 1890. The decline of this has been continuous ever since, though there was a notable rise in its popular acceptance between the two world wars. It seems now most unlikely that any thorough or intellectual rehabilitation of Wagner will take place until the wave of his box-office popularity shall have subsided.

And so for the present there is no reason why he shouldn't provide sport for his enemies as well as delight for the faithful. Most of all, right now, his music needs debunking and deglamorizing, so that some unprejudiced analysis of its virtues may eventually be possible. The question is not whether Wagner is one of the "larger musical phenomena." Of course he is. Or whether he is one of the prime numbers in music, which he certainly is not. The question is simply how do the scores stand up page by page beside those of other standard dramatic composers from Mozart to Massenet. When the parishioners take up that little bingo game, there will be surprises for all, I promise, many of them agreeable.

March 7, 1943

Strauss and Wagner

THREE of Richard Strauss's operas — *Salomé, Elektra,* and *Der Rosenkavalier* — have provoked world-wide admiration. Their musical style has long been called by the vague term "post-Wagnerian." Their whole method, musical and dramatic, seems to me, however, to merit a more specific denomination. The German æsthetic most current in poetry, painting, and the theater arts during the epoch of their composition has always been known as expressionism or, in German, *Expressionismus.*

Considering the important role played in the very creation of these works by literary and theatrical modernism, it is only just to their composer to credit him with having something on his mind beyond a mere continuation or extension of the Wagnerian musical technique. Two of them were made in close collaboration with a poet, Hugo von Hofmannsthal. The other, *Salomé,* uses as libretto the translation of a tragedy written originally in French by Oscar Wilde. It is not to be denied, I think, that however old-fashioned this sort of literature may seem nowadays, all three plays have a linguistic style and a moral (or amoral) consistency that make them more distinguished entertainment than any of the mythological poems that Richard Wagner (who was not properly a man of letters at all, in spite of his large literary production) ran up for himself. Wagner's best works are full even of musical inequalities, and the contrast between their musical vigor and their religio-philosophico-poetic flaccidity has always been a scandal. Strauss's three great ones (I do not know his others well) are all of a piece. You can take them or leave them, but you cannot separate their music from what it expresses.

Strauss's concept of dramatic composition, though derived from Wagner's, turns out in practice to give a quite different result. It begins, of course, by accepting the Wagnerian formulas of the convulsive accompaniment and of the expansion of time. I do not know where Wagner picked up the idea of scrapping all accompanimental formality, of eschewing, I mean, all orchestral figurations of an abstract character. Neither Gluck nor Beethoven nor Weber nor Meyerbeer nor Berlioz, from all of whom Wagner appropriated theatrical procedures, ever did anything of the kind. They made their accompaniments appropriate and expressive, but it never occurred to any of them to destroy their function as a sort of auditory proscenium by whose static structure the more sensitive and personal music of the characters themselves is framed.

Characterization and all personal expression are classically the role of the vocal line and take place on the stage, just as atmosphere and dramatic emphasis are that of the orchestra and belong in the pit. In Wagner, and even more in Strauss, the orchestra takes over the work of characterization, as well as that of emotional analysis and amplification, leaving little for the singing actors to do beyond a certain amount of intoned speech-imitation in the low register, punctuated by intensely pushed-out cries in the upper. Not appearing ridiculous while they stand around waiting for their emotions to be described by the orchestra has always been the acting problem of Wagnerian singers. Nobody minds the eight to twelve minutes of relative immobility during which the Countess Almaviva in Mozart's *Marriage of Figaro* sings her "Dove sono" or Charpentier's Louise describes her own love life in an aria beginning, "Depuis le jour." But when Sieg-linde, in the first act of *Die Walküre*, has nothing to do but cross the stage once while the orchestra plays a fifteen-minute footnote, it becomes evident to all that something should really be arranged to keep her occupied.

Strauss avoided this kind of situation by choosing stories about people who were not too dignified — who were, indeed, human-all-too-human (preferably outrageous) — and by putting the play-writing of these into skilled hands. He did not ask his artists either to stand around doing nothing or to do very much contin-uously expressive singing (they've enough to do getting the notes right). He gave them instead a literary and orchestral blue-print for acting all over the stage. Hence it is that, though the vocal line is always rather static and often musically nondescript, the visual drama, like the auditory orchestral one, is constantly and intensely convulsive. The convulsiveness all round is greater than in Wagner; can afford to be so because Strauss, a composer of much experience in the concert forms, can always make an act hold together, give it shape, progress, and conclusion, no matter how much violence goes on, even at a length, as in *Elektra*, of nearly two hours.

It is not my thesis that Strauss is the greater composer of the two. He is not. His thematic invention is too often bromidic and careless. He is a better musician than Wagner, yes, though not nearly so original or powerful a musical mind. His operas (or music-dramas) are certainly made after the Wagnerian model. But what happened to the Wagnerian model in Strauss's hands is something like this: He kept the convulsive accompaniment and the augmentation of time; but, feeling a need to correct the em-barrassment to actors and to the public that Wagner had caused by taking most of its dramatic responsibility away from vocal expression, he called in expert literary men, who tightened up the plays, while they searched in legend and in abnormal psy-chology for subjects suitable to convulsive orchestral treatment by a master hand.

It is exactly this research into the lurid and its rendering in the cataclysmic style that constitutes the kind of German art known to its practitioners as *Expressionismus*. Musically and musico-dramatically Strauss is its world master, and the Metropol-itan Opera Company's present *Salomé* I recommend as a vigorous production of one of its masterpieces. It is not incorrect to call

Strauss's music post-Wagnerian; it is merely insufficient. Because expressionism represents a rebirth rather than a mere survival of the Wagnerian music-drama, the term is sufficient only if we admit, as I see no reason for not admitting, that the whole expressionist movement, which was larger than any one man's contribution to it, came into existence spiritually, as well as temporally, after Wagner.

December 13, 1942

Mahler and Boston at Their Best

BOSTON SYMPHONY ORCHESTRA, *Serge Koussevitzky,* conductor.

SYMPHONY NO. 9	MAHLER
PRELUDE TO KHOVANSTCHINA	MUSSORGSKY
BABA-YAGA	LIADOV
CAPRICCIO ESPAGNOL	RIMSKY-KORSAKOV

GUSTAV MAHLER is to Richard Strauss as Bach to Handel or Debussy to Ravel. All such pairs of contemporaries have a common background of style and material that gives to their contrasted temperaments the ability to define and enclose an epoch, as the heads and the tails of a coin define and enclose between them its content.

Mahler's music is the more introspective. It is meditative, visceroemotional, all about himself. Strauss's is declamatory, objective, descriptive of everything in the world but himself. Mahler's has the power of attracting fanatical devotion to itself and to the personality of its author. Strauss's gives a ripsnorting good time to all without provoking the slightest curiosity anywhere about its author's private life. Mahler wrote as if the material of Viennese music itself were so bound up with his own soul that only by integrating the two in a practically marital union could a work be created that would be a valid expression of either. Strauss wrote his pieces very much as a theatrical producer cooks up a show.

And yet the musical material and technique of the two are almost identical. Their themes might have been written by either, so characteristically do they consist of descending appoggiaturas

and upward skips of the sixth. The two have an equal freedom
of modulation and the same habit of playing their chromatics
wild, not limiting the use of these to modulatory or to melodic
purposes but throwing them in anywhere they feel like it for any
reason whatsoever.

Both orchestrate, of course, with a sure hand and with wide
resources of imagination and fancy. Mahler's orchestra, however,
is the more elegant of the two by far, as is likewise his harmonic
and contrapuntal fabric. His concentration on personal sincerity
gave him an integrated manner of expressing himself, at his best,
that is stylistically more noble than anything Strauss, with all his
barnstorming brilliance, ever achieved. The Strauss heavy doublings and unashamed use of mere orchestral hubbub belong
to a less refined and a less responsible order of musical expression. Mahler keeps his colors clean, and he never writes a middle
part that hasn't in itself some intensity of expression or some grace.

The Ninth Symphony (considered by most Mahler devotees
to be the finest of his works, though *Das Lied von der Erde* has
its worshippers and so have the *Kindertotenlieder*) is beautifully
made and beautifully thought. It is utterly German and Viennese
and strangely not so at the same time. In reviewing *Das Lied von
der Erde* some time back, I opined that there were some French
influences in the particular contrapuntal approach Mahler employed. Naturally, I pulled down on my head a flood of abusive
correspondence from the Mahlerites, who will have no analyzing
of their idol and certainly no aspersions cast upon his hundred-
per-cent Germanism. I suppose they don't count his Israelite birth
or his professional travels (he conducted here at the Metropolitan
Opera House and at the Philharmonic for something like three
years) as factual evidence of a certain internationalism in his culture. Nevertheless, as I listened to the Ninth Symphony last night,
I was still aware of French influences. Certain of these are technical, like the no-doubling orchestration. Others are æsthetic. I know
the protest mail I shall get for saying this, but I must say it. Mahler has a great deal in common with the French impressionists. As
an Italian musician to whom I mentioned the matter put it, " He
comes as near being an impressionist as a German could."

Mr. Koussevitzky's reading of the work was highly satisfactory to this listener, who had only recently listened to Bruno Walter's recorded rendition of it with the Vienna Philharmonic Or-

chestra. Walter was slow and sentimental, and his unsteady tempos made a muddle out of Mahler's refined exactitude of notation. Koussevitzky let the piece move and kept the rhythms in place. In addition, the orchestral playing was of the beauteous kind that only Boston gives us regularly any more. Fluffy Russian savories done to a turn lightened and ended the evening's musical repast.

March 14, 1941

Close Communion

ORIGINAL BALLET RUSSE, *Col. W. de Basil,* director general, at the Fifty-first Street Theater.

I, Cotillon, music by Emmanuel Chabrier, orchestrated by *E. Chabrier, F. Mottl,* and *Vittorio Rieti;* choreography by *Georges Balanchine;* scenery and costumes by *Christian Bérard.*

II, Balustrade, ballet in four movements based upon the Concerto for Violin and Orchestra by Igor Stravinsky; choreography by *Georges Balanchine;* scenery and costumes by *Pavel Tchelitcheff;* violin solo, *Samuel Dushkin;* the composer conducting. (First performance.)

III, Aurora's Wedding, ballet in one act, music by P. Tchaikovsky; choreography after *Marius Petipa,* choreography for "The Three Ivans" by *Bronislava Nijinska;* scenery by *Leon Bakst;* costumes by *Alexandre Benois.*

The Stravinsky Violin Concerto turns out to be good ballet music by the same qualities that made it a not very good violin concerto. In no sense a conversation between soloist and ensemble, it is rather a monologue for violin to which other instruments play a continuous accompaniment, an insistent monologue as of someone improvising stubbornly and not caring whether anybody is trying to accompany him or not. The result lacks brilliance as a concerto. Toughly, hard-headedly poetic as music, it is not the least bit "grateful," as soloists would put it, for the violin.

It is exactly because of its lack of soaring cantilena and of sparkling passage work, cadenzas, show-off matter in general, that it is ideal for continuous choreographic composition. It is as tightly woven as a bird-cage. As four bird-cages, to be exact, because it consists of four tight and tough little movements, each of them minutely massive. Excepting the last. That is more loose-hung, more dependent on mimicries of Tchaikovskian charm than the other three.

These are as naïvely dogmatic as a first-prize violin student from the Paris Conservatory, for whom, indeed, the work might well have been composed. Its evocations of the violin classroom, combined with its willful avoidance of anything that might possibly imply a connection with that tradition of Baroque and Romantic musical culture that is the only possible excuse for playing the violin at all, give to the work a tense and heartrending charm.

This concentrated emotional quality, an emotional quality concentrated in and expressed by structural ingenuity, seems to have given Mr. Balanchine his first chance in several years to do what he loves to do best, to build long choreographic "variations," as the dancing world calls them, of a tightly knit continuity. I should not care to opine regarding their æsthetic value, nor should I feel technically competent to describe them further than by saying that they seemed to me of a piece with the music. They seemed to have come out of the music and to walk in close communion beside it, the closeness of this spiritual communion providing an independence, so characteristic of Balanchine, that relieved the dancers from any pedestrian obligation to keep step with the measure.

The composer conducted handsomely and Mr. Dushkin executed the violin solo role with accuracy and comprehension, as if the piece belonged to them jointly, which, as a matter of fact, it rather does. Something in the nature of an ovation was their reward; and they shared this fraternally with Mr. Balanchine, Mr. Tchelitcheff, the decorator, being absent on account of a seasonal grippe. The whole occasion, indeed, shone with that white light of mutual artistic understanding that has made ballet as practiced by Russians in our century something a good deal more incandescent than any other kind of dancing spectacle.

I should like to add, as a footnote to my recounting of the evening, that the orchestra played extremely well under Mr. Antal Dorati for the two other ballets. Also that the score for *Cotillon*, pieced together out of Chabrier, has lost none of its loveliness since first I heard it in 1932, though I thought at the time and still think the finale needs a more sonorous instrumentation.

January 23, 1941

Stravinsky's Symphony

LAST Sunday afternoon Mr. Leopold Stokowski and the NBC Symphony Orchestra gave us a performance that was notable in every way of Igor Stravinsky's Symphony in C major. Local musicians and music-lovers are grateful primarily to these gentlemen for the work's being done at all. But to have heard it in a rendition marked by such detailed clarity and so much over-all comprehension gives double reason for the proffering of public thanks.*

The piece has been in existence for more than two years; it was written to celebrate the fiftieth anniversary of Chicago's orchestra, and it has been played in various Western cities. Our local conductors have all read the score and turned it down. They have mostly considered it to be a weak work. In refusing to expose it to us, while giving us many another new symphony that has turned out to be weaker, they have presumed that a stricter standard of excellence is applicable to the work of a famous author than is appropriate to apply to that by composers of lesser prestige. This is reasonable enough, though contrary to the usual practice of program-makers. They have taken for granted also that conductors' judgments in this matter should satisfy the musical public.

It is true that we expect a high quality of musical workmanship from writers who have all their lives employed a high quality of musical workmanship, and Igor Stravinsky has never let us down in that respect. Moreover, any conductor can see from looking at the score of the Symphony in C major that it is not a piece likely to attract crowds or to win the conventional epithet "moving" (which means box-office). Neither is it, on the other hand, especially difficult of comprehension. If it had been played by everybody within the season of its Chicago première, as it most likely would have been had it been the work of Rachmaninoff or Shostakovich or Prokofiev or any other composer of world-wide fame excepting Stravinsky, an estimate of its intrinsic value would probably have been made without much delay by the musical pub-

* The composer was displeased at the non-observance of his strictly marked tempos.

lic itself. It is difficult to understand on what grounds the Eastern conductors have neglected an obviously well-written work in large form by a composer of such high repute. Their private reserves about its spiritual or æsthetic value would seem to me interesting as opinion but hardly valid reason for refusing to expose it to general judgment.

Well, Mr. Stokowski and the radio people have finally fulfilled a cultural obligation that in former times would have been considered a privilege of the non-commercial agencies. It is not the first time this has occurred. Alfred Wallenstein, of WOR, Howard Barlow and his guest conductors at Columbia, have frequently shown more confidence in their nation-wide public than the leaders of our resident musical foundations have in the taste of their local subscribers. It may be that the country at large is more curious about new music, more open-minded and more advanced than the elite of the Eastern cities. The history of the Stravinsky symphony and also that of the Milhaud symphony, which was written at the same time and which has had many successful performances in the Middle and Far West without yet reaching us, would seem to indicate that the Atlantic seaboard has lost much of its former cultural leadership.

After all this build-up by avoidance, the Stravinsky symphony turns out to be no wild and woolly he-bear at all. It is an elegantly written piece in the author's own especial version of the neo-classic manner. It is a companion work to his Piano Concerto of twenty years back, to his Octette, to his Piano Sonata, to a whole series of compositions that aim to evoke the amenities of late eighteenth-century Vienna.

To expect an expansive rendering of his subjective emotional life is to prepare oneself for disappointment in listening to Stravinsky's music. He has never gone in for that; he has, on the contrary, for thirty years insistently expressed his disdain for it in print and in person. He has always worked objectively, directing his whole talent and mind toward as impersonal a rendering as that of a painter or of a dramatist. He has frequently varied the object of his expression, and he has invariably chosen a manner of writing suitable to that object; but his æsthetic of musical composition has not altered since he first began to write, some forty years ago.

He has always been a man of the theater, and he has always thought like one. When writing for the stage he is directly atmospheric; he makes musical décor. When writing for the concert platform he is evocative. His symphony is no less theatrical a conception than the early piece called *Fireworks* or the opera about a Chinese emperor and a mechanical nightingale. It evokes the Austrian court symphony as deliberately as *Le Baiser de la Fée* evokes the Imperial Opera of Saint Petersburg and the ballets of Tchaikovsky or as *Petrouchka* represents the sights and sounds of a village carnival. It could be made into a ballet tomorrow, and probably will be before the decade is done.

There is no question that this particular piece, like many another of Stravinsky's platform productions, is stiff and a little prim. Its thematic material is impersonal, its syntax formal, its harmony and instrumentation wholly elegant and well bred. The author has done his best to make it as dry as champagne, as neutral as distilled water. It is not detrimental to the work, however, that in spite of his almost academic intentions, the Russian balletmaster in him does take over from time to time. Indeed, what breadth the piece has is due to the incompleteness of its voluntary stylization. It is no sugar-tit. And it has little ambition toward the *genre chef-d'œuvre*. But in its quiet way it is something of a masterpiece, all the same. When one compares it with its author's other works of the last twenty years in similar vein, one can hardly fail to recognize that it is the most ample of all his efforts to evoke the Austrian court style. Whatever the value of doing that may be, it is undeniably an achievement to have done it and to have bestowed thus on twenty years of labor so adequate a crown.

The legitimacy of the author's intention is no less open to question than is the legitimacy of any other æsthetic intention of our time. The intrinsic worth of the piece (aside from the clear mastery of its writing and rhetoric) and its possible influence on history are impossible of contemporary estimation. But that it presents a high degree of musical interest is undeniable. It does seem a little timorous of our Eastern conductors to have neglected it for two years while giving us constantly new works by minor Slavic symphonists (and others) that are certainly no better box-office. It was either overtimid of them, if the box-office is all they were afraid of, or overconfident about their own taste, if they thought their lack of personal liking for the work entitled them to avoid the clear responsibility of communicating it to us without delay.

February 28, 1943

Stravinsky's Late Beethoven

CELIUS DOUGHERTY and VINCENZ RUZICKA, duo-pianists.

PRELUDE AND FUGUE	BUXTEHUDE-DOUGHERTY
FANTASIE, OP. 103	SCHUBERT
SONATA OF FOUR PARTS	PURCELL
MUSIC FROM SEAS AND SHIPS, an American Sonata	DOUGHERTY
(First New York performance)	
CONCERTO PER DUE PIANOFORTI SOLI	STRAVINSKY

DOUGHERTY and Ruzicka, who played two pianos in recital last night at Town Hall, are enlightened program-makers. It is unfortunate that irresponsible tempos and a good deal of slappy tone-production marred what might otherwise have been one of the season's musical treats. Schubert's great F-minor Fantasy, a sonata by Purcell and a Prelude and Fugue of Buxtehude gave the concert a high degree of classical interest, while a new work of Mr. Dougherty's composition on American sea chanties offered a not unpleasant repose before the modern-style severities of Stravinsky's Concerto for Two Pianos Alone. The latter work in particular needs a charming, even an urbane, interpretation if it is to be absolved by contemporary audiences from the charge of gratuitous ugliness, its very abstruseness being a sufficient unpleasantness for many.

It is abstruse because, as in most of Stravinsky's music from the last twenty-five years, its style is its subject. And music-lovers brought up on the Romantic tradition of music, in which the style is supposed to derive from the subject, are confused by any other approach to the art. Nevertheless, the use of style as subject, the evocation of past periods, the modernistic usage of ancestral furniture and formulas, is as vigorous a practice in contemporary music as it is in contemporary theater, contemporary architecture and decoration. The whole æsthetic of Johannes Brahms, indeed, whom many consider the bulwark of musical conservatism, is based upon nothing less. Stravinsky cannot be reproached for his masterly distortions of classical shape and phraseology without the same indictment being held valid against the original neo-classic composer of them all, Brahms, who invented the looking-backward business, the taking of a style as his subject.

Brahms's preferred subject-matter was the style of Beethoven's middle period. The subject-matter of Stravinsky's Concerto for Two Pianos Alone is, if I mistake not, the style of Beethoven's later period, in particular that of the last four or five piano sonatas. It contains a stormy sonata movement, an air with coloratura ornaments, and a set of extended variations ending with a fugue. The melodic material is angular and strong, the emotional content violent. The calmer passages are static and more than a little mannered. Transitions are operated brusquely and without grace. There is a certain willful barbarism about the relation of theme to accompaniment. The whole picture of the later Beethoven music, as you can see, is complete, with all its mannerisms and all its perfectly real seriousness. And Stravinsky's music has here, just as Beethoven's did beneath the mannerisms he had inherited from Mozart and Haydn and those he had acquired in the course of his own composing life, an undeniable integrity of expression.

I should like to say also a certain grandeur of expression, were it not for the fact that grandeur, just as in many of Beethoven's later works, is as much the *modus operandi*, the conscious manner of the piece, as it is a result of inherent excellence. It is even more than in Beethoven the subject-matter, because the concerto is a study of another man's stylistic achievement. In Beethoven's case that achievement consisted in the extended expression of grandiose sentiments in a vocabulary of such astounding directness that musical scholars have never yet been able to agree how far plain rudeness, a deliberate avoidance of the amenities, was of the essence. I think last night's audience, though certainly impressed by his talent, felt equally uncertain about Mr. Stravinsky's desire to please.

March 23, 1944

Shostakovich's Seventh

WHETHER one is able to listen without mind-wandering to the Seventh Symphony of Dmitri Shostakovich probably depends on the rapidity of one's musical perceptions. It seems to have been written for the slow-witted, the not very musical and the distracted. In this respect it differs from nearly all those other symphonies in which abnormal length is part and parcel of the composer's concept. Beethoven's Ninth, Mahler's Ninth and Eighth, Bruckner's Seventh, and the great Berlioz "machines" are long because they could not have been made any shorter without eliminating something the author wanted in. Their matter is complex and cannot be expounded briefly.

The Shostakovich piece, on the other hand, is merely a stretching out of material that is in no way deep or difficult to understand. The stretching itself is not even a matter of real, though possibly unnecessary, development. It is for the most part straight repetition. The piece seems to be the length it is not because the substance of it would brook no briefer expression but because, for some reason not inherent in the material, the composer wished it that way. Of what that reason could possibly be I have only the vaguest notion. That the reason was clear to its author I have not the slightest doubt, however, because the piece all through bears the marks of complete assurance. It is no pent-up pouring out of personal feelings and still less an encyclopedic display of musical skill. It is as interminably straightforward and withal as limited in spiritual scope as a film like *The Great Ziegfeld* or *Gone with the Wind*. It could have said what it says in fifteen minutes, or it could have gone on for two hours more. The proportions of the work seem to this auditor, in short, wholly arbitrary.

They do not seem, nevertheless, accidental. Nothing seems accidental in the piece. The themes are clearly thought out and their doings are simplified with a master's hand. The harmonies, the contrapuntal web, the orchestration show no evidence of floundering or of experiment. If the music has no mystery and consequently no real freedom of thought, neither does it contain any obscurity or any evidence of personal frustration. It is as objective as an editorial, as self-assured as the news report of a public ceremony.

Heretofore this author's music, whether theatrical or symphonic, has been animated by an instinct for easy theatrical values. He has put into his works with never-failing effect crowd scenes, barcarolles, burlesques, and patriotic finales, holding these all together with a kind of neutral continuity-writing in two-part counterpoint. The most entertaining of these numbers have always been the burlesques of bourgeois musical taste, which were the more charming for their being purged, as it were, of bitterness by the optimism of the final patriotic and military passages. One could always feel in them the rambunctious but gifted boy whose heart was really in the right place. In spite of the static and not very significant character of the incessant two-part counterpoint between, his "production numbers," if one may call them that in symphonic music, have always been bright, full of gusto, and genuinely characteristic of their composer. They have put us in contact with a real person.

The Seventh Symphony has the same formal structure as the rest of its author's work. It is a series of production numbers, interspersed with neutral matter written chiefly in that same two-part counterpoint. There is a mechanized military march and the usual patriotic ending, neither of them quite as interesting or imaginative as it might be. And the rest of the episodes are even tamer. The pastorale and the Protestant chorale are competent routine stuff, no more; and the continuity counterpoint, though less static than usual, just sort of runs on as if some cinematic narrative were in progress that needed neutral accompaniment. The opening passage, which is said to represent the good Soviet citizen, is bold and buoyant. But nowhere is there any real comedy, which is what Shostakovich does best.

It is no reproach to an author to say that one of his works is the kind of work it is. And this work is certainly of more sober mien than most of its author's others. It is very long and very serious, and both these qualities are certainly deliberate observances. The facile competence and the assurance of the whole thing, moreover, eliminate the possibility that any auditor find the struggle between the artist and his material a major subject of interest. It is easy to listen to the piece, equally easy to skip any part of it without missing the sense of the whole. It is excellent journalism, and some of it can even be remembered. But it will probably not make much difference to anybody's inner musical life whether he hears it or doesn't.

Shostakovich is an abundant musician, a "natural" composer. He is also an experienced and perfectly assured one. Heretofore he has manifested a boyish taste for low comedy (redeemed by patriotic sentiments) that gave gusto to his writing and made listening to it sometimes fun. The present work shows a wish to put boyish things behind him and an ability to do so without losing confidence in himself. That it is less amusing than his previous works is not to its discredit. That it is, in spite of its serious air and pretentious proportions, thin of substance, unoriginal, and shallow indicates that the mature production of this gifted master is likely to be on the stuffy side. That he has so deliberately diluted his matter, adapted it, by both excessive simplification and excessive repetition, to the comprehension of a child of eight, indicates that he is willing to write down to a real or fictitious psychology of mass consumption in a way that may eventually disqualify him for consideration as a serious composer.

October 18, 1942

More of Same

SHOSTAKOVICH's Eighth Symphony, which was performed at yesterday afternoon's broadcast concert of the Philharmonic-Symphony Orchestra in Carnegie Hall, has been hitherto surrounded by its protectors with an air of mystery. The Columbia Broadcasting System has encouraged one to believe that a certain sum was paid for the performing rights and then refused to admit or deny the figure. The Russians themselves have refused to make any formal statement about the work at all. Though performed with public success in Moscow as early as November of last year, the newspapers that reflect official opinion there, *Pravda* and *Izvestia*, have never reviewed it. The piece itself, however, is as plain as the nose on your face. Why Russian government circles should reserve judgment on it is as difficult to imagine as any loyal reason why its American backers should go all kittenish about what they have done to deserve it.

The symphony, in four movements, lasts sixty-three minutes. Its melodic material is interesting; and if this is not always of the highest expressivity in degree, there is never any doubt about the nature of its expressive intent. The formal continuity is loose, but quite sufficient for a work of broad and simple character. There is no diffuseness; there is, as in the Seventh Symphony by the same author, merely extension. The orchestration is thin but tense. Its effects, like the melodic and contrapuntal ones, are easy to follow, both because many of them employ only one or two instruments and because all of them are insisted upon at some length.

This symphony is typical of its author's recent work. It is economical in the sense that matter ordinarily sufficient for a twenty-minute piece has been stretched out to last an hour. It has been stretched by the use of lengthy instrumental solos and other kinds of thin writing, but not by any abuse of literal repetition. There is little in the piece that need have taken very long either to compose or to score. Yet for all the spreading thin of its substance, the musical interest of this is sustained and homogeneous. Here is no carelessly thrown-together construction, but a rather remarkably stretched-out one.

The political value of launchings such as those the recent works of this composer have received is not a question requiring opinion from this department. But if symphonic music has any real value as national propaganda, it is difficult to imagine a contemporary composer better suited than Shostakovich to the producing of it for this purpose. No one else writes so seriously, so simply, so plainly. No one else makes an impression of sincerity with so little effort. Very probably length is a help to him in making this impression, since nobody ever takes a long piece for wholly meretricious. It is hard to see otherwise what that length accomplishes. Certainly it is a deliberately adopted device. Its texture is too skillfully attenuated for it to be the result of mere abundance. And anyway there is no abundance in it; but there is, on the other hand, every device of economy known to musical composition.

April 3, 1944

Smetana's Heir

THE BOSTON SYMPHONY ORCHESTRA under *Serge Koussevitzky's* direction.

Symphony No. 1 (first performance)	Martinů
Symphony No. 3. ("Eroica")	Beethoven

What a pleasure! What a pleasure to hear the Boston Symphony Orchestra again! Yesterday afternoon's concert in Carnegie Hall was substantial and delicious, with two symphonies for fare, an old and a new — the Beethoven "Eroica" and a First by the brilliant Czechish composer Bohuslav Martinů. The music was inter-

esting, and the renditions couldn't have been more elegant. Just
think of it! An ensemble that sounds like an ensemble playing
music that sounds like music! It restores one's faith; it really does.

The Martinů Symphony is a beauty. It is wholly lovely and
doesn't sound like anything else. Original is not the word for it,
because the thematic material is not quite that. The best of this,
moreover, is folklorish in the good Czech tradition. The harmonic
underpinning is a little plain, too, solid enough but not imaginative. Personal or individual would describe the work better. Because these words describe style rather than substance.

Personal indeed is the delicate but vigorous rhythmic animation, the singing (rather than dynamic) syncopation that permeates
the work. Personal and individual, too, is the whole orchestral
sound of it, the acoustical superstructure that shimmers constantly. It doesn't glow like Debussy or glitter like Ravel. It is
more like Berlioz in its translucency or like Smetana, Mr. Martinů's compatriot. It is like Smetana because the shining sounds
of it sing as well as shine; the instrumental complication is a part
of the musical conception, not an icing laid over it.

The shimmer I speak of is produced acoustically by mixing
acid sonorities with sweet ones. There is always an oboe around,
a muted trumpet or horn, violin harmonics, or light tremolos
played near the bridge. Against these are sweet flutes rising in
thirds, or clarinets. Often the strings play subdivided, high and
tenderly; and what they play is not sugary, but a shade acidulous
in its harmony. Consistently the whole is pointed up by delicately
percussive harp or piano. One would not have dreamed that after
fifty years' vulgarization of this kind of writing anybody could
make it sound so fresh, so lovely, so varied, so entirely personal.
One wouldn't have thought, either, that a composer could keep it
up through a whole symphony, that he could find enough variants
to make it interesting.

Martinů has kept it interesting, however, and made it deeply
expressive. He has amplified his taste for acid-sweet mixtures into
a full stylistic outlet for personal thoughts. He has had no need of
demagogy from the brass or of sob stuff from the strings. He uses
both as musical instruments of an ensemble that constantly sings.
It sings in many timbres and many colors, but always the colors
are clean and bright and always they are integrated into a shimmering pattern. The symphony is beautiful music and beautiful
workmanship. And if, in spite of its impersonal subject-matter (I

take it to be a meditation about his native land), it is highly individual music nevertheless, that fact places Martinů already above
his predecessor Dvořák and in the high company of Smetana,
greatest of all those symphonic composers in whose work patrio-
tism is of the essence.

November 22, 1942

Repeating Pattern

PHILHARMONIC–SYMPHONY ORCHESTRA, *Artur Rodzinski*, conductor, with *Robert Casadesus* as piano soloist.

MARCH IN TIME OF WAR (first performance)	HARRIS
SYMPHONY NO. 2 (first New York performance)	MARTINŮ
PIANO CONCERTO NO. 5 ("Emperor")	BEETHOVEN
TILL EULENSPIEGEL	STRAUSS

MARTINŮ's Second Symphony, which received its first local performance last night at a Philharmonic concert in Carnegie Hall,
is less fresh than his first. Its melodic material is a little too plain
and sensible for the ornate figurations in which it is embedded.
The themes are immobilized, like flies in amber; they are repeated
prismatically, but they do not expand or go anywhere. The piece
has the stamp of high-class workmanship, but it follows a formula
that is already becoming monotonous.

Like the shimmering sonorities of his master, Albert Roussel,
the glittering and note-heavy textures of Bohuslav Martinů are,
for all their transparency, an inflexible medium of expression. They
suit best exotic or fanciful subjects. Applied to straightforward
melodies of songlike character or to the semi-abstract motifs that
are the basis of symphonic continuity, they create a dichotomy of
style that suggests a photograph of your Aunt Sophie in front of
the Taj Mahal. Neither the subject nor the background appears
to advantage in such an arrangement. The background goes a little tawdry, and the subject does not express itself completely.
The Second Symphony last night sounded mechanical, repetitive,
overelaborate, and essentially trivial.

Far from trivial was the piano-playing of Robert Casadesus.
Utterly clean without any hardness, it had no sloppy edges any-

where and no ugly tone. Alone among the great virtuosos, Mr. Casadesus has preserved the tenderness of intimacy in the framework of power-projection. He has also preserved the French rhythmic tradition (which is the ancient and basic European one) in the rendering of German music. Never a quantity out of line; never a stress but for rhetorical reason. Many a passage of considerable length is executed, loud or soft, without any dynamic alteration of any kind; and the meter is clearer than if it had been thumped out. His was an extraordinary performance of the "Emperor" Concerto, extraordinary for its beauty, its power, its physical perfection, its intellectual distinction, its musical *élan*. Its only fault was a tendency to hurry along (largely the fault of the orchestra) in the waltz finale.

December 31, 1943

The Hindemith Case

PAUL HINDEMITH's music is both mountainous and mouselike. The volume of it is enormous; its expressive content is minute and not easy to catch. His output is voluminous; that implies a certain facility. His tonal grammar and syntax are perfectly clear; that is evidence of care taken. His work has style also; and that is proof of its artistic integrity, of an integration between what its author feels and what his listener hears.

There is nevertheless a good deal that is obscure about it. How often has one sat through pieces by Hindemith that seem to make sense musically but little or no sense emotionally! Even so ingratiating a piece as the Third String Quartet sounds more like the work of a composer who had nothing better to do one morning than like something that had got itself born out of inner necessity. His work could hardly be called hermetic, because hermetism is usually pretty compact. I should say that the obscurity one encounters in it is due rather to the diffuseness of its thought than to any especial concentration of meaning or any rigidly novel technique.

It is not, properly speaking, academic music. It is too loosely put together for that. It is cleanly written down but not much polished, and it meanders more than is considered good "form" in academic circles. Also, its instrumentation, though completely

sure-handed, is rarely brilliant or "effective" in the way that the
work of celebrated pedagogues is likely to be. He does not seem
to be interested in stylistic or cultural showing off any more than
he is in emotional expansiveness or emotional concentration.

His music exerts a great fascination, however, over music students; and it is not without a certain impressiveness for the music
public in general. It is obviously both competent and serious. It
is dogmatic and forceful and honest and completely without
charm. It is as German as anything could be and farther removed
from the Viennese spirit than any music could possibly be that
wasn't the work of a German from the Lutheran North. It has no
warmth, no psychological understanding, no gentleness, no *Ge-
mütlichkeit,* and no sex-appeal. It hasn't even the smooth surface
tension of systematic atonality. It is neither humane nor stylish,
though it does have a kind of style, a style rather like that of some
ponderously monumental and not wholly incommodious railway
station.

Having reflected in this vein for some years about Hindemith's
non-programmatic music, it was with the hope of maybe finding
I was all wrong that I went to hear the National Orchestra from
Washington play symphonic excerpts from *Mathis der Maler* last
Tuesday evening. I wanted to see what the least picturesque composer alive would do with the most picturesque subject imaginable. I remembered his having tried his hand some years ago at a
picturesque subject drawn from modern life in an opera called
Neues vom Tage, and I remembered having been amused at the
way he had managed to write music for that work that was ponderous and cute at the same time.

Mathis der Maler turned out to be more of same, only more
serious in tone, on account of its subject-matter, which has to do
with three religious pictures by Mathias Grünewald — a *Descent
of Angels,* an *Entombment,* and a *Temptation of Saint Anthony.*
The subject is an ambitious one and presents a problem of musical
method for which there is no precedent in musical tradition.

There are several classic procedures for representing visual
images by means of music. There is the ancient and simple one
employed by Rameau and Handel and Sebastian Bach, which is to
imitate in the melodic contours either the silhouette or the characteristic motion of the thing one wishes to describe, valleys being
exalted, for instance, the crooked being made straight and the
rough places plain, Adam falling out of paradise, troupes of

angels tripping down the major scale, and gentlemen attempting from love's sickness to fly-y-y-y-y-y-y-y-y in vain. There is also the Romantic procedure of adding to this auditive and kinetic vocabulary of visual suggestion a subjective description of the emotional effect of it all on some sensitive observer or participant. Bacchanalian routs, debauches in Venusberg, Swiss mountain weather, graveyard ballets, and visits to hell on Walpurgisnacht are common in nineteenth-century music.

Mendelssohn's contribution to landscape technique consisted in making the observer always the same man, himself. In Scotland, in Italy, in fairyland, he is always Mendelssohn, sympathetic and sensitive and strictly non-participant. The modern French technique of musical landscape painting, of which Debussy was the most skillful practitioner, is essentially Mendelssohnian, though the expressive range and psychological intensity of Debussy's work are greater than those of Mendelssohn's because it is not bound to the German conception of thorough bass or to the idea of "developing" the thematic material. It conceives any melodic line as a self-sufficient expressive unit, counterpoint as a plurality of such units, harmony and rhythm as coloristic ornamentation to melody. "Form" in the German sense of harmonic progress is something to be avoided, since it implies that the author is either going somewhere or trying to make a point, instead of receiving and transmitting a series of related impressions from some point of view where he is supposed to remain motionless, his will immobilized by the intensity of the visual-auditive photographic process. Musical landscape painting does not need "form" in the sense of progress. It needs, on the contrary, a static musical unity based on sequential statement of all the things that need to be said in order to make the piece a proper description of its subject.

All these procedures exist as known ways of translating sight into sound. There is no known way of translating into sound visual pictures that have already been translated into so stylized a medium as painting. A composer's version of a painter's version of the Church's version of scenes from sacred history is what *Mathis der Maler* purports to be. As such it is naturally not very successful. It couldn't be. When one considers, in addition, that Hindemith has never properly liberated himself from the German bass, that his rhythm is constrained and unimaginative, that whenever he can't think what to do next he writes imitative counterpoint, that his melodic contours, though dignified enough, are inexpressive, that his creative concentration is too diffuse to allow him to write either visual music or subjective emotional music effectively, it is surprising that the *Mathis* tryptich should come off at all.

It comes off, just as all his music does, in spite of everything, by good intentions and by being playably orchestrated. The *Entombment* has a certain directly expressive quality, though the influence of Grünewald would seem to be present more as private stimulus to the composer's invention than as anything a listener need take cognizance of. The *Descent of the Angels* and the *Temptation of Saint Anthony* are not handled as convincingly, on the whole, as the Romantic masters handled similar subjects. Saint Anthony's victory over temptation, for instance, is represented by a routine Lutheran chorale harmonized for brass in a routine manner that might just as well represent Mr. Hindemith's satisfaction at getting to the end of his piece as a saint's triumph over his lower nature.

Mathis der Maler is typical of North Germany at its best and of modern scholastic facility at its worst. It is complex, ineffective, unpolished, lacking in both grace and expressive power. All the same, it has a moral elevation and a straightforward, if clumsy, honesty that make it impossible not to respect and to admire it for being at all times unquestionably "good" music.

February 9, 1941

Serious Music

NEW FRIENDS OF MUSIC, first concert of the season yesterday in Town Hall with the Budapest String Quartet (*Josef Roismann*, first violin; *Alexander Schneider*, second violin; *Boris Kroyt*, viola, and *Mischa Schneider*, cello); *Louis Bailly*, viola; *Benar Heifetz*, cello; *Mordecai Bauman*, baritone, and *Milton Kaye*, accompanist.

QUARTET IN D MINOR (posthumous)   SCHUBERT
Budapest Quartet
Songs by CHARLES IVES: EVENING, ANN STREET, TWO LITTLE FLOWERS, GENERAL BOOTH ENTERS INTO HEAVEN, THE GREATEST MAN, CHARLES RUTLEDGE
Mr. Bauman
Sextet, OP. 4, VERKLÄRTE NACHT   SCHÖNBERG
Budapest Quartet, Messrs. *Bailly* and *Heifetz*

CITY dwellers are at their best in early winter between five and seven of an afternoon. No time is more propitious for the projection of high musical thought; none finds the devoted listener more completely in possession of his faculties. Yesterday's concert of the New Friends of Music was a delight to the ear and to the mind, and I fancy the audience at Town Hall must have offered equal delight to the executants.

Franz Schubert's "Death and the Maiden" quartet is a deeply tragic, lyrically impassioned meditation on the death of Franz Schubert, provoked by his having contracted an incurable disease. The work is Schubert at his most inspired and most sustained. The Budapest String Quartet played it with comprehension of its emotional poignancy as well as of its musical values.

Chamber music in a hall that seats 1,500 people is, of course, a contradiction in terms; and string-quartet sonorities are likely to come out pretty false under such conditions. Even if forced fortissimos are avoided, there is a constant temptation to make overpowerful accents and a certainty that no matter what happens the tone of the ensemble will have a certain deadness laid on it.

The reason why public string-quartet playing is such a difficult art is that in the clear, dead acoustic of such halls every musical fault is audible; and at the same time no auditory glamour, no sharpness of sensuous delight, is there to charm the listener through a work or passage that isn't quite all it should be in rhythm or intonation.

The Budapest Quartet has a satisfying cellist to build its tonal structure on. Mr. Mischa Schneider's tone is never groany, never waily, rarely hoarse. He keeps his fortes within the limits of what can be made to sound; and his rhythm is a live thing, a breathing thing, a sustaining pulse for the whole musical musculature.

Mr. Boris Kroyt's viola and Mr. Alexander Schneider's second violin are delicate, higher distillates of the same essential timbre. The first violin does not blend so well, stands out a trifle by its too thin, acid tone and by being every now and then squarely off pitch.

Charles Ives's songs have a certain sincerity and worthiness about them. On the whole they are pretty kittenish. The texts are kittenish; the tunes are kittenish; the accompaniments are practically kitty on the keys. Only short passages of "Evening" and "Charles Rutledge" have any musical or prosodic inevitability about them, and they sound more like improvisation than like organic composition. The finale of "General Booth Enters into Heaven," however, the part built around the hymn-tune "There Is a Fountain Filled with Blood," is first-class music. The double harmonies are not just a blur, as Ives's harmonies so often are. They are like a prism that defracts, a lens that amplifies; and their notation and placing are as precise as a good job in optics.

Verklärte Nacht, far from being an isolated example of something or other in Arnold Schönberg's career, as is commonly supposed, is a work that embodies all that composer's finest and corniest qualities. The finesse of its string-writing makes it a joy to play and to hear. The seriousness of its emotional content is unquestionable. Its slithery chromaticism is the emotional and technical diving-board from which a young man of such gift and power (he wrote it at twenty-five) could only plump off square into the mud-puddle of atonality. Atonality was already being theorized about in Vienna in those days (1889). The young Schönberg slipped, plumped, embraced, stayed.

The most individual among Schönberg's many gifts as a composer is his ability to enlarge an emotional experience without going to town sentimentally about it. He blows it up, not to hit you over the head with it, but to inspect it. His *Verklärte Nacht*, no less than his *Gurrelieder* and his *Pierrot Lunaire*, is a microscopic examination, a psychic analysis of its stated poetic text. Schönberg is a late Romantic, if you will; but not for nothing did he spend his first fifty years as a fellow citizen and contemporary of Dr. Sigmund Freud.

October 21, 1940

Real Modern Music

NBC SYMPHONY ORCHESTRA, *Leopold Stokowski*, conductor, in Studio 8-H, Radio City, yesterday afternoon with *Eduard Steuermann* as piano soloist.

"Tu mancavi a tormentarmi"	Cesti-Stokowski
Unfinished Symphony	Schubert
Piano Concerto, Op. 42 (first performance)	Schönberg

ARNOLD SCHÖNBERG'S Piano Concerto, which received its first performance anywhere yesterday afternoon by the NBC Symphony
Orchestra, Leopold Stokowski conducting and Eduard Steuermann playing the solo part, is the first original work for large
orchestra by this master to be heard in New York since quite a
long time back. For many of our young music-lovers it is no doubt
their first hearing of any orchestral work of its kind. One cannot
be too grateful to Mr. Stokowski for giving himself the trouble to
prepare it and for paying his radio listeners the compliment of
presuming their interest. It is an honor paid not only to one of
the great living masters of music but to the American public as
well; and the General Motors Corporation, which sponsored the
broadcast, should be proud of the event.*

The piece, which lasts a shade under twenty minutes, consists
of four sections neatly sewn together and played without pause —
a waltz, a scherzo, an adagio, and a rondo. All are based on a
single theme, though there is considerable development of secondary material in the scherzo. The musical syntax is that commonly known as the twelve-tone system, which is to say that the
employment of dissonance is integral rather than ornamental. The
expression of the work is romantic and deeply sentimental, as is
Schönberg's custom and as is the best modern Viennese tradition.

The instrumentation, too, is characteristic of its author. It is
delicate and scattered. The music hops around from one instrument to another all the time. It sounds like chamber music for a
hundred players. There is plenty of melody, but no massing of
instruments on any single line for giving the melody emphasis,
as is customary in oratorical symphonic writing. The work is not
oratorical, anyway. It is poetical and reflective. And it builds up
its moments of emphasis by rhythmic device and contrapuntal
complication, very much as old Sebastian Bach was wont to do.
Its inspiration and its communication are lyrical, intimate, thought-
ful, sweet, and sometimes witty, like good private talk. At no point
is there grandiloquence or theater. The work derives much of its
impressiveness from its avoidance of any attempt to impress us
by force.

Its great beauty is derived partly from the extreme delicacy
and variety of its instrumentation and partly from the consistency

---

* Leopold Stokowski's contract as conductor of the NBC Orchestra was
not renewed for the following year. His assiduity toward modern composition
is considered in musical circles to be the chief reason for this change.

of its harmonic structure (a result of its systematic observance of the twelve-tone syntax). Its particular combination of lyric freedom and figurational fancy with the strictest tonal logic places it high among the works of this greatest among the living Viennese masters (resident now in Hollywood) and high among the musical achievements of our century. With the increasing conservatism of contemporary composers about matters harmonic, many of our young people have never really heard much modern music. Radical and thoroughgoing modern music, I mean. It is too seldom performed. Well, here is a piece of it and a very fine one, a beautiful and original work that is really thought through and that doesn't sound like anything else.

Eduard Steuermann played the piano part with all delicacy and love. There isn't much in it to show off with (only two brief and fragmentary cadenzas, and they are not written for brilliance), but the piano is there all the time. It weaves in and out rather in chamber style, and Mr. Steuermann never overplayed it or underplayed it. Everybody gave his serious best to this serious and far from easy work. One came away almost not minding that it had been preceded by the inexcusably long (nearly five minutes) commercial plug that is the NBC hour's present sacrifice to commercial sponsorship.

February 7, 1944

A Wealth of Dissonance

INTERNATIONAL SOCIETY FOR CONTEMPORARY MUSIC, Church of St. Mary the Virgin, last night. Participants: *Rudof Kolisch*, violinist; *Eduard Steuermann*, pianist; *Bennington String Quartet*; *Carl Weinrich*, organist.

SONATA FOR VIOLIN AND PIANO   JANÁČEK
Rudolf Kolisch, Eduard Steuermann
STRING QUARTET IN B FLAT   IMBRIE
Bennington String Quartet
TOCCATA   MUFFAT
VARIATIONS (first performance)   SCHÖNBERG
FUGUE IN E (first New York performance)   LAMB
Carl Weinrich

MUSIC of dissonant texture is a particular cult of the International Society for Contemporary Music. The music of Arnold Schönberg is the prayer book for dissonance-lovers, especially those brought up in the central-European rite. The Church of St. Mary the Virgin has long been the seat, if not of dissonance, of dissidence from the banal in musical practice. Last night it housed a concert of the International Society that was pretext and framing for a new work by Schönberg, written for that most dissonant of all instruments, the organ, and played to perfection on New York's most brilliant-sounding organ by Carl Weinrich.

The organ is a dissonant instrument because it contains rows of pipes tuned to furnish the entire harmonic series, or most of it, upon the pressing down of any one key. The simplest major chord under such an arrangement becomes a highly complex sonority. Many churches, especially those with stone interiors, those with more height than width and those that contain complex sound-reflecting surfaces in the form of transepts, vaults, tribunes, and side aisles, are in themselves highly dissonant sound-boxes. The dying away of any sound in such resonant buildings being somewhat slower than instantaneous, the playing in them of rapid organ music, even though this be composed according to classical harmonic syntax, produces a complexity of reverberation that is virtually complete. Modern music does not sound one whit more discordant at St. Mary's, for instance, and didn't last night, than a toccata by the seventeenth-century composer Georg Muffat.

This is not to say that all organ music sounds alike. Music differs in tune and rhythm and progress (or form); and one harmonic sequence differs from another in glory, as well as in significance. But since any music played on the fuller combinations of a rich and bright-toned organ in a reverberating enclosure makes all the tones of the chromatic scale all the time, the calculated dissonance of modern writing adds little to the effective dissonance that is inherent to the acoustical set-up.

Schönberg's Variations for Organ, opus 40, finished in 1943, is not a twelve-tone piece. It is squarely, though chromatically, in D minor. It is coloristic in conception and gives opportunity for diversified registration. Rhythmically it is a bit halting, like most of this author's music. Harmonically and contrapuntally it is full of fancy. The whole effect is that of musical impressionism, an accumulation of fancy being its aim rather than an impressive build-up.

Hugh Lamb's Fugue in E, on the other hand, though equally dissonant, is not a color-piece; it is a line-drawing that builds to a climax of complex sound by the march of unrelenting counterpoint. Both works are rich to the ear; but the Schönberg is lighter, wittier, more romantic in feeling, and intellectually the more distinguished. Lamb's is a sound church piece; Schönberg's is poetry.

A String Quartet in B flat by Sergeant Andrew Imbrie preceded these organ pieces. It is a skillful work, dissonant in sound, oratorical in its gesture, with good melodic material and a serious poetic tone. It, too, profited from the resonant acoustics of the church; but even in a dry concert hall I am sure it would have sounded well, because no amount of acoustical glamour can conceal musical poverty. Sergeant Imbrie's work showed no such poverty. It showed original musical thought, sound workmanship and dignified, highly personal sentiments.[*]

April 11, 1944

[*] Sergeant Imbrie's String Quartet in B flat was later awarded the New York Music Critics' Circle award as the best new piece of American chamber music first performed in New York in the 1943–4 season.

French Music Here

DARIUS MILHAUD has communicated to me the catalogue of an exhibit held recently in the foyer of the Music Building at Mills College, Oakland, California, for the two weeks from November 27 through December 11, 1940, of Erik Satie's manuscripts. These manuscripts, the property of Monsieur Milhaud, were brought by him last summer from France at some inconvenience, since the traveling facilities available at that time did not always include transportation of unlimited personal impedimenta. That Monsieur Milhaud should have made room for these at the cost of leaving behind manuscripts and orchestral material of his own for which he might have need during his stay here is evidence of the esteem in which he holds the unpublished works of the late Sage of Arceuil.

The catalogue, which contains 105 items, mentions fourteen bound booklets that average forty pages each and fourteen paperbound booklets that run as high as twenty-five pages each. In addition, there are the twenty-four-page orchestral score of *Five Grimaces for "A Midsummer Night's Dream"* and a score of fifteen pages of a piece called simply *Danse*, dated December 5, 1890, later incorporated into the longer work entitled *Three Pieces in the Shape of a Pear*. There are sketches for three ballets, *Jack-in-the-Box*, *Relâche* and *Mercure*, and for the marionette opera *Geneviève de Brabant*. Also songs, famous ones like "Le Chapelier," from *Alice in Wonderland*, and "La Statue de Bronze," and dozens of unpublished waltz-songs and other such light matter written during the eight (or was it twelve?) years that Satie earned his living by playing the piano at a small theatrical establishment called The Harvest Moon (La Lune Rousse), an enterprise of the type known as *cabaret Montmartrois* or *boîte de chansonniers*.

There are counterpoint exercises, too, and fugues and chorales from his second student days when, already forty, he enrolled at Vincent d'Indy's Schola Cantorum and for four years went through all the scholastic musical grind he had skipped in youth. And there are letters, forty-three of them, to Monsieur Milhaud, photographs, programs, clippings, and accounts. Item 47 is a first edition of *Images*, by Claude Debussy, bearing a dedication to Satie from his lifelong friend.

The collection, as one can see from the above brief digest, is an extensive one. Its importance depends on what one thinks of Erik Satie as a musical figure. This writer is in agreement with Darius Milhaud and with some of the other contemporary French composers in placing Satie's work among the major musical values of our century. He has even gone so far in print, nearly twenty years ago, as to parallel the three German B's — Bach, Beethoven, and Brahms — with the three S's of modern music — in descending order of significance, Satie, Schönberg, and Stravinsky.

That is a personal estimate, of course, though one agreed to by many musicians in France and some elsewhere. I should not wish to force my personal musical tastes on anyone, any more than I should want anybody else's forced on me. If you love Mahler, for instance, Mahler is your oyster; and the same goes for Strauss, Sibelius, Palestrina, and Gershwin. But there are certain key personalities without some acceptance of which it is impossible to understand and accept the music of the place and epoch that they dominated. Erik Satie is one of those.

French and other Parisian music of the 1930's has been but

little performed in America. (That is an old quarrel of mine with
the League of Composers.) Such of it as has been performed
here is usually considered to be mildly pleasant but on the whole
not very impressive. This estimate is justified only on the part of
persons initiated to its æsthetic. And its æsthetic, as was that of
Debussy, is derived directly from the words and from the works
of Satie, whose firmest conviction was that the only healthy thing
music can do in our century is to stop trying to be impressive.

The Satie musical æsthetic is the only twentieth-century musical æsthetic in the Western world. Schönberg and his school are
Romantics; and their twelve-tone syntax, however intriguing one
may find it intellectually, is the purest Romantic chromaticism.
Hindemith, however gifted, is a neo-classicist, like Brahms, with
ears glued firmly to the past. The same is true of the later Stravinsky and of his satellites. Even *Petrouchka* and *The Rite of
Spring* are the Wagnerian theater symphony and the nineteenth-
century cult of nationalistic folklore applied to ballet.

Of all the influential composers of our time, and influence even
his detractors cannot deny him, Satie is the only one whose works
can be enjoyed and appreciated without any knowledge of the
history of music. These lack the prestige of traditional modernism,
as they lack the prestige of the Romantic tradition itself, a tradition of constant Revolution. They are as simple, as straightforward, as devastating as the remarks of a child.

To the uninitiated they sound trifling. To those who love them
they are fresh and beautiful and firmly right. And that freshness
and rightness have long dominated the musical thought of France.
Any attempt to penetrate that musical thought without first penetrating that of Erik Satie is fruitless. Even Debussy is growing
less and less comprehensible these days to those who never knew
Satie.

When Satie used to be performed here occasionally, the works
were found difficult to understand. French music in all centuries
has been rather special, not quite like anything else. In our century it has become esoteric to a degree not currently admitted
even in France. It has eschewed the impressive, the heroic, the
oratorical, everything that is aimed at moving mass audiences.
Like modern French poetry and painting, it has directed its communication to the individual.

It has valued, in consequence, quietude, precision, acuteness
of auditory observation, gentleness, sincerity and directness of

statement. Persons who admire these qualities in private life are not infrequently embarrassed when they encounter them in public places. It is this embarrassment that gives to all French music, and to the work of Satie and his neophytes in particular, an air of superficiality, as if it were salon music written for the drawing-rooms of some snobbish set.

To suppose this true is to be ignorant of the poverty and the high devotion to art that marked the life of Erik Satie to its very end in a public hospital. And to ignore all art that is not heroic or at least intensely emotional is to commit the greatest of snobberies. For, by a reversal of values that constitutes one of the most surprising phenomena of a century that has so far been occupied almost exclusively with reversing values, the only thing really hermetic and difficult to understand about the music of Erik Satie is the fact that there is nothing hermetic about it at all.

It wears no priestly robes; it mumbles no incantations; it is not painted up by Max Factor to terrify elderly ladies or to give little girls a thrill. Neither is it designed to impress orchestral conductors or to get anybody a job teaching school. It has literally no devious motivation. It is as simple as a friendly conversation and in its better moments exactly as poetic and as profound.

These thoughts occurred to me the other evening at a League of Composers concert of recent works by Milhaud. Not a piece on the program had a climax or a loud ending. Nothing was pretentious or apocalyptical or messianic or overdramatized. The composer's effort at all times was to be clear and true. And when I saw the catalogue of the Satie manuscripts and learned how Milhaud had brought them to America at the cost of not bringing all his own; when I remembered, also, the brilliant and theatrically effective works of Milhaud's youth, *Le Bœuf sur le Toit* and *Le Train Bleu* and *La Création du Monde,* I realized that after Satie's death he had been led, how unconsciously I cannot say, to assume the mantle of Satie's leadership and to eschew all musical vanity. That, at any rate, is my explanation of how one of the most facile and turbulent talents of our time has become one of the most completely calm of modern masters; and how, by adding thus depth and penetration and simple humanity to his gamut, he has become the first composer of his country and a leader in that musical tradition which of all living musical traditions is the least moribund.

January 5, 1941

Better Than it Sounds

LEAGUE OF COMPOSERS, concert of works by Latin-American composers at the New York Public Library, with *Francisco Mignone*, composer-pianist; *Liddy Mignone*, soprano; *Hugo Balzo* and *Tapia-Caballero*, pianists; *Isaac Feldman*, violinist; *Carleton Sprague Smith* and *Gerald Rudy*, flutists, and *Sydney Beck*, violist, as soloists in the following program.

SECOND SONATA FOR PIANO   JOSÉ MARÍA CASTRO (Argentina)
Mr. Balzo
SONATA A TRES, for two Flutes and Viola   JOSÉ ARDÉVOL (Cuba)
Messrs. *Smith, Rudy* and *Beck*
THREE PIECES FOR VIOLIN AND PIANO:
CANCIÓN, RECITATIVO, ARABESCO   DOMINGO SANTA CRUZ (Chile)
Messrs. *Feldman* and *Tapia-Caballero*
Songs: BERIMBAU ("Jew's Harp"); A ESTRELA ("The Star"); PASSARINHO ESTA CANTANDO ("The Bird is Singing"); DONA JANAINA
FRANCISCO MIGNONE (Brazil)
Mme Mignone; Mr. Mignone at the piano
PIANO SONATA (1941)   MIGNONE
Mr. Mignone
MUSIC FOR CHILDREN: ("Zapateado"; "Quenas"; "Pericón"; "La Morochita"; "Popular Tune"; "Arroro Indigena"; "Danced Song")
LUIS GIANNEO (Argentina)
DANZA CRIOLLA   HECTOR TOSAR (Uruguay)
Mr. Balzo
SONATA NO. 2 FOR VIOLIN AND PIANO   CAMARGO GUARNIERI (Brazil)
Messrs. *Feldman* and *Balzo*

THE LEAGUE OF COMPOSERS CONCERT of works by living South American composers at the Public Library yesterday afternoon was a good deal of a disappointment. Both the works and their execution were animated by the best intentions and pulled off in some cases with no small skill, but somehow a proper ambiance for musical acceptance was missing. Decidedly a new formula is needed for the presentation of South American music. I have read and heard privately a great deal of this music. There is a large repertory of interesting stuff, but every time it is staged in the North American concert manner it is a flop. My acquaintance with the music leads me to believe that the fault is ours.

The South Americans seem to have a functional conception of

music, as all the Latin peoples do. Their music is written to be used rather than to be inspected. A great deal of it is reflective. This kind is pleasant to read or to play for two or three musical friends; it loses its intimacy and its gentle communication when it is subjected to concert expounding. Most of the Brazilian work is in popular vein. Miss Elsie Houston has made a success of this kind of music by singing it with its own kind of vocalization, keeping all flavor of the vocal studios out of it. Every time the works of Villa-Lobos and his school are performed without an air of informality and of spontaneity, they lose the quality of spontaneity that is their chief charm.

Between the frankly popular style and the wholly intimate style South Americans seem to have found no middle ground save that of virtuosity. Their theater music and their night-club music and their carnival music and their magic incantations are in every way admirable. The Brazilians are especially good at all these. The intellectual music of Uruguay, Argentina, Chile, and Peru is of a sincerity and a gentle loveliness unmatched, to my knowledge, elsewhere in the world. I have never yet heard a piece of South American music from anywhere that was written with any obvious awareness of a concert public, however intelligent that public might be, that did not fall into the ways of virtuosity and end by sounding hopelessly provincial. Because virtuosity is always provincial unless it is the flower of a decaying great tradition.

Now, South America, like North America, is musically very young. It has not had time yet to go to seed and fluff. Musical expression in this hemisphere is still a serious matter, even when it is gay and folksy. The concert hall is at best a mortuary chamber, most of all for living music. When that music is written, as the northern Europeans do it, with full consciousness of audience psychology, it becomes as formal a thing as a mythological opera or a learned lecture. Now, mythological operas and learned lectures are perfectly good things; but they both presuppose a public, or at least a patron and his guests. They are objective. The constant tendency of South American music to go either popular (which implies no public, only participants) or utterly intellectual, reflective, and private (which shows a clear indifference to impressiveness) makes me think that perhaps there isn't much public down there for any intellectual product more profound than salon meditations and facile virtuosity. In any case there is a great deal of music written in those parts that has the perfume of integrity. Some of this is folklorish and some of it is contrapuntal and abstract. None of it does itself justice in the columbarium-like layout of our professional concerts.

March 9, 1942

Harris and Shostakovich

BOSTON SYMPHONY ORCHESTRA, *Serge Koussevitzky*, conductor,

Overture-Fantasia, Romeo and Juliet	Tchaikovsky
Prelude to the opera Khovanstchina	Mussorgsky
Symphony No. 3	Roy Harris
Symphony No. 6	Shostakovich

AMERICA's most popular symphonist, Roy Harris, and Russia's best-known one (and we gather he is as popular at home as abroad), Dmitri Shostakovich, shared honors and applause at yesterday's concert of the Boston Symphony Orchestra in Carnegie Hall. Both composers are disputed about in professional circles, but the fact is scarcely controvertible that they have won the affection of a large musical public. The fact that yesterday's performance of Harris's Third Symphony was the thirty-third (all told) in three seasons means that the work has passed out of the novelty stage and that it is something more than a fillip to the musically curious.

Since any programmatic juxtaposition renders comparison inevitable, it is fair, I think, to consider yesterday's two symphonies and their authors as at least momentarily parallel. Mr. Harris's work appeared to me yesterday as the more original of the two, Mr. Shostakovich's as the more facile. Harris's Third Symphony has goodly melodic material; but its structure and instrumentation, though in no way banal, are somewhat naïve. Their naïveté, indeed, is the source of much of their intensity of expression. Shostakovich's material is less noteworthy, and his contrapuntal style lacks tension. But he orchestrates with some brilliance, and he builds a climax with professional smoothness. The notes of Harris are more significant than they sound, for their resonance is, even in the loudest tuttis, always muffled by unidiomatic instrumental writing and ungrateful chord dispositions. The Shostakovich score sounds at all times sonorously confident; but the notes themselves, though charming enough in the animated passages, are not nearly so convincing to this listener as the sound they make is agreeable.

It is possible that my greater interest in the music of Harris is due to nothing more recondite than the fact that we are fellow countrymen and that his musical thought is consequently sympathetic to my own instincts and sentiments. Even the greatest of the Russian musicians (and I do not consider Shostakovich one of these) owe much of their power over us to certain strangenesses of thought and manner. Harris's work is not strange at all; or if it is, it is so only because of its rather unprofessional surface tension. Inside, it is as familiar and as welcome as something that oft was felt (and deeply) but never said before.

There has been a great deal of effort made to interpret Harris as an American master of the (essentially European) heroic style. I think the idea is false, because I do not consider him a master of anything, least of all of that (even in Europe) foolish and decadent manner. Grandiloquent he is, and clumsy as a technician and hopelessly lacking in objectivity. Heroics are a form of theater, and Harris is without theatrical instinct. His one film score proved that. His is a reflective nature, lyrical and introspective and quietly fanciful. My interpretation of his qualities is, of course, no better than anybody else's; but I am moved by his music, and I feel, therefore, an obligation to describe it in my own way. Whatever its exact nature is, I believe it to be beautiful and more than skin-deep. I am not so convinced in the case of Shostakovich, for all his gaiety and gusto and sound facility.

The Boston orchestra played admirably, as usual. It occurred to me, listening to the Tchaikovsky *Romeo and Juliet,* that Mr. Koussevitzky's way of playing the works of this composer is more eloquent than what the others do with them because, in addition to his consistent avoidance of forced instrumental tone, he makes practically no alterations of the basic rhythm. Such as he does make are of a formal nature, like a slight retard before a new section. He never allows the expressive nature of a Tchaikovsky melody to interrupt the firm rhythm over which it flows. This reticence seems to me to clarify the music and to augment its significance.

April 5, 1942

Superficially Warlike

BOSTON SYMPHONY ORCHESTRA, *Serge Koussevitzky*, conductor.
assisted by HARVARD GLEE CLUB and RADCLIFFE CHORAL
SOCIETY, *G. Wallace Woodworth*, conductor.

A FREE SONG (*Secular Cantata No. 2*)	SCHUMANN
(First New York performance)	
ESSAY No. 1	BARBER
A LINCOLN PORTRAIT	COPLAND
(*Will Geer*, speaker)	
SYMPHONY No. 5	BEETHOVEN

THE BOSTON SYMPHONY ORCHESTRA offered yesterday afternoon in
Carnegie Hall a program without much inner unity. Such exter-
nal cohesion as it had consisted of indirect references to the war.
But musically the works played seemed rather to contradict one
another than to set one another off.

The title of Mr. William Schuman's secular cantata, *A Free
Song*, refers, I take it, since the composition is partly fugal in
style, not to musical freedom but to freedom of some other kind,
economic, social, religious, amorous, or political, no doubt.
The times being what they are, one would probably be safe in
betting it was the latter, though of certain evidence I have none,
the chorus's effective enunciation of the text being zero in row U.
The music's intrinsic interest seemed also to this listener to add up
to a not high figure.

Private Samuel Barber's Essay for Orchestra, No. 1, is a pretty
piece but not a very strong one. It resembles more a meditation
than it does the kind of logical exposition one usually associates
with the classical prose form of that name. Perhaps Mr. Barber
thinks of the word *essay* in its contemporary sense of a reflective
composition on some relatively trivial subject. Certainly his musical material here is not striking. Neither, unfortunately, is his
development of it, though there is, as always in this composer's
music, grace. The military note was added to this performance by
the composer's presence, bowing, in uniform.

Mr. Aaron Copland's *A Lincoln Portrait* consists of a pastorale,
a scherzo, and a melodrama. The first is plain but pleasant; the

second, a sort of county-fair scene made up of phrases out of Stephen Foster, is brilliantly picturesque. Lincoln himself comes into the portrait only by quotation, when an actor (yesterday it was Mr. Will Geer) speaks, as finale, over a slight orchestral accompaniment selected passages from the addresses of the great President. Even if Mr. Geer had not seen fit to utter these in the flat and twangy accent used in theatrical productions to characterize Vermont storekeepers, they would still have seemed, for all their grandeur, an unhappy ending to a musical work.

It is not easy to make a portrait of a person no longer living, as any artist will tell you. But the problem, difficult or not, is what it is; and Mr. Copland has chosen to essay it. By leaving off in the middle and simply inserting quotations from Lincoln's speeches, he has achieved a result comparable to what a painter would achieve if, after sketching in a period background of some kind, he were to substitute for a full rendering of his subject a half-dozen snapshots taken at various epochs of the latter's life, including something from the war period, of course.

The afternoon ended with an excellent performance of Beethoven's Fifth Symphony, of which the principal motif is currently thought to resemble the letter V in Morse code — three dots and a dash. This motif really consists, in its most frequent statement, of four dots, and in its initial, or motto, form of three dots and something the length of about fifteen dashes, a signal not admitted, so far as I know, in any telegraphic alphabet. Yesterday's rendition was a fine one, all the same.

April 4, 1943

More Barber

BOSTON SYMPHONY ORCHESTRA, *Serge Koussevitzky,* conductor.

EINE KLEINE NACHTMUSIK (K. 525)	MOZART
SYMPHONY NO. 2, OP. 19 (dedicated to the Army Air Forces)	BARBER
SYMPHONY NO. 3, F MAJOR, OP. 30	BRAHMS
EXCERPTS FROM THE DAMNATION OF FAUST	BERLIOZ

NOT in several years has your announcer heard Serge Koussevitzky in such fine form as at last night's concert of the Boston Symphony Orchestra in Carnegie Hall. The orchestra itself is always in such perfect condition that one gets to thinking it doesn't make much difference how the conductor feels. It does, though. Because with him, too, at his best and well cast as to repertory, the music he plays can be as memorable an experience as the sound it makes.

Mozart's *Kleine Nachtmusik* is not perfect casting for the good Doctor. The rhythm of Mozart, his meter, his varied phraseology, the relation of ornament to melodic line, the function of off-beat accents and of surprise modulations all seem to escape him. The music comes out, in consequence, palid and more than a little nervous. But once this work was out of the way, the concert took on color. I have seldom heard a reading of the Brahms Third Symphony (by far his best, in my modest opinion) that was at once so poetic, so gracious and so transparent. The Berlioz selections, ending as usual with the *Rakoczy March*, were so happily equilibrated in every way and so utterly delicious as sheer sound that their memory will remain, I am sure, for many years as a model of the way they can and should be performed.

Samuel Barber's Second Symphony is a broadly conceived work full of variety and emphasis. I admit some uncertainty as to what it is all about. If his First, which we heard on Wednesday at the Philharmonic, represents, as I think it does, a Hamlet-like backward yearning toward the womb of German Romanticism, this one may well be Hamlet in modern dress. I've a suspicion they are really the same piece. The new one is modernistic on the surface; at least an effort has been made to write in the dissonant style. But the melodic material would have been set off just as well, probably better, by a less angular harmonic texture. Also, Mr. Barber does not handle dissonant counterpoint with freedom.

The work seems to lack striking melody and contrapuntal life. There is lots of emphasis, but it is all of inferior material; and it is operated chiefly by instrumental weight rather than led up to by logic or by tonal rhetoric. Even the instrumentation, though competently calculated, is lacking in character. The constant abuse of instrumental doublings for purposes of emphasis has produced a muddiness of texture that weighs down further a piece already top-heavy with oratorical paraphernalia. Mr. Barber at his best is songful and elegiac. His harmonic instincts and training, though elegant, are conventional. Pending further acquaintance with his Second Symphony, I am inclined to think that the commission to write a work glorifying the Army Air Forces has led him to try his hand at a publicity task for which he had little taste and less preparation.

March 10, 1944

Bernstein in Boston

BOSTON SYMPHONY ORCHESTRA, *Serge Koussevitzky,* conductor, with *Leonard Bernstein* as guest conductor and *Jennie Tourel,* mezzosoprano, as soloist.

LA PROCESSION NOCTURNE	RABAUD
SYMPHONY No. 3 ("Rhenish")	SCHUMANN
SYMPHONY No. 1 ("Jeremiah")	BERNSTEIN
EL SALÓN MEXICO	COPLAND

THE BOSTON SYMPHONY ORCHESTRA at home seems always less ostentatious than on tour. In the hall where it has rehearsed (a hall of well-focused rather than diffuse acoustic properties) and in front of its own well-washed and well-mannered audience, it strikes one as only natural that the cultural amenities should have taken on so high a polish, as of good wood long regularly waxed and rubbed. Not the least of this orchestra's cultural amenities is its gracious hospitality to that which is novel and of good report in the world of music.

Leonard Bernstein, who conducted his own First Symphony today, is nationally of good report as a conductor. He is less well known as a composer, though the present work, which has already been received well by both press and public in Pittsburgh, will no doubt go far toward correcting this situation. It is not a masterpiece by any means, but it has solid orchestral qualities and a certain charm that should give it a temporary popularity, not the least of its charms in today's concert being Mr. Bernstein's excellent directing of it and Jennie Tourel's resonant intoning of its Hebrew text.

Unlike Robert Schumann (his Third, or "Rhenish," Symphony was played just before the new work, Mr. Koussevitzky conducting), who composed with genius but who was not a master of instrumentation, Mr. Bernstein orchestrates like a master but does

not compose with either originality or much skill. His piece lacks
contrapuntal coherence, melodic distinction, rhythmic progress,
harmonic logic, and concentration of thought. On the other hand,
it has by moments a certain lyrical intensity; and at the beginning
of the middle, or scherzo, section there is a sort of dance passage
that evokes most poignantly the Jewish Near East. Also, the instrumentation makes lovely sounds. The loud and soft contrasts are
probably more extreme than they need be, but the placement of
the instruments is at all times sonorous.

There is no useless instrumental doubling anywhere. Solo
passages are placed in grateful ranges for each instrument. And in
the tuttis he writes his brass a little high, just as Berlioz did. The
result is one of shining brilliance and vibrant juxtapositions of
color. Aaron Copland's *El Salón Mexico,* which Mr. Bernstein conducted at the end, itself a fairly brilliant piece of orchestration,
sounded muddy by comparison with the Bernstein score. Neither
his sure-handed scoring, however, almost too sure-handed for a
young man of twenty-five who is going to be a real composer, nor
the diffuse and improvisatory character of the composition inspires
the confidence in Mr. Bernstein's original gifts that this reviewer
entertains towards his genius as an executant and an interpreter.*

February 19, 1944

* The "Jeremiah" Symphony received, nevertheless, the award of the
Music Critics Circle of New York City as the most distinguished new orchestral work of American authorship played there during the season of 1943–44.

Our Musical Tom Sawyer

NBC SYMPHONY ORCHESTRA, *Leopold Stokowski,* conductor, concert broadcast from Studio 8-H, Radio City.

THE ENGULFED CATHEDRAL	DEBUSSY
A SHROPSHIRE LAD	BUTTERWORTH
SYMPHONY NO. 4	ANTHEIL

GEORGE ANTHEIL, whose Fourth Symphony was given its first performance anywhere by Leopold Stokowski and the NBC Symphony Orchestra yesterday afternoon, has long been a problem
child among musicians. Extravagantly gifted but imperfectly

trained, he was publicized in Germany, in France, and in the United States during the 1920's as a boy genius; and some of the most influential literary figures of the time — notably James Joyce and Ezra Pound — hailed him as a musical messiah. Of late years he has been engaged in diversified journalistic activity (he has written musical criticism, a syndicated column about endocrinology for the lovelorn, political prophecy, and military analysis), as well as the composition of film scores. Yesterday's performance of the Fourth Symphony marks his return to the serious music world. At forty-four, though a far more expert workman than he used to be, he is still something of a problem child, because his qualities are unusual.

He is also a problem child because he is not quite aware of his qualities. Twenty years ago he posed as the heir of Igor Stravinsky; today he is clearly making a bid for the Shostakovich trade. But he is not any kind of a Russian composer. He is an American composer, probably the most thoroughgoing American of us all. He is a musical Tom Sawyer, gay, fanciful, ingenuous, self-confident, and comical. It is the courageous comicality of his work, in fact, that has long endeared it to the literary mind. He is not in the stuffy sense an imitator of anybody; he is a humorist, a parodist, a clown.

The Fourth Symphony, though surely this was not its author's intention, is about the most complete musical picture of an American circus that has ever been made. There is everything in it — military band music, waltzes, sentimental ditties, a Red Army song, a fugue, eccentric dancing, every kind of joke, acrobatic turn, patriotic reference, and glamorous monstrosity. It is bright, hard, noisy, busy, bumptious, efficient, and incredibly real. It is "Columbia, the Gem of the Ocean" orchestrated in red, white, and blue, with three cheers for the same every five minutes and plenty of pink lemonade. By moments it is thin of texture, but at its best and busiest it makes a hubbub like a live crowd and five brass bands. And its tunes can all be remembered.

This is not to say that the work is a masterpiece. But it is hard, clean, humane, outdoor fun and not at all timid in its manipulation of the higher musical skills. If you like your music sanctimonious, or even logical, you will probably be shocked by it. But if you like tunes, rhythms, discords, and bright sounds for themselves alone, you will find its brash complexity as rewarding as yesterday's audience seemed to do. Myself, I have always found An-

theil's serious music (excepting his operas) invigorating. I consider him a powerful musician and a healthy spirit. And once
again Mr. Stokowski and the General Motors Corporation merit
our thanks for giving us music that makes sense here and now.

February 14, 1944

Levant Tough and Tender

NBC SYMPHONY ORCHESTRA, *Alfred Wallenstein* conducting, concert broadcast last night from Studio 3-B, Radio City, with *Oscar
Levant*, composer-pianist, as soloist in the following program.

SYMPHONY NO. 2	SPOHR
CONCERTO FOR PIANO AND ORCHESTRA	LEVANT
LA VALSE	RAVEL

IT is amazing the amount of good music-writing and careful music
execution that gets lost over the radio. I listened last night to a
concert of the NBC orchestra from one of those seating arrangements where one sees the performance through glass but hears it
through an electrical receiving mechanism. This mechanism gives
normally a result not inferior to that of the bedside box and truer
acoustically than what most household receiving sets produce. I
heard the strings most of the time, excepting for the cellos, which
were rarely audible. I heard the flutes and clarinets pretty regularly and the trumpets. Oboes, bassoons, and trombones were
never audible except in solo work. Horns and double basses came
into the softest passages like added atmospheric pressure on the
eardrums. The whole auditory effect was so distorted, so false to
reality, that I don't wonder at the necessity radio companies seem
to feel of sort of excusing the whole serious music business and of
bolstering it up with unashamed sales-talk before and after.

The Spohr Symphony No. 2 is inoffensive. Its lively scherzo
and schottische finale would make good background music in a
refined beer hall or in any American home. Ravel's *La Valse* is
known to most of my readers, though few, I suspect, would have
recognized it through the fog of radio distortion that made it sound
less like *La Valse* than like an orchestra tuning up to play *La
Valse.*

Oscar Levant's Piano Concerto is a rather fine piece of music. Or rather it contains fine pieces of music. Its pieces are better than its whole, which is jerky, because the music neither moves along nor stands still. The themes are good; and if they are harmonically and orchestrally overdressed, they are ostentatiously enough so that no one need suspect their author of naïveté. The rhythm is lively, too, and the expression, for the most part, direct and easily comprehensible.

I suspect its piecemeal character of being due to lack of a central musical idea or dominating emotional urge. Its most obvious single communication is the composer's desire, determination, even, to write a piano concerto. Maybe a too long working over destroyed its original unity. As music it is honest and charming and, for all its pseudo-complexity, straightforward. At least, each passage is straightforward. It is the spiritual isolation of the passages one from another that gives the whole a reserved and compartmental quality that weakens its impact.

Nevertheless, the impact of Mr. Levant's battling personality is not absent. His music, like his mind, is tough and real and animated by a ferocious integrity. Its off moments are like the Sunday afternoon of a pugilist, all dressed up and no place to go. But even so, biceps are visible through the flimsy suiting of Hollywood atonality; and whenever he makes a spontaneous movement, he bursts the none too solid ready-made seams. I have mentioned all the faults I could find in the Piano Concerto, because he would expect that of me, as I should of him. But the same professional loyalty impels me to dwell also for a brief paragraph (though strength is far harder to describe than weakness) on its real excellence, because, for all its not being, I think, a completely successful work, it is friendly music and good music, all of it. It is even, beneath its trappings of schoolboy homage to Gershwin and Schönberg, hard and lonely and original music, full of song and solitude. I sometimes wish Levant would not work so hard at being a composer. He seems afraid to relax and let music write itself. But every man must scale Parnassus in his own way. Maybe the hard way is the only one he would feel right about taking.

February 18, 1942

The Budding Grove

FOURTH ANNUAL CONCERT OF ORIGINAL COMPOSITIONS
BY STUDENTS OF THE HIGH SCHOOL OF MUSIC AND ART,
given yesterday afternoon at the school, with the following program.

Compositions for piano (composers performing):

CONCORD AND DISCORD	HARRIET GARILL
MELODY IN A MINOR	MILTON KRAKOWER
MODERATO	JOSEPH LIEBLING
PROMENADE ALL	ADELE LEVIN

Samuel Scheiner, caller

Compositions for instruments:

TRIO FOR VIOLIN, CLARINET, AND PIANO (first movement)   CHARLES SCHIFF
Hyman Shulman, violinist; Meyer Kupferman, clarinetist; Jesse Beller, pianist

DUET FOR CLARINETS	ARTHUR LEFKOWITZ, ARTHUR STRACHER

Performed by the composers

DUET FOR CLARINET AND CELLO	MIRIAM GOLDENBERG

Charles Van Doren, clarinetist; Leonard Freiser, cellist

WOODWIND SEXTET	MEYER KUPFERMAN
DANCE OF THE LEAVES, for string ensemble	JANET CHILDS

Conducted by the composer

Compositions for choral ensemble (Senior Ensemble performing):

PEACE	ADELAIDE ROBBINS

Albert Sly, conductor

SPEAK TO ME	LAURA GOLDMAN

Albert Lightfoot, baritone; conducted by the composer

100TH PSALM	ALBERT SLY

Composer at the organ; Jason Goldman, conductor

Compositions for orchestra (Senior Symphony Orchestra performing):

CHORALE FOR ORCHESTRA	SEYMOUR SHIFRIN

The composer conducting

MINUET	GERARD JAFFE

The composer conducting

OVERTURE IN A	WILLIAM BLANK

The composer conducting

NEW YORK's High School of Music and Art is a public high school
to which students, stemming from all classes of society and resident in all neighborhoods, are admitted on a basis of musical or
artistic aptitudes. This is not to say that literary and scientific
studies are neglected or that any deficiency in these is tolerated.
On the contrary, the academic work of this admirable institution

ranks higher than that of most high schools. But its work in
music and art is, of course, its specialty; and this must be seen to
be believed. Yesterday afternoon in the assembly hall a fourth
annual concert was given of original compositions written and
performed by students.

These varied from simple pianoforte pieces to works for full
orchestra. There were duets, trios, a wind sextet, a piece for
string ensemble, and others for choir, including a full anthem for
chorus, soloists, and organ. The soloists played and sang beautifully; the conductors led with vigor and exactitude; the orchestra
performed in excellent style and with lovely tone, and the chorus
sang real English words with all beauty of sound and with correct intonation. The young people seemed, moreover, to understand and to believe in one another's work. From the beginning
to the end there was pleasure in being present at the skillful
accomplishment of sincere musical acts. There was joy and friendliness and spontaneity of collaboration and no lack whatever of
an intelligently critical attitude in the reception of the different
works.

The pieces were by students aged thirteen to eighteen, at all
different stages of advancement from the first to the ninth semes-
ter of theory instruction. They were not classroom exercises but
free compositions, uncorrected by any instructor and chosen com-
petitively for this performance. Their musical language was the
basic musical language of educated America, roughly the language of European Romanticism from Schumann to Tchaikovsky.
There was little of Wagnerian insistence or of Brahmsian intro-
version. Mozart and Beethoven, however, had certainly been con-
sulted as models of formal procedure. The choral pieces were
based on less classic models, though in no case was there any
departure from acceptable style. The farthest any piece strayed
from mid-nineteenth-century harmonic syntax was the moderate
but wholly neat and charming French impressionism of Mr. Meyer
Kupferman's Wind Sextet.

All this is normal and usual. Youth is conservative, and mild
Romanticism is its oyster. One does not expect consistent revolu-
tionism or radical research from adolescents. Neither does one
expect to encounter much unconscious influence of backwoods
American folklore in the music of urban New York. The spirit
of yesterday's work was one of respect for classic methods and
the emulation of classic beauties. What one had not quite ex-

pected was the air on everybody's part, both authors and interpreters, of being completely at home in the writing and performing of music. It was all as natural as a school play or magazine.
And when Americans, even a few hundreds of them in New York
City, can express themselves in music as easily and as well as
that, we may rest assured that America's musical future is as solidly based as her present distinction in the divers branches of
literature.

April 17, 1942

OPERA

Mozart on Love

THE POPULARITY of the New Opera Company's *Così Fan Tutte* performances and the general acknowledgment of their musical excellence have stimulated the following reflections on the part of this reviewer.

First of all, let it be reiterated that the singing itself is, by any standard of contemporary opera singing, very good singing indeed. Paris, Dresden, Vienna, Milan, and our own Metropolitan are lucky when they can get together a Mozart cast of that quality. Miss Milanov, who sang Donna Anna last year in *Don Giovanni,* is not the mistress of her voice nor of the musical content of her roles that Miss Ina Souez is, for instance, who sings Fiordiligi in the present production. And that role, written for Madame Ferrarese del Bene, demands a compass far from ordinary. Miss Kuzak is not so good a singer as the Metropolitan's Miss Sayao, but she has a distinguished personality. Mr. Marshall, whom I heard on the opening night in the tenor role, has a voice not unfavorably comparable to that of the Met's Mr. Kullmann. And Fritz Busch, who conducted, is a better conductor and a far finer musician than most of those Thirty-ninth Street has been offering. Even the scenery and the costumes and the heavy-handed stage direction were better than what new productions get at most of the big houses nowadays. For all their carelessness and crudity, they were high art beside what was exhibited last year with Gluck's *Alceste.* There is no getting around it or laughing it off, *Così Fan Tutte* at the Forty-fourth Street Theater, though far from ideal, is none the less a high-class operatic performance.

The pleasure it has been giving, let me repeat, is nearly one hundred per cent musical. (Or, at least, musico-literary, since da Ponte's libretto constitutes a far from negligible element in the enjoyment to be derived from Mozart's psychologically quite elaborate setting of it.) And the person obviously responsible for the high musical level of the production is Mr. (or, in the German style, Dr.) Fritz Busch. One can scarcely overemphasize the pleasurable effect of witnessing an opera that has been really rehearsed; and one can never be too grateful to a conductor who nursemaids six soloists, at least one of whom has never been on a stage before, through the opening night of an extremely difficult work without any of them either losing his head or taking the bit in his teeth. With a smallish and not really first-rate orchestra, with inexperienced soloists, with scenery so carelessly designed and executed that nobody could tell what any of it was going to do next, with none of the ladies' costumes capable of being got through any of the doors without the skirt having to be tipped up on its side, with all these stimuli to pity and terror and with a show to be got across of a work fantastically famous and difficult, Mr. Busch produced a performance in which all the orchestral notes were in their proper places and in which no singer trembled or got tight in the throat. More than that, he gave a rendition that was good entertainment and that was dramatically convincing.

Making convincing dramatic entertainment out of *Così Fan Tutte* has not been one of the specialties of our century. Indeed, it has long been considered impossible to do anything approaching this. One is used to seeing the play treated as a bit of not very funny eighteenth-century smut and the music as a set piece of the Rococo charm school. The libretto has rarely been interpreted for what it is, a serious farce-comedy in the Molière vein by an extremely gifted poet whom Mozart had already honored twice with his collaboration. But unless the libretto is so interpreted, it is impossible to give to the musical rendition of it a dramatic expression any more profound than what one might give to a musical version of *Twin Beds*.

Fritz Busch knows better. He knows that Wolfgang Amadeus Mozart did not waste his music on trash. Mozart never, in fact, wrote an opera of which the theme was not a plea for tenderness, for humane compassion, and for an enlightened and philosophic toleration of human weakness. And, although some of his librettists were more skillful littérateurs than others, Mozart himself manifested no small sense of literary values in his choice of subjects and of authors. His first opera, *La Finta Semplice*, was written at the age of twelve to a play by Goldoni. *Mitridate* is made from an Italian translation of Racine. *La Clemenza di Tito* is by Metastasio. And *Le Nozze di Figaro* is both Beaumarchais and da Ponte. Even if *Così Fan Tutte* were not the work of Mozart's favorite librettist, one should be able to tell from the complexity of the musical fabric that the composer had a certain interest in what he was doing.

What he was doing was showing that infidelity can strengthen love. He had reason to know, whose own wife's conduct was definitely on the promiscuous side. And he was showing also that one needn't be especially high-minded in order to be both loving and sensible. His characters are people of quite conventional mentality who behave as almost any of us might. Also, like almost any of us, they learn from jealousy, torment, and amorous disillusionment that love can go on just the same (perhaps even better) when pride has been got out of the way.

Now, the trouble with the representation of all this in music is that as Mozart's carefree young lovers draw closer to the real facts of life, their music becomes progressively less brilliant. His second act runs richer and deeper than the first, but it is at no time so sparkling. The first is all concerted pieces, the second mostly arias. It is customary to knock the audience cold by the speed and precision of the first and to let the second bog down into sentiment. Mr. Busch has sacrificed the brilliance of the concerted pieces in order to build up to a genuinely moving quality in the heart pains the young men suffer at proving their mistresses false.

This novel attitude toward the story helps to save for us some of Mozart's finest music at no disadvantage to the always delightful first act. Not that Busch's first act tempos aren't more than a bit on the slow side. I think they are mostly slower than is really necessary. But, as I explained in reviewing the performance a week ago last Tuesday night, I don't think Mr. Busch is particularly good at finding perfect tempos anyway. What he has done here is to find the sense and the seriousness in this beautiful work and to show them to us with the aid of his vocal collaborators. Now that he has shown us that *Così Fan Tutte* can be made to make sense all the way through by not allowing it to run away with itself at the beginning, it should be not at all difficult for other conductors to adjust this conception to a pace (a pacing, rather) that will preserve the very high level at once of anima-

tion and of expressivity that makes Mozart's operas different from
all the other operas in the world and far more powerful than
most.

October 25, 1941

Confusion Ordered

THE MAGIC FLUTE, opera in two acts, music by WOLFGANG AMA-
DEUS MOZART; book by *Emanuel Schickaneder,* presented last night by
the Opera Department of the Juilliard School of Music at the Juilliard
Auditorium in *Edward J. Dent's* English version, with the following
cast.

Queen of the Night	*Rita Doubet*
Pamina	*Estelle Hoffman*
Papagena	*Vivienne Simon*
Ladies of the Queen of the Night	*Derna De Pamphilis*
	Dorothy Hartigan
	Mary Frances Lehnerts
Genii of the Temple	*Janet Burt*
	Elsa Krause
	Mildred Talbot
Tamino	*Davis Cunningham*
Monostatos	*Robert Harmon*
Sarastro	*Phillip MacGregor*
Papageno	*William Gephart*
Speaker of the Temple	*William Dean*
Priests	*Roger White*
	Lloyd Lindner

Conductor, *Albert Stoessel.* Stage Director, *Alfredo Valenti.* Scenic Director, *Frederick J. Kiesler.*

MUCH has been said about the stupidity and the useless complexity
of *The Magic Flute's* libretto. It has certainly never made much
sense to this reviewer. Last night's performance at the Juilliard
School made it seem as simple as a Sunday-school pageant. And
when all is said and done, that is about what *The Magic Flute* is.
It is an allegorical fairy tale in praise of Freemasonry and the
brotherhood of man.

The locale of the action and the identity of the characters have
usually been represented as fanciful. Tamino, being a Japanese

prince, has been put into every imaginable kind of Oriental armor. Zoroaster is classically got up Persian. Pamina is likely to be vague in style. And the scenery is normally Biedermeier Egyptian. Is it any wonder we don't quite get the plot?

Frederick Kiesler has taken for granted that calling the high priest Zoroaster and at the same time having him pray to Isis and Osiris was not necessarily an anachronism on the part of the authors, but was rather simply the routine language of the Masonic Lodges, which pretended to trace their origin to Egypt and which certainly welcomed into their fold believers from all religions. The prince's Japanese birth he takes to be a simple literary masquerade, since it is highly probable that he represents the Emperor Joseph II, recently inducted to the Lodge, as the Queen of the Night represents Joseph's mother, Maria Theresa, who never approved of Freemasonry.

Kiesler has taken everybody out of masquerade except the Queen.* Tamino, Pamina, and the Priests are represented as eighteenth-century gentlefolk. The Bird-Man and Bird-Woman he has left in their feathers, as indeed they were left by the plot to live out their simple lives without the enlightenment of Masonic initiation.

He has used a permanent stage-set, indicating changes of locale by changing painted pictures that are framed in a sort of late eighteenth-century pavilion, upstage center, and indicating changes of weather by projecting clouds, flames, and other atmospheric effects on a cyclorama at the back. As a result we know not only that we are dealing with real people in the chief characters, but that these are living through a series of adventures and trials that take place in various real sites and climatic conditions, rather than merely going through a series of pretexts for singing on a stage a diversified series of songs in fancy dress.

It has long been a conviction of this reviewer that the best theatrical results are rarely obtained from professional stage designers, but rather from artists who practice professionally the more basic plastic techniques. To be specific, from oil painters, sculptors, and architects. The only real renovations of staging that have taken place in the last thirty years have been due to the collaboration of constructivist sculptors, cubist and post-cubist painters with opera and ballet. Kiesler has approached *The Magic*

* Mr. Kiesler informs me that his original project required that the Queen of the Night be dressed to represent Maria Theresa.

Flute as an architect. He has made the decorations clear and functional, and he has given them an unbelievable architectural solidity and a high seriousness of expression. Their lack of meretriciousness is astounding.

There is no malice in my spending my space today on the visual aspects of last night's *The Magic Flute*. The singing was excellent, the orchestra excellent, the whole auditory presentation an honor to the school and a pleasure to its hearers (and hearing *The Magic Flute* is no mean pleasure). But it does seem to me that there is more news value in Kiesler's having made the opera make sense than there could be in anybody's having sung it no matter how well.

December 12, 1940

Two-Star Matinee

LA TRAVIATA, opera in four acts by VERDI, first performance of the season at the Metropolitan Opera House yesterday afternoon with the following cast.

Violetta	*Licia Albanese*
Flora Bervoix	*Thelma Votipka*
Annina	*Helen Olheim*
Alfredo	*Charles Kullmann*
Giorgio Germont	*Lawrence Tibbett*
Gastone	*Alessio De Paolis*
Baron Douphol	*George Cehanovsky*
Marquis d'Obigny	*Louis D'Angelo*
Doctor Grenvil	*Lorenzo Alvary*

Conductor, *Cesare Sodero*. Stage Director, *Désiré Defrère*. Chorus Master, *Giacomo Spadoni*. Ballet Master, *Laurent Novikoff*.

IF the coronation of stardom for male actors is *Hamlet,* that for actresses is certainly *La Dame aux Camélias*. Licia Albanese won for herself a royal crown in that role yesterday afternoon at the Metropolitan Opera House, the version used being the best known of all the musical ones, Verdi's incomparable *La Traviata*. Her triumph was shared with Cesare Sodero, who conducted the work more beautifully than I have heard any other conductor conduct any opera in many, many years. The supporting cast and ensemble did good work, too; but the intensity and the delicacy and the animation of the whole were unquestionably centered in Miss Albanese and Mr. Sodero, and it was obvious during the curtain calls that the audience was fully aware of this.

Miss Albanese began by looking beautiful but singing with a tremolo that was no doubt due to nervousness. She had never sung the role before, I believe. After fifteen minutes the tremolo disappeared, leaving only beauty, both personal and vocal. She was as deeply touching in her gaiety as in her heartbreaks and in her tubercular agony. She used her limpid voice, her delicate person, and her excellent musicianship to equal effect in creating the character Violetta. I use the word *create* for her achievement because that is what she really did. She did not play or imitate or sketch. She created a complete personality that lived and loved and drank champagne and made decisions and died. She did this with skill, with art, with conviction, with beauty, and with all loveliness.

She lived her "Ah, fors è lui" as she sang it. And how well she sang it! As if she had no doubt of its musical and dramatic sincerity, as if she knew it were a part of the play. In the last scene her transition from low speaking (and what rich speaking!) to the full high B flat on which she dies was one of the most accomplished bits of vocalism it has been my pleasure to hear in some time. That it was as deeply moving as it was skillful to observe and lovely to hear is proof of Miss Albanese's high standards of musical and dramatic integrity. One has heard many Violettas. Miss Albanese's is, I should think, one of the great ones, because, like all the great ones, it resembles no other yet is wholly convincing.

That it was so convincing and pleasurable is due in large measure to the identity of conception that was manifest between herself and Mr. Sodero about the opera itself. From the delicate prelude to the last tragic chord, the conductor kept the whole piece lacy and light and sweet. Its background is the waltz, the Second Empire French waltz, sparkling and tender. And the oom-pah-pah of waltz accompaniment is both the abstract musical material of the opera's continuity-foundation and the theme of which the work is an expressive development. Only Beethoven, among all the other composers of opera, knew as Verdi did the gamut of drama that lies in abstract musical formulas, in scales, arpeggios, and neutral accompanying figures. He filled *Fidelio* with them, played with them as freely as if they had been the equally abstract Fifth Symphony theme.

It was clear from the care with which Mr. Sodero brought in the first statement of the oom-pah-pah basic chords, as they first appear wholly uncovered in the prelude, that he knew what Verdi was up to. Mysterious and dramatic they were, a first fore-shadowing of the merry waltz motifs that permeate the opera and give it its special tone of mundanity and of penetrating personal sentiment. On a basis like that anything can happen. For four acts on that basis drama did happen, and personal sentiments grew into personal tragedy.

Always the waltz was present; always Mr. Sodero knew it was present and each time for what reason. The whole moved expres-sively and with animation. The tempos were always right for the drama, the rhythm always right for the music, the orchestral and vocal balances always right for full clarity and emphasis. I have rarely heard opera directed so satisfactorily. One could hear everything that went on in the pit and on the stage. Neither seemed assertive or subservient. And neither made any special effort at loudness. I do hope we shall have lots more of Mr. Sodero before the season is out and of Miss Albanese, too. This reviewer could do without the radio introduction that still holds up the Saturday matinee curtain for ten minutes to read the cast out loud and to recount a bowdlerized version of the plot.

December 6, 1942

Negro Traviata

NATIONAL NEGRO OPERA COMPANY, in a performance of VERDI's LA TRAVIATA in Madison Square Garden last night. The cast:

Violetta	*Lillian Evanti*
Flora Bervoix	*Minto Cato*
Annina	*Lillian M. Smith*
Alfredo	*Joseph Lipscomb*
Germont	*William Franklin*
Gaston	*Oscar Griffin*
Baron Douphol	*Edward Boatner*
Marquis d'Obigny	*Wilson Woodbeck*
Doctor Grenvil	*Horace Wilson*
Conductor, *Frederick Vajda.*	

THE NATIONAL NEGRO OPERA COMPANY, which made its first local appearance last night in Madison Square Garden before an audience estimated at 10,000 persons, looks like a praiseworthy singing group. What it sounds like is more difficult to say, since any opera company working under what amount almost to outdoor conditions, including the use of electrical amplification, sounds very much like any other opera company. What it would sound like in a theater of reasonable proportions is even harder to imagine. About all one could hear in undistorted form was rhythm and pitch. Nevertheless, it was clear that two, at least, of the soloists are singers of some value and that the choral work was solid.

Lillian Evanti, who sang the role of Violetta, has certainly a voice of wide range and many colors. Her control of those colors appeared to be at times a little precarious, but she has an ear for pitch and an instinct for dramatic expression. I should like to hear her sing without microphonic aid or interference. I fancy that Miss Evanti, though perhaps not fully mistress of her extraordinary vocal resources is capable of brilliance and beauty.

William Franklin, who sang Germont, has a ringing baritone voice of excellent placement; and his enunciation of words is unusually clear. He has an unaffected dignity of presence, too, though his personal dramatic projection is not great. I have not seen his Porgy, but I can imagine it as more convincing than his Germont, who is a bit of a stuffy character anyhow.

It has never seemed to me that Negroes had much to gain from attempting to adopt the theater of Romanticism. They are not a Romantic people, and they do not understand bourgeois violence. The Baroque in tragedy, in comedy, and in religion is their home town. They understand its afflatus and its pageantry, its conventions, its excesses, and all its humane elegance. The operas of Handel are made for them. They could make real spectacles out of these, and they could sing their grandiloquent airs and choruses with the most touching dignity.

If there is any future for Negro opera (and I am convinced there is a great one), that future depends on the choice of a repertory that is congenial to Negro thought and attitudes, that exploits the Negro's gift for noble sentiments and sustained vocal outpourings. Nineteenth-century Italian opera does not do justice to his enormous but somewhat impersonal dramatic and musical talents. It is as unsuitable to him and as difficult for him to do convincingly as the Baroque repertory has become for contemporary white people.

March 30, 1944

The Verdi Case

HEARING last Monday Verdi's *The Masked Ball* at the Metropolitan Opera House has led me to wonder why that work, so satisfying orchestrally and so brilliant in its vocal writing, has never moved much the layman's simple human heart and why, even among musicians, it is more admired than deeply loved.

It is easy enough to pick flaws in the book, for these are many and grave. The heroine has no character; she is a lay figure. The hero has little more, not enough to make him interesting. An opera can get away with a vague tenor (Mozart's *Don Giovanni* does) if the heroine is a real live woman and the villain sufficiently wicked. It is hard to interest an audience in two lovers whose personalities are so imprecise and whose passion itself is so trivial.

The lovers are further thrown into shadow by the lady's husband, Renato. This future regicide is an extremely interesting person. He is kind, loyal, and passionate. All one's sympathy goes out to him. It seems a pity that such a tactful and forbearing spouse, once he had got his silly wife home from a midnight expedition where she had gone to gather a magic herb some fortune-teller had told her about and where she had ended by compromising her husband in front of his political enemies, it seems really too bad that after their long walk home in the snow he didn't sit down with her and quietly, by some straight-from-the-shoulder questioning, find out what really had or hadn't been going on and then decide on some sensible course of action. I was sorry to see a good man's home broken up so uselessly.

Oscar, the king's frivolous page, whose indiscretions betray his master's interests every time he opens his mouth, was a favorite of Verdi himself among his dramatic creations. Musically this preference is understandable, because rarely has a composer expressed so well pretty frivolity and light-hearted empty-headedness as they are implied in Oscar's staccato coloratura airs. The

trouble with this role nowadays is the necessity of its being sung
by a woman. Italian stage conventions are more precise than ours
about femininity and masculinity. Consequently travesty is easier
to get away with in Italy than here. It is virtually impossible on
the Anglo-Saxon stage for a woman to represent an effeminate
youth without seeming merely to be playing a male role ineffec-
tually.

The opera's libretto is not its only fault. Its very musical
strength is its weakness. The expressive nature of the orchestral
accompaniments, the appropriateness of the contrapuntal writing, the sustained characterization of individual parts in the concerted numbers, the thematic unity of the whole work, are justly
celebrated. Neither Meyerbeer nor Rossini ever etched a theatrical
design more deeply. Richard Wagner himself, though a more
sumptuous painter of psychological traits, was less accurate in his
timing. Verdi did an A-1 professional job on *The Masked Ball*.

But music never lives by its professional quality. It lives by
its tunes. And the tunes in *The Masked Ball* are every one of them
tricky. Let us except the baritone aria "Eri tu," Oscar's "Saper
vorreste," and just possibly the Laughing Chorus. All the others
fall somewhere between broad simplicity and full, complex expression.

La Traviata and *Il Trovatore* are full of simple melodies that
depict character and feeling in elementary but universally acceptable music. Wagner, at his best, and Mozart wrote melodies that
express the same broad values but that comment more profoundly on the drama at the same time.

The orchestral accompaniment of *The Masked Ball* is a more
elaborate auditive picture of the play than is the orchestral accompaniment of any opera Verdi had previously written. It sounds
like the best French contemporary work, bearing little resemblance
to the previously current Italian style that Wagner describes as
"making the orchestra sound like a big guitar." The trios, quartets, and other ensemble pieces are equally fine. The melodic material all these are made out of is simply not good enough. The
tunes are pretty — little more. They lack the grand and elementary plainness of those in the earlier works. And they lack the
penetrating accuracy of great stage music. They are affected and
soft, like the libretto.

One could put the blame for the whole trouble on the libretto
if one didn't know that Verdi's career was always dominated by

the same problem. In *Aïda* he went back to broad writing. But he was obsessed by the desire to make Italian operas that would be as penetrating psychologically as French operas and as sumptuous musically as the German. He mastered psychological penetration instrumentally and wrote, in *Otello* and *Falstaff,* two of the most sumptuous musical works of the century. He could write big simple melodies and magnificent vocal bravura passages. He never learned how to build a melodic line that would be at the same time monumental and penetratingly expressive of the text. This inability to interpret character delicately is what gives to *Otello* and *Falstaff* a certain air, in spite of their instrumental delights, of banality. The same inability gives to *La Traviata* its rough and massive grandeur.

The lack of really delicate delicacy in Verdi's melodic contours, compensated though it be by pungent orchestration and the soundest dramatic building, makes the whole body of his work seem just a bit commercial. One is more often tempted, in fact, to take off one's hat to his triumphs of pure musical theater than one is to bare one's head before any revelations of the subtleties of human sentiment or of the depths of the human heart.

December 8, 1940

Hokum and Schmalz

LA FORZA DEL DESTINO, opera in a prologue and three acts, music by GIUSEPPI VERDI, book by *Francesco Maria Piave;* first performance of the season at the Metropolitan Opera House yesterday afternoon. The cast.

Marquis of Calatrava	*Frederick Lechner* (debut)
Donna Leonora	*Stella Roman*
Don Carlos of Vargas	*Lawrence Tibbett*
Don Alvaro	*Frederick Jagel*
Preziosilla	*Anna Kaskas*
The Abbot	*Ezio Pinza*
Father Melitone	*Salvatore Baccaloni*
Curra	*Thelma Votipka*
The Alcade	*Lorenzo Alvary*
Trabuco	*Alessio De Paolis*
A Surgeon	*John Gurney*

Conductor, *Bruno Walter.* Stage Director, *Herbert Graf.* Chorus Master, *Giacomo Spadoni.* Ballet Master, *Laurent Novikoff.*

THE METROPOLITAN OPERA's first broadcast performance of the season was a thoroughly uninspired walk-through of Verdi's *La Forza del Destino*. Not that the work itself is particularly inspired, either. It suffers from a libretto that is little more than a stringing together of all the nineteenth-century Italian theater hokum that its author, Piave, had ever heard of; and that means practically all there was. There are murders and maledictions and tavern gaieties and transvestitism and mistaken identity and a battle and a storm and an eating scene and a comic monk and a paternal abbot and a male chorus dressed up as Franciscans and several duels and at the end a general carnage of all the principal persons. Underneath all this there is no real conflict of character and no general theme beyond that suggested in the title, which might well be translated, "Tough Luck."

Verdi wrote some skillful and rather grand music to this hodgepodge, though not his most touching by any means. It is hard and brilliant theater music, and unless it is performed with a hard and brilliant timing it sounds absurd. A few moments yesterday were so performed, notably the duet between Pinza and Baccaloni, as Abbot and friar. Stella Roman gave the stage a lift, too, whenever she was on it, through the strange and commanding beauty of her voice. It is too bad that an interesting and highly personal timbre should be almost her whole stock in trade as a star. I say *almost* because she does sing on pitch, too. But she has no personal warmth on a stage and no tension. She creates no drama. Also, her work lacks continuity. She doesn't sing in phrases, only in single notes. These she exploits with her own spectacular technique of crooning and crescendo; and very agreeable they are to hear, I must say. But her work has no architectural line, either as drama or as music.

Architectural line is what Bruno Walter's reading of the score seemed chiefly to lack, too. Instead of pathos and emphasis, he achieved only sentimentality and clatter. Rarely have I heard the Metropolitan orchestra sound so ill-balanced, its strings so thin, its brasses so tinny. And that exactitude of timing that is the very essence of melodrama was nowhere present, save in the Baccaloni-Pinza duet.

Frederick Jagel and Lawrence Tibbett were ineffective, to say the least. The former sang throatily and without rhythm, the latter painfully and constantly flat. I am afraid Mr. Tibbett has become in recent years a vocal liability to whatever opera he appears in. The resonance is gone; he is almost never up to pitch; it makes one's throat ache to hear him. Even his dramatic power seems to have deserted him. Yesterday he moved about with as little of ease and freedom in his limbs as in his voice, though his static appearance was that of youth.

The full telling of yesterday's sad story requires my recording that the chorus work was ragged, unresonant, and frequently off pitch. Also that the crowd scenes contained too much milling around for either musical accuracy or dramatic significance. On the whole, however, I am inclined to blame the general ineffectiveness of the performance on the conductor. I felt no radiation of power from him except during the playing of the Overture; and the singers gave no evidence of being held firmly to the rocket-like trajectory that that work requires in order to be convincing. It is possible, of course, that Mr. Walter had felt impelled out of loyalty to management and public to go through with his seasonal début at a time when he was not yet fully recovered from his recent illness.

November 28, 1943

Vocalism Victorious

DIE WALKÜRE, music-drama in three acts, book and music by RICHARD WAGNER; second performance in the Wagner cycle, last night at the Metropolitan Opera House with the following cast.

Siegmund	*Lauritz Melchior*
Hunding	*Emanuel List*
Wotan	*Julius Huehn*
Sieglinde	*Lotte Lehmann*
Brünnhilde	*Helen Traubel*
Fricka	*Kerstin Thorborg*
Valkyries —	
Helmwige	*Maxine Stellman*
Gerhilde	*Thelma Votipka*
Ortlinde	*Irene Jessner*
Rossweisse	*Lucielle Browning*
Grimgerde	*Mary Van Kirk*
Waltraute	*Hertha Glaz*
Siegrune	*Helen Olheim*
Schwertleite	*Margaret Harshaw*

Conductor, *Erich Leinsdorf*. Stage director, *Lothar Wallerstein*.

WAGNER continues to bring out the vocalism fans. Last night's
Walküre was heard by a full house at the Metropolitan with
many standing, and applause ran high. Vocalism ran pretty high,
too, with Lotte Lehman leading the field, Lauritz Melchior placing. Helen Traubel ran well. Julius Huehn, limping vocally from
the start, was about to run in the third act, in spite of his disabili-
ties, when your reviewer went off to write his piece.

The first act was the more satisfactory of the two that he
heard, partly because the singing was more expert and partly
because it is a better piece of music than the second, which, in
spite of the pleasant bravura of the Valkyrie's whoop and some
most ingenious storm music, is long, labored, and fragmentary.
The first contains some of the best musical conversation there is
anywhere. This is quiet and delicately varied; and last night Miss
Lehmann and Mr. Melchior enunciated it with all clarity, intoned
it with all beauty of sound. The tenor cavatina, or Spring Song,
too, was delivered with a rhythmic alacrity most agreeable to follow; and the final curtain was built up to with great skill and much
restraint by both artists.

Mr. Leinsdorf's conducting of the orchestra under all this was
of no small aid to the protagonists on the stage. He kept the accompaniment alive and mostly soft all the way through, a beautiful job. Naturally, since singing was the subject of the evening,
it didn't occur to anyone to offer the conductor even a teensy-
weensy curtain call.

The second act was loud and coarse, as is its nature. Miss
Traubel's handsome voice was displayed *grosso modo* without
much refinement of expression, and so was Miss Thorborg's. The
former lady wore a flat coiffure and an exasperated expression
not unlike those of a comic-strip character named Inna Minnie.
The latter looked angry and acid in her yellow silk wrapper. Mr.
Huehn looked well, but his throat was in no state to sing Wotan.
The orchestra was raucous, the trombones being particularly
unpleasant in their inability to achieve a round tone or a correct
balance in chords.

Wagner as a young man was angry against Donizetti's music
and jealous of its success. It is one of the neater ironies of fate
that his own operas, after a hundred years, have come to fulfill the
exact function in repertory that Donizetti's used to. They are vehicles for vocalism and nothing else. Nobody cares who conducts
them or very much what the orchestra sounds like, provided it

remains subservient to the singers and makes a clatter at the climaxes.

Vocalism is the thing sought, not dramatic sense nor vicarious emotional experience nor any kind of audio-visual spectacle. Stage direction and scenic effects are unimportant. Even symphonic pacing has ceased to count. But the whole art of singing, as that is understood today, is exemplified in the work of the great Wagnerian vocalists. People go to hear Flagstad and Traubel and Melchior and Lehmann exactly as they used to go to hear Melba and Sembrich and Caruso and Adelina Patti.

They listen raptly and applaud with vigor. They get their money's worth, too, because the Wagner productions nowadays, though often carelessly conducted, have more good throat work on display than we are likely to find in the productions of Italian pieces that were written with vocal display in mind. These have become virtually impossible of correct execution in the present decline of vocal art. But Wagner can still be sung.

February 17, 1943

Carmen à l'Aimable

CARMEN, opera in four acts, libretto by Henri Meilhac and Ludovic Halévy based on *Prosper Merimée's* story; music by Georges Bizet; performed yesterday afternoon at the Metropolitan Opera House with the following cast.

Carmen	*Gladys Swarthout*
Micaela	*Licia Albanese*
Frasquita	*Thelma Votipka*
Mercedes	*Helen Olheim*
Don José	*Charles Kullmann*
Escamillo	*Leonard Warren*
Dancaire	*George Cehanovsky*
Remendado	*Alessio De Paolis*
Zuniga	*Louis D'Angelo*
Morales	*Wilfred Engelman*

Conductor, *Wilfred Pelletier.* Stage Director, *Désiré Defrère.* Chorus Master, *Fausto Cleva.* Soloists with the ballet, *Monna Montes, Ruthanna Boris, Grant Mouradoff.* Scenery designed and painted by *Joseph Urban.*

YESTERDAY'S matinee, being a broadcast performance, would seem to have been cast for vocal effect. Very successfully, too. Such an abundance of beautiful singing is not to be heard every day. The acting was not much, though the climaxes were solid, thanks to Mr. Kullman; and the spectacle in general was sumptuous.

Miss Swarthout's voice is warm and beautiful and friendly, and her usage of it is far from unrefined musically. In the role of Carmen that friendliness seems to get in her way, excepting for the passages of pure anger, which she does well. Carmen is classically considered to be a sexy role, and it is not easy to be friendly and sexy at the same time. She is jolly; she is athletic; she grins constantly. She is as pretty as a moving picture and, in the "healthy" American sense, attractive; but she has about as much direct sex-appeal as a Chesterfield cigarette advertisement. She is all charm and innuendo, and she has far too much energy.

She has, however, a fine and full stage presence whenever she manages to keep still; and her dead pan is utterly beautiful and terrifying. She overdresses the part less than most stars, and some of her studied "business" is excellent. Her card scene is good. The death scene is good too, though a shade violent. She might have been quieter and left the violence to Don José. Her dancing in the second act was more convincingly Spanish and more distinguished than anything the ballet troupe did yesterday. Her whole rendition, in addition to its auditory opulence, showed evidence of great pains and much sincere effort to get things right. Working thus against nature to achieve melodrama, the result could hardly be expected to rank among the world's great Carmens. It was due purely to Miss Swarthout's vocal warmth that a characterization otherwise fairly frigid ended by being acceptable as the cause of so much amorous conflagration.

Mr. Kullman sang well and looked well. Also, as I mentioned before, it was due to his dramatic foresight that the climaxes all came off adequately. Miss Albanese's French is of the sketchiest and her comprehension of French style equally so. So she did the only thing possible with the rule of Micaela; she sang it in the Italian style. But being a singer of refinement in the Italian style, nothing she did was offensive. She took every occasion to display her beautiful voice, even adding a *messa di voce* on high B flat in the third-act aria; but at no time did she destroy the cantilena or falsify the expression of Bizet's lovely music. Her singing was distinguished and, as always, beautiful.

Equally distinguished and beautiful was that of Mr. Leonard Warren as Escamillo. He neither looked nor even pretended to act the part; but oh, how beautifully he sang! What vigor of musical line! What refreshing variety of *demi-teints*! What constantly accurate resonance, at all times placed squarely in the upper part of the face! The Misses Votipka and Olheim, the Messrs. Cehanovsky, De Paolis, D'Angelo, and Engelman did solo bits and the celebrated concerted numbers with style and full resonance.

The stage direction was mostly not very good, especially for the chorus. The Joseph Urban scenery is still excellent. The conductor gave us a real French *Carmen,* but a second-class one. That is to say that his conception was correct but that the adjustments of tempos one to another were often a bit crude. The delicate ones came out overemphasized, the sharper ones a little fuzzy. The tempos were mostly on the fast side, a fault that did little harm to the performance except in a few places — animated it rather. The orchestra itself sounded well. On the whole, a vigorous performance of a vigorous work, a *Carmen* memorable for real singing in every role.

March 16, 1941

Paris Forever

LA VIE PARISIENNE, comic opera, with music by JACQUES OFFEN-BACH, new English text based on libretto by MEILHAC and HALÉVY by FELIX BRENTANO and LOUIS VERNEUIL, with lyrics by MARION FARQUHAR, produced by the New Opera Company last night at the Fortyfourth Street Theater with the following cast.

Comte Raoul de Gardefeu	*Ralph Magelssen*
Baron Bobinet	*John Tyers*
Metella	*Carolina Segrera*
Mr. Hutchinson	*Clifford Newdahl*
Evelyn Hutchinson	*Ruby Mercer*
Jackson	*George Rasely*
Gabrielle	*Ann Lipton*
Gontran	*Hugh Thompson*
Georges	*Norman Roland*

Gaston   *Leon Lischiner*
Alphonse   *Paul Best*
    Conductor, *Antal Dorati*. Stage Director, *Felix Brentano*. Chorus Master,
Herbert Winkler. Choreographer, *Igor Schwezoff*. Settings and costumes de-
signed by *Marco Montedoro*.

IN the French version, a Swedish family is the protagonist of
that love affair with Paris that seems to come once into the lives
of so many people from so many lands. In the A. P. Herbert
version it is an English household. Messieurs Felix Brentano and
Louis Verneuil have for the present adaptation brought their
visitors from Chicago, which is appropriate and charming of
them. The real subject of the piece, however, is the homage that
Offenbach himself, a German from the Rhineland, was offering to
the city which he loved and which loved him.

    Paris has always been good for foreign musicians and some-
times good to them. To none was ever it more generous than to
Jacques Offenbach, né Levy, from Offenbach-am-Main. And no
musician, foreign or French, not even the Gustave Charpentier of
Louise, ever placed at the feet of his mistress a fresher or a lovelier tribute than *La Vie Parisienne*. It is a crown of waltzes picked
out with polkas and quadrilles and interwoven with melodies that
distill the tender sentiment, the whole tied up with a great big
lacy ribbon in the form of a cancan. And the melodies are as
fresh as the day they were picked; the rhythm pops like champagne; the gaiety is as genuine as anything I have ever seen on a
stage. Every company that acts that operetta has the time of its
life and communicates its effervescence. This production is certain
to sell lots of fizz-water for the tonier bistros of the town. And to
leave happy memories with all. The grand quadrille and cancan
that end the third scene are a very ocean of lace and of legs.
As Jean Cocteau, himself no mean lover of the Lutetian strand,
once said of such an occasion, "Venus herself, nascent, could not
have kicked up more foam."

    One has one's reserves about any transformation of a text one
loves. I regret the omission, on silly moralistic grounds presumably, of the flirtatious wife. I regret the omission of the traditional
gesture with which the nymphomaniac widow ends her number,
"Es-tu content, mon colonel?" which is a lifting high of the hoop-
skirt to expose black panties worn in memory of the departed
mate. I regret the omission of the patter song, "Repeuplons les
salons du Faubourg Saint-Germain," and of the father's chop-

licking, "Je veux m'en fourrer jusque-là." Also the virtual omission of the theme song: "Je serai votre guide dans ce ville splendide." Nevertheless, this version is a good one. The spoken text is less ingenious than Mrs. Farquhar's rhymed lyrics, which are tiptop. All in all, it is difficult to imagine a better adaptation and translation job of a musical play, or to remember one.

The star of the cast is Clifford Newdahl, who both sings and really troops. The others are better vocally than dramatically, though Miss Ruby Mercer does her love stuff with much charm, and Miss Carolina Segrera has a genuinely powerful stage personality. Miss Ann Lipton, the soubrette, is my favorite among the ladies of the cast, both vocally and personally. The men are all right but sort of stuffy, like all singing heroes.

From the specially hand-painted curtain in the Chéret manner to the last detail of gloves and footwear, the stage-sets and the costumes are sumptuous and witty, rich in material, designed and combined with both taste and brilliance. So are the dancing and the stage movements. As a musical show *La Vie Parisienne* makes the rest of Broadway both look and sound silly; and this applies to the Thirty-ninth Street crematorium as well, whenever that ancient and honorable institution tries to do light opera. I do hope the New Opera Company can keep the show running. Or possibly sell it to a producer. It would not surprise me if there should turn out to be gold in those trills and furbelows.* If the Paris of Offenbach, which is, after all, about as near to the eternal Paris as any, not excepting that of the late Third Republic, can sell bubbly in the bars and put other operas at the Forty-fourth Street over the spring, she will have made a pretty return for the love that New Yorkers and musicians have long borne her.

November 6, 1941

* This production closed shortly afterward.

Melody and Tears

LA BOHÈME, opera in four acts, Italian libretto based on *Henri Murger's* LA VIE DE BOHÈME, by GIUSEPPI GIACOSA and LUIGI ILLICA, music by GIACOMO PUCCINI; special performance for the benefit of the New York Protestant Episcopal City Mission Society yesterday afternoon at the Metropolitan Opera House with the following cast.

Rodolfo	*Armand Tokatyan*
Schaunard	*George Cehanovsky*
Benoit	*Salvatore Baccaloni*
Mimi	*Jarmila Novotna*
Parpignol	*Lodovico Oliviero*
Marcello	*John Brownlee*
Colline	*Ezio Pinza*
Alcindoro	*Salvatore Baccaloni*
Musetta	*Annamary Dickey*
A Sergeant	*Arnold Gabor*

Conductor, *Gennaro Papi.* Stage Director, *Désiré Defrère.* Chorus Master, *Fausto Cleva.*

YESTERDAY's performance was a ripsnorter for gaiety, vigor and general run-around. Few effects in the theater are more thoroughly delightful than that of chorus ladies' maternal physiques in gamins' wigs and trousers. Everybody loves it, even the chorus ladies themselves, who cavort and tussle enthusiastically. Few theatrical devices are so completely ineffective, on the other hand, as that of hiding youthful love behind a beard.

Yesterday's gamins were jolly. Yesterday's youthful lovers seemed, on the whole, more boisterous than passionate. Mr. Tokatyan sang Rodolfo on short notice in an improvised costume that consisted of a modern tail-coat such as gentlemen wear as customers to the opera and a pair of equally modern, quite snappily cut, in fact, trousers of a light, checked material. He sported above these a neat black beard trimmed in a style resembling at once that commonly associated with graphic representations of Our Saviour and that indubitably worn by Napoleon III. His singing was good, though the voice is a little harsh.

Miss Novotna was dressed in the least glamorous colors, excepting for a little red jacket in the first act. At the Café Momus festivities she wore an infant's hood of white lace with streamers that tied under the chin. Already tall, the get-up made her look like Charlotte Greenwood. She sang at all times handsomely, though her voice has a veil on it, a slight buzz that prevents it from being the movingly beautiful thing it would be if she could give it a clearer and more ringing sound. Her musical style yesterday and her acting were the afternoon's most distinguished. In a cast that overacted and whooped up the show incessantly, she remained calm and convincing at all times. Her death was genuinely touching, though Mr. Tokatyan's behavior with the corpse was anything but.

Miss Dickey, as Musetta, sang and acted well, in spite of a wig that suggested 1900 blondined hair more than it did anything associated with the Latin Quarter of the 1840's, and in spite also of a rather silly pink dress that stood out too much in the ensemble. Her last act was admirable.

After having been to a number of comic works at the Metropolitan this season, it was good to hear an opera with a tragic ending. The deployment of all the singers and all the instrumentalists that opera in a big house requires, the setting up of so much scenery and the designing of so many costumes, all the paraphernalia of what my colleague Mr. Richard Watts referred to last week as "so tumultuous a dramatic medium," are likely to seem futile unless the subject-matter of the work that uses them all is something more essentially serious than what can be arranged into a happy ending.

In the case of *La Bohème* the touching quality of the work is not due to the mere presence of death. It is due as well to the genius of Giacomo Puccini. I call his musico-dramatic gift genius because no one has ever been able either to analyze its power away or to laugh it off. Say what you will, and present that opera how you like, it is a truly sad story that makes people cry. After all, is anything in the world more poignant than youth and love and tuberculosis?

January 4, 1941

Mildly Dissenting

DER ROSENKAVALIER, opera in three acts, libretto by HUGO VON HOFMANNSTHAL, *music by* RICHARD STRAUSS; last performance of the season at the Metropolitan Opera House last night with the following cast.

Princess von Werdenberg	*Lotte Lehmann*
Baron Ochs von Lerchenau	*Emanuel List*
Octavian	*Jarmila Novotna*
Von Faninal	*Walter Olitzki*
Sophie	*Marita Farell*
Marianne	*Thelma Votipka*
Valzacchi	*John Garris*
Annina	*Irra Petina*
Commissary of Police	*John Gurney*

Major-domo of the Princess   *Emery Darcy*
Major-domo of von Faninal, Innkeeper   *John Dudley*
A Singer   *John Carter*
Notary   *Gerhard Pechner*
    Other roles performed by *Maxine Stellman*, *Mona Paulee*, *Mary Van Kirk*,
Annamary Dickey, *Sari Montague*, *Lodovico Oliviero*, *Wilfred Engelman*,
Michael Arshansky and *Ludwig Burgstaller*.
    Conductor, *Erich Leinsdorf*. Stage Manager, *Désiré Defrère*. Chorus
Master, *Konrad Neuger*.

"THE KNIGHT OF THE ROSE," or *The Rose Cavalier,* as the Metropolitan Opera program so drolly translates it, was the operatic fare
of last evening. The audience adored it and the singers seemed to
be having a good time. The performance all through was remarkably even and smooth. I am sure it is a personal shortcoming that
I did not find myself taking much interest in the affair.
    If I may be permitted the confession, I have never been able
to keep my mind on *Der Rosenkavalier*. It does not bother me
and it does not amuse me. I can take a cat nap here and there
without seeming to miss anything, because when I wake up the
music is always doing exactly what it was when I dropped off.
It is full of waltzes that all sound alike and that have nothing to
do with the play, which is about mid-eighteenth-century Vienna.
It is full of broken-up vocal lines that have no musical necessity,
because the orchestra always has the tune anyway, and that always have to be sung loud because the orchestration is thick and
pushing, owing to Strauss's constant overwriting for the horns. I
think it is really an acting opera, because the vocal line is not very
interesting and the orchestral writing, though elaborate, is to my
ear wholly inconsequential. I make exception vocally for the final
trio, which is as pretty as can be, and instrumentally for the well-
known passage where the celesta comments in another key.
    From the acting point of view the work has many good roles.
The Marschallin, the Baron, the Knight of the Rose himself and
the Italian intriguers are all well characterized by the librettist
and easy to play. The Marschallin is not easy to do with distinction, but fortunately we still have Lotte Lehmann for that. Oc-
tavian, the Knight, is not easy to do with elegance, either, but
Miss Novotna saved us last night from the embarrassment one
so often feels at the all too feminine shape and manners of the
Marschallin's young lover. My favorite actress in the cast was, as
usual, Irra Petina. I love what she does with her hands. I also
love the way she sings and found her vocally the most satisfactory

artist in the cast. Lehmann's voice is lovely but faded. Novotna is musically stylish but sometimes lacking in tonal beauty. Miss Farell's work is not quite ripe. Emanuel List is competent but rough. And the rest of the singers hadn't enough to do to make them vocally noticeable last night. Everybody's singing was all right; but nobody's, except Miss Petina's, was anything to cherish in the memory as sheer sound.

Erich Leinsdorf conducted all right, too, though an ideal rendition would have been rhythmically more flexible. Also, if the orchestra is not to force the singers in this work to sing always loud and monotonously, especial care must be used to secure a highly transparent string tone and the woodwinds must be discreet. Otherwise the sound gets thick and absorbs the voices instead of setting them off. Leinsdorf didn't bother much about this. His work had a certain zip and go about it, however; and he got a clean response from his orchestra. Defrère's stage direction was excellent, and the thirty-year-old sets of Hans Kautsky are still acceptable. With so many quite good elements involved, and with the whole performance operating on such a high level of presentability, it seemed a shame that I couldn't get up anything like the enthusiasm about it that the audience did.

March 14, 1942

Free Love, Socialism, and Why Girls Leave Home

LOUISE, musical romance in four acts by GUSTAVE CHARPENTIER, first performance of the season at the Metropolitan Opera House for the benefit of the Free Milk Fund for Babies. The cast.

Louise	*Grace Moore*
Julien	*Raoul Jobin*
The Mother	*Doris Doe*
The Father	*Ezio Pinza*
Irma	*Maxine Stellman*
Camille	*Thelma Votipka*
Gertrude	*Irra Petina*
The Apprentice	*Lillian Raymondi*

Elise	*Annamary Dickey*
Blanche	*Helen Olheim*
Suzanne	*Lucielle Browning*
The Forewoman	*Maria Savage*
Marguerite	*Mary Van Kirk*
Madeleine	*Anna Kaskas*
The Painter	*Wilfred Engelman*
First Philosopher	*Lorenzo Alvary*
Second Philosopher	*Walter Cassel*
The Sculptor	*Lodovico Oliviero*
The Poet	*John Garris*
The Student	*John Dudley*
The Song-Writer	*George Cehanovsky*
A Street-Sweeper	*Maria Savage*
A Newspaper Girl	*Mona Paulee*
A Young Ragpicker	*Lucielle Browning*
A Milk Woman	*Maxine Stellman*
A Coal-Picker	*Anna Kaskas*
A Noctambulist	} *Alessio De Paolis*
The King of the Fools	
First Policeman	*Emery Darcy*
Second Policeman	*Gerhard Pechner*
A Ragpicker	*John Gurney*
A Junk Man	*Louis D'Angelo*
A Street Arab	*Lillian Raymondi*
An Old-Clothes Man	*John Dudley*
A Bird-Food Vendor	*Tony D'Addozio*
An Artichoke Vendor	*Mona Paulee*
A Watercress Vendor	} *Anna Kaskas*
A Chair Mender	
A Carrot Vendor	*Alessio De Paolis*
A Rag Vendor	*George Cehanovsky*
A Green-Peas Vendor	*John Dudley*
Act III — "La Muse"	*Nina Youchkevitch and the Ballet*

Conductor, *Sir Thomas Beecham*. Stage Director, *Désiré Defrère*. Chorus Master, *Konrad Neuger*. Ballet Master, *Laurent Novikoff*.

YESTERDAY afternoon's performance of *Louise* at the Metropolitan Opera House was one of mounting power. It began rather weakly with Mr. Jobin singing throatily and off pitch and Miss Moore posing around in attitudes derived from still photographs of Sarah Bernhardt. It picked up with the entrance of Miss Doe, and it became a real dramatic exposition when Mr. Pinza arrived. The sweeping musical conception of Sir Thomas Beecham, who conducted, and the great beauty of the symphonic passages made it evident, too, that a musico-dramatic occasion of some magnitude was in progress.

The second act belonged to the conductor and to the ensemble, as it should, with Miss Maxine Stellman adding a handsomely sung solo in the dressmaking scene. The third act was everybody's. Miss Moore began it with a good "Depuis le jour." She and Mr. Jobin then got through the conversation about socialism and their love-duet and had just gone into the house when the surprise party arrived with lanterns and dancers and a brass band. Here Sir Thomas and the chorus took over again and did a rousing "Coronation of the Muse," with Miss Youchkevitch dancing most prettily. Then Miss Doe came on; and everybody else left but Louise and Julien, the alto Mother giving at this point a well-sung and excellently acted summons for Daughter to come home and console sick Father. One felt one had been through quite a bit of excitement by this time, but the height of it was yet to come.

The last act was a triumphant rendition dramatically, vocally, and musically by Miss Moore, Miss Doe, Mr. Pinza, Sir Thomas, and the orchestra of one of the most shocking family brawls I have ever witnessed. Everybody was superb. Indeed, this climactic summary of all the reasons why girls leave home was of a sweep and power that marked the afternoon as a memorable one. It also brought to this reviewer's notice the fact that the whole plot and libretto of *Louise* are literature.

It has long been supposed that Gustave Charpentier wrote his own text for this opera; and, indeed, no other author is named on the title page of the score. I do not know exactly how much work the composer did on the libretto; but Max Jacob once told me that the plot of it was conceived and much of the dialogue written down in one evening at a dinner of Charpentier and some literary friends in a Paris restaurant, Jacob himself being present and participating in the communal creation. Also that the poet Saint-Pol-Roux was the one writer there who remembered to put his name to the work. He may also have done more on it at a later time, because Jacob assured me that Saint-Pol-Roux received performing-rights fees regularly for *Louise* from the Society of Dramatic Authors and Composers.

Whatever may be the exact history of this libretto, however, it is certainly not the work of a literary amateur. Its intrigue is tightly woven; its characterization is powerful, and the dialogue is simple, direct, and stylistically pure in a way hardly to be expected of a composer who has never shown elsewhere any unusual literary mastery. What is his and characteristic, of course, is the musical mastery, manifest throughout the opera, of all the implications of a brilliant literary text. The opera is built up with clear musical characterization, an intense expression of the atmosphere of its subject, and a sound respect for the plain language of plain people. Its musical continuity is symphonic in character without being overcomplex; and its orchestral coloration is fanciful, appropriately picturesque and expert. If it were not for the trumpery musical quality of two of the chief leitmotives — Louise's and Julien's — and the consequent monotony of their subsequent developments, the work might almost rank beside *Carmen* and *La Traviata* in operatic literature. Even so, when conducted with understanding and acted with some style, as it was yesterday (not to speak of much excellent singing), it is a pretty poignant piece of musical theater.

January 16, 1943

The Grace Moore Case

ONE has watched in the past Miss Grace Moore's operatic career with amazement and sometimes with impatience. Her faults were so abundant, her talents, musical and dramatic, so limited, that it has often been occasion for wonder that so much energy and hard work should be deployed on so seemingly hopeless an errand. After seeing her in *La Tosca* the other evening, I am inclined to think that the expenditures were not wasted, after all, and that she has "arrived," as people used to say, at a quite indisputable and authentic stardom.

Her faults have not diminished nor her qualities changed. Both, indeed, have matured. It is the complete visibility of all the factors involved that makes it possible for us to accept her as a finished artist. It is probable also that the realization by Miss Moore herself that her voice will never be any more beautiful than it is today nor her acting any more effective that causes her to give so careful, so conscientious a performance. Few, indeed, are the operatic *prime donne* whose work bears evidence of such good will toward art and such workmanlike integrity.

Miss Moore's musical gifts are modest but well schooled. Her voice, once almost overbrilliant, has lost its surface glamour but none of its real fire; and Miss Moore has improved considerably of late years at the handling of it. It always had more flame in it than sheer beauty. Nowadays this warmth is supplemented by a technical assurance that is none the less welcome for being, alas, all too rare among vocalists of the French school.

Miss Moore's musicianship is difficult to diagnose, because her roles have so far all been such as to require no especial refinement of musical understanding. She seems to have had sensible coaching, and she sings mostly on pitch and in fair rhythm. The musical instinct, I should say, is adequate and the technique solid, so far as it goes, the only element of Miss Moore's musical equipment that goes beyond good training being the very personal timbre of a voice that is the more penetratingly affecting from having lost the impersonal brilliance and bloom of its youth.

Miss Moore's shortcomings at the creating of dramatic illusion are well known. No amount of coaching has been able to make an actress out of her. And yet her performances are far from ineffective. She goes through the motions of acting with such gusto and beams at the audience with such obvious pleasure that no one can resist her wholly. I have often thought she misunderstood her talent, that she is essentially a comedienne and that her proper role is that of the buxom lass with arms akimbo, apple cheeks, and a merry wit. Certainly her stage comportment has not the somber intensity we are accustomed to associate with humorless amour and tragic outcome. In whatever role, she seems always to be playing Madame Sans-Gêne. Her physical advantages themselves are scarcely those of the tragic actress. She has a face that records no darker sentiment than that of well-being. Her arms wave cheerfully at all times. Her smile is what is known as infectious. And yet she plays *femmes fatales.* How does she get away with it?

She gets away with it by giving, however inadequate as illusion, a completely careful and studied performance. No audience can resist such a compliment. She also gets away with it because the nature of her studied performance is such as to recall a great tradition of operatic acting. She has been coached by Garden in the routine of pose and plastic attitude. Her whole concept of stage action is pre-First-World-War — 1900, even. It is derived from the sculpture of Rodin. It has never heard of modern stage style, which is static and low in relief, like contemporary sculpture. Like Garden, she moves in spirals and adopts, wherever possible, robes that lend themselves to vorticism. The contrast between her rounded feminine pantomime and the angular masculinity of Mr. Sved, who plays Scarpia to her Tosca, is advantageous to the plot and to both artists.

There is no doubt that Miss Moore's face and figure are ill adapted to tragic expression. Nevertheless, the choreography of her performance is not without interest or dignity. Its very artificiality is proof of its authenticity. It is a detailed reconstruction, worked out in some of the roles under Garden's own tutelage, of the best French tradition of operatic acting. It is not animated by genius, as Garden's work was; nor has Miss Moore, for all her blandness and cheerful spirits, any erotic projection comparable to Miss Garden's somber fire and intellectual sensuality. But, for all that, her work is made after a great model.

The spirit of great workmanship can never be copied, but its technical shape and framework almost can. I am inclined to think Miss Moore's position in the operatic world, quite apart from the mere agreeableness of her performances, which, at their worst, never let one down, has something to do with her relation to a great tradition. In an epoch when operatic style is little understood and its practice more and more improvisational, Miss Moore gives a thoroughly worked-out rendition of whatever she does. That working out, moreover, is done on no eclectic precept or personal basis. It is a sincere attempt to observe a great tradition. And somehow, by sheer good will, hard work and intellectual modesty, Miss Moore manages to produce the best performance now available in that tradition.

Her work is old-fashioned, if you like. And her personal shortcomings are enormous. But these are so frankly not concealed that we can easily discount their effect on us. And her consistent avoidance of anything vocal or dramatic that might possibly be considered contemporary is proof of a passionate devotion to one of the grandest periods of operatic rendition. I share her admiration for the operatic style of the Third Republic. And I take off my hat to a contemporary artist who has gone back to the highest decades of that period for models to copy and to emulate.

February 22, 1942

Mélisande

THE CHARACTERS in *Pelléas et Mélisande* are correct, well-to-do French people. They don't talk about their business much; but they own property, wear good clothes and seem to be running some sort of kingdom. They have strong passions, kind hearts, good manners, and an intense family life. They understand about love and approve of it. What they cannot deal with is any vagueness on the subject. Mélisande's attractiveness for them seems to be due partly to the fact that she has no family ties (they can thus adopt her completely) and partly to the fact that her affections and her amorous tendencies are both powerful and imprecise. She fascinates them; they never know what to think of her. She keeps them guessing not through any plan but simply through the fact, astounding and incredible to them, that she has no plan, no conscious motives of any sort.

This lack of project, of intention on her part does not prevent her from acting with utter straightforwardness. Her one interest in life is being loved; she demands love from everybody and gets it. She pays willingly any price asked and suffers cheerfully all the consequences involved, early marriage, childbirth and death. She will do anything to avoid not being loved. She lies about a ring she has lost; she submits to a thorough beating from her husband; she refuses to hold a grudge against anyone at any time. Her famous remark at the end of the flagellation scene reveals how egocentric is all her sweetness. "I am not happy here" is her whole comment on the incident. A lonely girl with a floating libido and no malice toward anyone can cause lots of trouble in a well-organized family.

Her husband sees trouble coming quite early, goes to bed of a minor ailment, and tries to think the situation out. "Mélisande, be reasonable!" is his last plea. She doesn't know what he means. After that, tragedy is inevitable. Attempts on the husband's part to discipline her and to spy on her friendship with his younger brother merely bring out the relentless quality in her character, her inability to accept any discipline whatsoever. He tries to murder his brother. Then he pleads with him as man to man. But by that time the brother's sentiments are sufficiently definite so that he cannot, as an honest Frenchman, go back on them. Mélisande wouldn't have collaborated on a noble renunciation, anyway. She would never have got the idea. So the young man is ordered away on a trip. When his departure provokes a real love scene (husband having impatiently shut them both out of the house one evening), there is at last a visible justification for running the deceiver through with a sword.

Nevertheless, Mélisande has the last word. She gives birth to a child, forgives her husband his violence by saying there is nothing to forgive, and dies sweetly, like Little Eva, after refusing to answer all direct questions about her love life. The husband, reasonable and logical to the end, has wanted to know whether he has killed his brother unjustly. Also, with a legitimate curiosity, whether there is any chance he is not the father of the baby. Her reply is equivocal, "We have done nothing to be blamed for." The aged father, an observer from the beginning rather than an actor in the tragedy, thereupon brings out the following pearl of wisdom and of comfort for his bereaved son: "It's terrible but it's not your fault." The French family is thus juridical-minded to the last.

This recital has one purpose only, to remind my readers and all who saw the lovely performance of this opera last week at the Metropolitan that the role of Mélisande is not an easy one to play. It has never been easy, and very few singing actresses have ever made a success of it. Mary Garden and Maggie Teyte were memorable. I have heard others do it, but none convincingly. Mélisande must be childlike on the surface and amorous underneath. She must be both affectionate and self-centered. She must radiate an unaware sexual preoccupation. And she must move delicately. The opera is her show, hers and the conductor's.

Bidu Sayao, in the present production, comes nearer to making the opera her show than any other singer I know of has done, excepting always Garden and Teyte (and I never saw Teyte in it). She has worked out a visible line of movement that is expressive, and her fragile youth is most touching. It is the first star role I have seen her carry off at all, her whole previous effectiveness having been in the domain of the soubrette. She has not learned yet to project her amorous feelings and her sorrows in heroine style, as if the future of the cosmos hung upon them. But she seems to have made a beginning. Also she has created a

Mélisande that, if it is not one of the great ones, is convincing, nevertheless.

Martial Singher, as Pelléas, overpowers her in every way. His vocalism, his declamation, his stage presence, his whole musical and dramatic equipment are of another magnitude. Their scenes together are his scenes, though there seems to be no intention on his part of making them so. All the same, Miss Sayao does a good Mélisande. Her characterization represents not only a step forward for her as a serious actress but also a contribution second only to that of Mr. Singher to a beautiful performance of a great work. When one remembers how many fine sopranos have made no effect at all in the role (though they have dreamed all their lives of singing it), one is obliged to recognize Miss Sayao's achievement as being a far from minor one.

January 30, 1944

Porgy in Maplewood

AFTER six years George Gershwin's *Porgy and Bess* is still a beautiful piece of music. Its faults are numberless; but its inspiration is authentic, its expressive quotient high.

I went to Maplewood, New Jersey, last Monday night to hear its reopening. Cheryl Crawford has produced it with almost the original cast, Alexander Smallens conducting, as before. Happily, the Mamoulian scenery and stage movements have not been reconstituted; they were always too ponderous and too complex to be advantageous. Also, Mr. Smallens has taken occasion to diminish the thickness of the instrumentation and to make some further musical cuts. Gershwin would not have minded, I am sure. He was, if anything, too complaisant about permitting changes in his scores. And his orchestration, at best, was never very skillful or very personal, this particular score, which he probably made without assistance, being heavily overcharged with useless doublings.

As to musical cuts, a considerable number of these had already been made, with Gershwin's consent, during the opera's original run. Others have been incorporated in this production, with the purpose of speeding up certain badly timed passages and with that of eliminating, where possible, the embarrassments due to Gershwin's incredibly amateurish way of writing recitative. In some cases spoken dialogue has been substituted for intoned speech. Without being entirely certain from one hearing whether all these excisions, instrumental and textual, are exactly the right ones to have made and whether perhaps even more of them might be desirable, I approve heartily their having been made at all. It seems to me that that kind of correction, carried out by a skillful musician who knew the composer well and respected his genius, is exactly what the work needs right now. By making it as good a show as possible, as easy to execute and to listen to as is consistent with Gershwin's own writing (nobody has altered his actual notes), the work has, I fancy, more chance of becoming a part of standard operatic repertory than it would have in its original rather clumsy version. Conductors at the Metropolitan do far worse distorting of European classics. Anyway, there will always be time later to revive the original version, if anyone feels passionately about it.

Porgy and Bess is a strange case. It has more faults than any work I have ever known by a reputable composer. There are faults of taste, faults of technique, and grave miscalculations about theatrical effect. It remains, none the less, a beautiful piece of music and a deeply moving play for the lyric theater. Its melodic invention is abundant and pretty distinguished. Its expressive power is impeded by no conscious stylization of the musical means. Gershwin's lack of any intellectual orientation, even the most elementary, toward musical style and his positive ignorance about everything that makes opera opera seem only to have thrown the more into relief his ability to write beautiful and expressive melody and his childlike sincerity. When one considers one by one the new works that the world's greatest opera houses have produced with ballyhoos and hallelujahs in the past forty years and the almost unvarying pattern of their failure, one is inclined to be more than proud of our little Georgie. He didn't know much about musical æsthetics and he couldn't orchestrate for shucks; but his strength was as the strength of ten because his musical heart was really pure.

It was so pure that he could put music to a piece of phony white folklore about Negro life in Charleston, music which is itself about as Negroid as Broadway, and still get Negro artists to perform it without sticking their tongues in their cheeks. They perform it movingly and sincerely. Miss Ruby Elzy, as Serena, gives the loveliest single performance in the cast; Mr. Avon Long, as Sporting Life, replacing the original Bubbles in that role, gives the most brilliant. Miss Helen Dowdy as the Strawberry Woman is perfect both vocally and dramatically, and Miss Georgette Harvey is complete as Maria. I have never cared much for Miss Anne Brown or for Mr. Todd Duncan, who play the name parts. She is vocally not quite top-drawer and rather wooden as an actress. He is a good singer, and he has a stage personality of great sweetness and warmth. But he hams and mugs and overplays and misses most of his best effects by underestimating his own simple power. Mr. Edward Mathews, as Jake, though vocally excellent, makes the same mistake. Miss Harriet Jackson, as Clara, began a little nervously and got better; vocally she was quite lovely. Mr. Jack Carr, who played Crown, was handsome to behold; but he is both vocally and dramatically insufficient for this weighty part. The goat was the most beautiful animal of his species I have ever laid my eyes on.

Rumor hath it that the production will be brought to town. I hope so. It is a good one, and the score itself has both musical distinction and popular appeal. It has a few weak moments, always did. These are invariably the scenes in prose dialogue. The set pieces, where George was working with Ira Gershwin's neatly metrical lyrics, are all excellent. In a year when American compositions are being searched out and honored, it would be not only just, it would be, I should think, good business to expose before our eager and friendly musical public a work which not only New York, the composer's natal city, but America, his native land, might well be proud to honor and happy to love.*

October 19, 1941

* This revival opened shortly afterwards on Broadway, where it ran for two years. In January 1945 the company was still touring.

Blitzstein's Operas

THE MORE comprehensive and grandiose any subject-matter, the more necessary it is to treat it theatrically in a stylized and conventional manner. Symbolic and legendary histories, as of gods, demigods and heroes, involving, as they always do, the prestige of some ethnic group and a whole panoply of the supernatural, have always required for their serious exposition as spectacle the conventions of poetic diction and of ceremonial choreography. From the Greek tragic theater to the contemporary opera there is no exception. There is only the corrective of comedy, which pokes fun when serious matters and noble conventions get out of hand and go pompous.

The conventions of serious theatrical style, once established as an observance by authors and spectators, require a steady supply of serious subject-matter for their continuance. The opera, for example, has in the 340 years of its existence roamed and combed indefatigably the fields of mythology, of military and political history, of religion, sexuality, and social unrest. Embedded and fossilized in the repertories of the most conformist opera foundations are subjects that, if treated less stylistically, would be even today social dynamite. Incest, revolution, suicide, miscegenation, black magic, religious heresy, pessimism, free love, and the abolition of private property are glorified and advocated nightly at the Metropolitan Opera House. In face of such a tradition, Mr. Marc Blitzstein's advocacy of militant trade-unionism as a self-protective measure for America's unemployed, in his opera *No for an Answer*, need not surprise, though the use of a serious art form for the presentation of a serious theme would seem to have shocked some.

This work is not Mr. Blitzstein's first offense, any more than it is the opera's first offense. If Goethe's *Faust* and *Werther*, in Gounod's and Massenet's musical investitures, seem little likely to provoke nowadays much psychological dither, Mozart's Freemasonry and Richard Wagner's philosophy of revolution still peer through their operatic trappings to give us pause. Even socialism is no newcomer to the musical boards. When we remember Alfred Bruneau's *L'Attaque au Moulin* and *Le Rêve* (both after Zola), Gustave Charpentier's *Louise,* and Dmitri Shostakovich's *Lady Macbeth of Mzensk* (in rising order of socialistic violence), it does seem a little foolish to be bothered by so orthodox an exposure of trade-union theory. *Louise,* for instance, not only expounds socialist principles at some length but throws in also a defense of free love and depicts the breaking of family ties by a respectable working girl for reasons of sexual unrest as proper behavior on her part.

What makes the Blitzstein work more pungent just now than these others is the fact that its locale is here and that its language is our own. It is also of some impact that Mr. Blitzstein's musical style, as contrastable with the morass of respected, academic American music-writing that bogged down our opera houses annually until these institutions got tired of losing money and stopped it, is itself pretty pungent and potent.

It is of no importance that I should esteem *No for an Answer* to be a slightly less interesting work musically than Blitzstein's earlier opera, *The Cradle Will Rock*. That is a personal estimate, and many musicians disagree with it. What is of importance to note, and very few musicians can disagree with this, is the fact that Mr. Blitzstein has proved himself in both works to be an opera composer of considerable power. I wish to insist, therefore, that no matter what happens to the present work in the way of commercial success or failure, it is a serious work on a noble subject by a major musical author. Nothing can wash that out.

As to the nature of the Blitzstein talent, the following observations seem to me possible ones to make:

His dramatic sense is strong and his timing of dramatic points accurate.

His musical invention is abundant and varied, his musical characterization appropriate and often sharply expressive. He can draw laughter and tears as few living composers can.

His musical procedure in the theater is based on stylistic parody. The parody of a torch song and the parody of a lullaby are particularly effective, though in different ways. The parody of a love scene, where the girl wants to talk but the man has only one thing on his mind, is touching indeed. The parody of a workers' chorus rehearsal is carried to the point of imitating Russian choral arrangements, à la Volga Boat Song, as these are currently indulged in by worker groups more or less Slavic in racial constituency. Whether the parody is always a conscious one I could not say. I should imagine that the *No for an Answer* theme song itself was not quite intended as a take-off on Robinson's and Latouche's *Ballad for Americans;* but it comes close to being funny, all the same.

Unconscious mocking of oneself is masochistic. It is the buffoonery of the father Karamazov. It is also a characteristic trait of Yiddish comedy. Conscious parody can be tender and humane, as in the love and lullaby scenes, as well as devastatingly ironical.

When Blitzstein parodies knowingly, his music has better tunes and better structure than when he is parodying unconsciously. In the latter case he gets sentimental; and the assumed vulgarity of his musical style, so really elegant at its best, comes dangerously close to the real thing.

It is not within my province or professional competence to estimate the literary value of the Blitzstein libretti. They seem sufficient to me, and I often remember whole scenes from them. To any who might opine that the characters are lay figures, I suggest that characters for musical treatment have to be pretty simple. Few operas have more than one or two real people in them. *No for an Answer* has at least two, the rich boy and the little tough, the spy.

The musical value of the Blitzstein scores I place quite high. I place that of *The Cradle Will Rock* higher than that of *No for an Answer*. I think the author got involved in handling a more complex literary situation and in consequence neglected to give the continuous build that the more complex literary situation demands. He counted too much on the drama's own build. Also, the accompaniments, especially to melodrama and action, are insufficient and inexpressive. They sound like parodies of Dwight Fiske.

I am not happy about this work, as I was about the other. There is material there, human, literary, and musical, to make a successful opera; but it needs reworking. I understand much has been done since last Sunday. Probably more will be done before next. That is good procedure. Gounod's *Faust* had to be quite radically rewritten before it became the successful work we know.

January 12, 1941

"Experimental" Opera

A RECENT production by the Columbia Theater Associates of an "operatic comedy" entitled *Pieces of Eight,* by Bernard Wagenaar and Edward Eager, has occasioned, in view of its generally unfavorable reception by the reviewing press, no small amount of reflection by all concerned. Not that there is anything grave about a group of serious artists having brought forth a work that has failed to please or even to impress. Everybody does bad work from time to time. It is rather that the results of all the autopsies, public and private, that have been performed over the piece have caused the directors of this and of many another similar artistic project to wonder, organic financial disease being not involved in this tragedy, whether there might not be some basic mental maladjustment in their own attitude toward musical theater that is capable of being corrected.

There are many establishments in the United States consecrated to the production with amateur, partly amateur, or student forces of something known as "experimental" theater. The words *experiment, workshop,* and *laboratory* are so frequently associated with this kind of effort that it is probably correct to assume that a pragmatic theory of style underlies the whole movement. It is my opinion that a pragmatic attitude toward style, though advantageous for audiences as a critical point of view, is not sufficiently dynamic to give force and direction to people involved in the making of art. Even for an entrepreneur such an attitude is dangerously close to the more brutal forms of commercialism. In enterprises operating under academic influence it is inevitable that a certain broad-mindedness about styles and techniques should prevail. But it is all the more necessary, hence, that the creative art projects of universities and colleges should espouse some particular æsthetic or other if they wish to avoid diffuseness. Eclecticism of taste is becoming to scholars, but eclecticism in style is not a forward-looking æsthetic for artists.

The whole concept of "experimental" art is probably a false one anyway. Certainly it is if by *experimental* is meant: "Let's try it out and see what happens." Artistic work proceeds, of course, just like any other, by trial and error. But by the time the public and the critical press are invited to witness a show, to use it, as Gertrude Stein would say, in the living that they are doing, the makers of the show, at least, should be fairly well satisfied that it makes a continuity. Performance at this point is an experiment only in the scientific sense of a demonstration, the chief hazard involved being the nature of the reception it will receive, which is not an artistic consideration.

Artists and producers are constantly risking both their prestige and their fortunes on a gamble for public favor, and nobody pretends for a moment that the public's and the critics' responses are without influence on subsequent production. But nobody in the

professional world thinks, either, that there is any advantage to be
derived from exposing work to the ultimate rigors of practical
usage that is admitted by its makers to be in an experimental
state. Design need not be perfect, and execution can be very
rough indeed; but art that is tentative in conception, that is uncertain about itself on the inside, is not art at all. It is student
work, and its faults can be shown up in the classroom or in private
performance without exposing its authors to public embarrassment. Heaven knows there are enough risks involved in any
public performance without adding to these the basic insecurity
of a let's-see-if-it-works theory of style.

Small art theaters do valuable work when they are committed
to a policy of æsthetic advance, particularly if that is limited to
one kind of æsthetic advance. They often do good work when
devoted to æsthetic stabilization, when they conserve traditional
techniques against erosion. They are useful also sometimes for
demonstrating to parents and others student work in authorship
or in elocution. They are not likely to be effective unless there is
a clear theory or a strong personality guiding them. And they
rarely work well when much music is involved.

The reason for this is that the musical theater is (excepting
only the cinema, which is a special form of it) the most complex
artistic entertainment known to man. Its production requires routine; it cannot be improvised. And small laboratory theaters are
for the most part not organized for this routine. They can produce successfully (and that is difficult enough) classical operatic
works of small format. They can produce modern works in a conventionalized manner provided there is plenty of skilled professional advice available. And they can handle the modern dance.
They do not do well with operatic first performances, on the whole,
because their methods are too tentative to be efficacious in dealing
with so recalcitrant a theatrical problem.

Any such theater needs a clear and simple line of policy. Its
aim can be the offering of singing and acting experience to students. Or it can be the offering of a modest theatrical outlet for
the work of directors and decorators too advanced for the commercial stage. Or it can be the providing of a means of production
to living composers and poets. But it cannot be all these things at
once. It must specialize. The musical theater is not only too complex a form of collaboration for small institutions to handle without specializing; it is also too little understood among us to make

any but the most prudent approach to it profitable. Dramatic composition for poets, musical declamation for composers, the projection of the English language (or of any other) for singers, all those basic trainings are weak in our pedagogy. No musical art theater can expect to be more than tentative till they shall have been built into solid and well-understood techniques.

It is the business of our small art-theater projects to do this. And they must take up the problems one by one. A theater specializing in vocal diction need not be pretentious in its repertory or its visual productions. The training of composers to write correct declamation depends on singers who can project consonants, but it does not require the production of operas based on pageantry or an atmospheric orchestral composition. And the drilling into poets of stage ways, of an ability to create character and to tell a story clearly in words that can be sung, is in no small degree dependent on the existence of composers and singers capable of making these unaccustomed practices worth the effort. In the present chaotic state of our musical theater it does not seem to serve any good purpose that singers none too well trained to the techniques of the stage should be asked, as they were recently at the Brander Matthews Theater, to interpret a text that was trivial, banal, and indelicate set to the music of an otherwise skillful composer who has little feeling for the theater, no experience in writing for it, and only the most elementary acquaintance with the quantities of the English language.

One thing at a time, gentlemen, please! And if you must try them all at once, just to see what happens, give yourself a break with a serious story. Don't complicate your "experiment" with the exigencies of farce timing!

May 21, 1944

Advice to Opera Singers

MARY GARDEN used to tell her students "Take care of the dramatic line, and the musical line will take care of itself." Sounder words were never spoken about the problems of the singing actor. Nothing is rarer today on the local operatic stage, however, than artists who work on this principle. Some of the Euro-

peans still do, like Pinza and Baccaloni, Petina and Novotna, and
some of the singers from elsewhere who have had sound European training and experience, like Brownlee and Sayao and Grace
Moore. But the mark of the outsider, of the provincial, is the purely
musical performance with a little acting stuck on.

There has been a good deal of this at the Metropolitan Opera
in the last few years. It was to be hoped that the New Opera
Company would provide a corrective. After two seasons (and I
have seen the whole repertory) it is possible to say with assurance that in spite of some excellent conducting and some very
good sheer vocalism, in spite also of appropriate-sized theaters
and an unhackneyed repertory, circumstances that would have
seemed to stimulate a more convincing dramatic approach than
usual, the New Opera productions, far from being an improvement over the stodginess of many at the Met, have been a field
day of everything that should not be done on an opera stage.

The first thing that should not be done is to treat the opera as
an impure musical form, as a sort of concert in which one also pretends to act a little bit and in which the presence of scenery and
an orchestra justifies an occasional attempt to bellow beyond
one's means. The opera is not a musical form, pure or impure. It
is a theatrical form and one of the most intense, most concentrated and most highly stylized of these. Singing is its medium,
of course, just as elocution is the medium of the spoken stage.
It goes without saying that unless one can sing correctly one has
no business appearing in it, any more than one should appear in
the "legitimate" theater without being able to read lines. Singing
is its medium, its fascination and charm, if you like, too; but singing is not its subject. Its subject is whatever the subject of the
play is. To approach any work of art otherwise than with a determination to give a clear and convincing rendition of its subject
is to approach it indirectly, impurely, insincerely.

Even concert music goes dead when an artist tries to interpret
a piece as if it were a mere vocal or instrumental example. There
is no such thing as *the* symphony, *the* fugue, *the* song. An aria is
not a piece of singing; it is a piece of music. Current pedagogical
methods tend to isolate voice placement from diction, both from
interpretation, and all three from dramatic rendering. As a result,
the vocalism of our young singers quite regularly breaks down
when it moves from studio conditions to the concert hall or to the
stage. The overlays act as complications rather than simplifica-

tions of the singing process, and an overcomplicated singing process makes it impossible to interpret music.

I recognize that analysis, the isolation of all the component elements, is essential to a proper learning of anything. It is right to practice vowel vocalization and to study languages. But the synthesis of the component elements is where technical practice ends and music-making begins. Now, when music-making begins, a wholly different range of values comes into play. A piece must be approached as an expressive thing; a role must be rendered as character. The artist must avoid vocal error, of course, as the actor must avoid stumbling and mumbling and as the painter must keep his colors clean. But the things to keep the mind on are character and meaning. Character and meaning rendered through correct vocalism are what make style in singing. And style is carrying-power.

Once a singer is sufficiently in command of verbal vocalism to appear on a professional stage at all, his duty to himself and to his public is to reduce his technical preoccupations to a sort of censorship and to put his main mind on positive expression. Also, since detailed expression is likely to lack continuity, he must put his mind on the progress of the play. That is what Miss Garden meant by the "dramatic line." She did not mean that good acting will enable any one to sing who doesn't know how to sing. She meant that attention to the meaning of a role will enable a singer who already knows how to sing to interpret both the *words and music* of that role.

The truth of this may seem obvious, once one says it that way. But it is surprising how many young singers have never envisaged operatic interpretation in terms of any obligation to dramatic sincerity. They think because Tetrazzini and Caruso appeared to be merely singing when they were on the stage that these artists were getting away with murder from a dramatic point of view. This is not true. These artists acted well in the statuesque Italian tradition. They rendered character convincingly, in spite of their monumental physiques; and their diction was not something stuck on, when they thought of it, to vowel vocalization. It was the essence of their execution, the binding substance that made the play clear and the vocalism expressive. They believed in the play. If they hadn't they would have been concert artists like John McCormack, who was marvelous in songs and separate arias but who could never get into a role.

My advice, therefore, to the singers of the New Opera Company and to many at the Metropolitan is the same as Miss Garden's. Get into your roles, sing the words, render character. If your vocal technique won't stand up under this, leave the stage at once and take more lessons. Otherwise you will have a public failure and injure your voice at the same time. Above all, take the opera seriously as a dramatic form. It is certainly the most serious one left since the demise of poetic tragedy.

November 29, 1942

Mugging at the Opera

No serious instrumentalist would dream of accompanying his public musical renditions with a play of facial expression. Something of the sort is occasionally indulged in by gypsy violinists in night clubs, the rapt countenance being supposed conventionally in such locales to indicate nostalgic or erotic transports. Sometimes a swing drummer, too, will bring to his eye an insane gleam as he goes into a cadenza, in order to make it seem as if the complications of his solo performance were wholly spontaneous and due rather to inspirational seizure than to art. But in spite of such showmanship of this nature as is met with on the lower levels of musical exploitation, it has never been considered good form for serious instrumentalists to make faces. Certainly not Hofmann nor Kreisler nor Rubinstein nor Casals nor any of the great conductors even, for all their graceful wavings of hair and wrist, ever indulged deliberately in anything of the kind. Heifetz's dead pan, indeed, is as complete as that of any reception clerk at the Ritz or of any salesman at an establishment dealing in Old Master paintings. The concert tradition everywhere is a firm one that no serious musician should accompany his instrumental execution with any play of facial expression whatsoever. He should not even smile too much when bowing.

A slightly greater liberty is allowed to vocalists. These may smile all they like when greeting the audience or acknowledging its applause. They can make friends with the house at all times except during the progress of a musical rendition. They may laugh, blow kisses, curtsy, or cavort; but when about to sing, they must compose the visage, take a correct stance, and get to work

For tradition requires that all concert music, even vocal music, be rendered as music and not as theater. Hence the vocalist is not expected to appear either amused or depressed by the substance of what he is singing. He is expected, on the contrary, to make his effects by musical means, not by pantomime. John Charles Thomas and Kirsten Flagstad and Alexander Kipnis and Helen Traubel, for example, all sing with a perfectly straight face, though Thomas does occasionally add a little staging to a cowboy ditty.

In the theater all is different. Opera singers are supposed to act, and almost any tradition of acting allows some facial pantomime. It is just as well not to overdo this at the opera, because it isn't visible very far away. What one must count on chiefly for carrying one's performance to the top rows is vocal expression amplified by movements and attitudes of the whole body. There is a certain range of facial expression that is permissible (when one is not actually singing), but that range is small and must not be counted on to carry. Most of the great singers have always dispensed with it entirely, preferring to use make-up as a tragic or comic mask that portrays the meaning of each role more clearly than facial play ever can.

Even in operatic comedy there is not much face play worth doing beyond eye-rolling à la Baccaloni and occasionally looking stupid. Opera is not realistic enough and our opera houses are not small enough to make it profitable for singing actors to work with the face. It is more like ballet, which is classically and correctly performed with a minimum of mugging.

The purpose of this preamble is to restate the principles of platform behavior that govern serious musical performance. I include comedy because that, too, is serious musical performance in so far as the performers of it wish to be considered seriously as musicians and as musical actors. The reason for restating these well known principles is that I have noticed a tendency on the part of certain singers at the opera this year to disregard them. This disregard may be due to lack of proper theatrical training in some cases and to a mistaken calculation in others, but in all cases it lowers the artist's musical and dramatic tension.

I refer to the tendency to grin constantly that mars the acting of Miss Grace Moore, of Miss Gladys Swarthout, and of Miss Josephine Tuminia. That tendency has been developed of late years in all those activities of our lives that it is considered proper to photograph. It has been encouraged by press photographers

particularly, because it is the easiest way to bring into the eye of
the subject that tiny sparkle that alone keeps him from looking
in any final overlit picture like a corpse. That photographers working under pressure of time and in unpropitious lighting should
sacrifice every other facial value to that light in the eye is reasonable enough. In the process of so doing, however, they have
filled our periodicals and our daily press with row upon row of
biting teeth and with faces that look as if they had lost all muscular control. The discomposed visage has even become a sort of
standard mask that people put on before entering a room at a
party. It has come to symbolize energy, pleasure, amiability, and
goodwill in front of any public whatsoever.

The artist who wishes to use this mask when saluting the public in his own person — when taking curtain calls, for instance —
is free to do so. Let him grin to his heart's satisfaction, if not to
ours. But in a dramatic role his face should be kept in place. It
does nothing at all toward animating a musical performance to
smile and show the teeth and turn the head vaguely toward the
house as if to indicate what a wonderful time everybody must
be having. It deadens the performance rather. It takes the singer
half-way out of his assumed character and makes a personal
appeal to the audience. It says in effect: "You may not like the
show, but you do like me. Don't you!" It is disloyal to the authors
of the piece and to the other artists of the cast. It deceives nobody
and only tends to make the audience suspicious about the artist's
self-confidence.

In the case of Miss Tuminia I fancy the constant smiling is
due simply to lack of stage training. In the case of Miss Moore
and Miss Swarthout, both of whom have sung in opera for years,
it is probably their Hollywood experience that makes them both
so conscious of their faces. In all three cases the grinning is unnecessary, because they can all sing very beautifully indeed and
do not need to make any special appeal. It is unbecoming, as
well, because they are all quite good-looking women when their
faces are in repose. But nobody is good-looking with his face in
explosion and all his molars exposed.

Flagstad and Novotna and Albanese and Lotte Lehmann let
their faces alone for the most part. When they do frown or smile,
it is at some other character on the stage. When they need to express something by pantomime they use their bodies. This tradition is the correct one. I am surprised that somebody in authority

at the Metropolitan Opera House, if there is anybody there who
has any authority over stage deportment, should not have put a
stop already to violations of it that mar the whole spectacle whenever they occur.

March 30, 1941

What's Wrong with the Met?

THE METROPOLITAN OPERA HOUSE has been full every night all
season, and so has every other Broadway theater. It would be a
mistake to consider the box-office reports of this one as meaning
anything beyond the fact that all entertainment is doing business.
Musicians and other experienced opera-goers have noted a number of excellent opera performances, nevertheless. On the whole,
or so it seems to this reviewer, who has been a fairly regular at-
tendant, the taking of a ticket has been perhaps a less hazardous
action this season than it has in previous years. But essentially
the Metropolitan hasn't changed much. Its policies and adminis-
tration have long seemed to him a muddle; and a muddle they
remain, in spite of good shows now and then.

If the Metropolitan performances were not so unpredictable
and so varied in quality there would be no reason for a music
critic to comment on the organization that produces them. But
being as they are — sublime, ridiculous, and everything in between — and being also the visible reason for existence of a corporation that raises money by public passing of the hat and that is
recognized by the state as of cultural utility, they make one wonder willy-nilly whether we, the public, are getting all we are
entitled to out of our contributions. Consequently, though I have
no intention of recommending specific changes in the personnel,
since my interest is only in policies, I do think it my privilege, if
not my duty, to point out that some kind of reform is desirable
in the running of that enterprise.

My argument is not based on information about interior fric-
tions, though everybody who knows anybody working there has
heard about those. It is based on the simple fact, clearly visible
to any regular patron, that the quality of the performances is undependable. Now, a business that puts out an undependable product is not a sound business, though it may for a time be a profitable

one. Still less is an intellectual or artistic establishment worth its investment unless its work is authoritative. That is what such projects exist for and why they enjoy the financial privileges they do. It is their business to establish real intellectual and artistic standards and to maintain them.

It is not as if the Metropolitan were a young institution of cultural value not yet proved. It is sixty years old and known throughout the forty-eight states to be of tremendous value to culture. The history of the establishment is too full of splendor (and I don't mean diamonds) for anybody to misunderstand what we expect out of it now. And we do not expect the impossible, either. If good singers are scarce, which they are, we can put up with the best available. If public taste is conservative, which it is just now, we can do without novelties. If American artists can't get to Europe, and they can't now, we will take them without previous operatic apprenticeship. But if the standards of everything in a grand old cultural house go erratic, we are entitled to complain, I think, that the house is being badly run.

Continuing establishments have their ups and downs, of course. But they also have their traditions. The Metropolitan's best tradition is one of going on. Its worst tradition is one of not having any very solid musical traditions at all. There is no proper library of annotated scores, for instance. There is literally no way for singers to study there great interpretations from the past of the works they appear in. There are some persons around who remember these things; but it is clear that they seldom get a chance to tell anybody about them, because, although the artists who have sung or learned their roles elsewhere frequently give an authoritative reading, those who have prepared their roles on the spot practically never do. The Metropolitan has a glorious history, but a history is not a tradition. A tradition is precise knowledge about the way something has been done in the past; a rich tradition includes knowledge about a great many of the ways that something has been done in the past. An ancient, conservative house needs to conserve something besides property values. It has no business dealing in improvisation.

The Metropolitan's conducting staff is first class. The singing company is an excellent troupe, a better troupe, indeed, than consistent miscasting often shows it up to be. The orchestra is second class but fair. The chorus is a disgrace. It sings in no recognizable language and habitually off pitch. That is, when it sings at all; one third of it comes in at about the fourth measure, usually. The stage direction is timid and, for new productions, pretty sketchy. There is a vast store of none too fresh costumes and of water-soaked scenery. Lighting is effected by equipment of antediluvian model and largely without rehearsal. All this is obvious to anybody who goes there often. And yet, in spite of it all, some beautiful performances turn up.

There is no reason to suppose that the beautiful performances are planned any more than there is to think the less fortunate ones are. An accident of balanced casting and a little extra care, in consequence, on the conductor's part will do wonders, especially with conductors like Beecham and Walter and Cooper and Szell or with artists like Baum and Castagna and Singher and Albanese, with Peerce and Branzell and Pinza. With brilliant but not wholly dependable singers like Milanov and Roman and Warren, with Traubel and Moore and Harshaw, that little accident makes all the difference in the world. That it is an accident one cannot doubt, since even the best-balanced cast rarely stays together for more than one or two performances. It is my reflected opinion, after four years of pretty steady attendance, that the best performances at the Met are more the result of spontaneous accord among musical artists than they are of office planning or of rehearsal. Such planning as shows up in performance is more likely than not to impress one as reflecting indifference, carelessness, irresponsibility, and boredom.

Either the above observations are sound or they are not. If they are, musicians and other experienced opera-goers will corroborate them. If not, then I don't know a right show from a wrong one. But if I am right, if the one quality manifested consistently in recent years by the Metropolitan Opera performances — underneath all the sincere effort exerted by the various artists and all the real talent, even genius, these have shown for putting over a show in spite of difficulties — is a lack of taste, of judgment, of showmanship, of style, then the institution's directorial and organizational staff is at fault. This does not mean that the staff should or should not be altered. It means that the institution's whole conception of what opera should be needs to be altered, and radically. There is too much inefficiency there and not enough idealism. *April* 9, 1944

RECITALISTS

Classical Beauty

JOSEF HOFMANN, pianist; recital last night in Town Hall.

SONATA, OP. 14 (Concerto without orchestra)	SCHUMANN
SONATA IN C MINOR, OP. 111	BEETHOVEN
SONATA IN B MINOR, OP. 58	CHOPIN

As long as one keeps to piano concerts, truly the town is teeming with delight. Last night it was Josef Hofmann's turn to feed our auditory nerves and to caress our intelligence.

His playing is less monumental and less streamlined than that of any of the other pianistic great in my memory, saving only that of the incomparable de Pachmann. The pillars and buttresses of its architecture are thin and strong. The rooms above are high, airy, clean, and eminently habitable. His forms, to change the figure, grow like trees. No leaf but is attached to stem and branch; no branch but leads us downward to the root. All is organic, orderly, straight-grown toward the light. The word *pedagogic* springs constantly to mind as one listens. Not pedagogic in any pejorative sense. But pedagogic as if each execution were an example to be preserved of how incredibly right piano-playing can be when it is right.

The Schumann sonata could have been taken down by dictation from his playing of it without so much as a sixteenth-note rest being lost or a doubled inner voice being obscured. The clarity of his articulation was as complete in every rhythmic detail as in the piece's main foundations. And heaven knows that piece is a tangle of finicky rhythms.

The Beethoven opus 111, despite the rival claims of various bravura compositions, remains, in my opinion, the most difficult piano piece in the world. Not only because the trills and tremolos

and stretches are ungratefully placed and unconscionably tiring
to play, but because the work presents as great a difficulty to the
mind as to the hand. To make anything consistent out of it is both
an intellectual and a technical achievement. Do not think I am
being flippant about a great piece of music, for I am not. I am
merely insisting that the work is hermetic, complex and knotty
from every point of view.

A good deal of this knottiness comes from the fact that Beethoven was experimenting with pianistic dispositions that he
could not hear very well, if he could hear them at all. Very few
pianists can ever make anybody hear them. Mr. Hofmann did
make them heard, and clearly. In addition, the whole gamut of
dynamic violence and delicacy and deep song, with its under-
current of musical meditation, that is the special palette of Beethoven's later works was richly set out before us, as though the
piece were as straightforward a sonata as the "Waldstein" or the
"Appassionata."

The Chopin B-minor Sonata was my completest enjoyment of
the evening. Mr. Hofmann has always put his super-best into
Chopin. So it is just as well to mention in that connection certain
technical and musical excellences that are the very substance of
Mr. Hofmann's piano-playing, because it is in his playing of that
composer's works that they are most sumptuously and completely
laid before us.

The sustaining force of his Grand Accent is always there, of
course, though without any undue heaviness in the bass. His
orchestral variety of kinds and heights of touch is large indeed.
But instead of orchestrating melodies and figures by using for
each a special kind of tone that is unvaried during the progress
of the phrase, as is the more common modern practice, he turns
and shades each part and phrase within the limits of the special
kind of tone that he has chosen for it. The result is less like the
sound of many mechanical instruments subject to one man's will,
as is the current taste in pianism, than it is like an orchestra of
living musicians subject to a conductor only in the main line of
the music's interpretation.

This living, non-mechanical quality is achieved by no exploitation of human frailty. His scales are as even as well-matched
pearls. No crescendo or diminuendo is ever made because that is
the natural or easy way of playing something. All is willed. But
it is willed to be shaped in the round. No phrase is ever flat or

plane. The result of this rich instrumentation is a musical beauty that is not only noble in its proportions but humane in all its aspects. It is a classical beauty, scaled to the measure of man.

November 7, 1940

Great Music

ARTUR RUBINSTEIN, pianist; recital last night at Carnegie Hall with the following program of music by FRÉDÉRIC CHOPIN.

POLONAISE FANTAISIE, OP. 61
FANTAISIE IMPROMPTU
ÉTUDES (posthumous) IN A FLAT AND F MINOR
ÉTUDE IN C SHARP, OP. 10
SONATA IN B MINOR, OP. 58
SCHERZO NO. 4, IN E MAJOR
BALLADE NO. 4, IN F MINOR
THREE MAZURKAS; NOCTURNE
SCHERZO IN B MINOR

IT is not easy to define what we mean by great music, but it is very easy to agree that the nineteenth century produced lots of it. It is also easy for musicians to agree that Frédéric Chopin was one of the great composers of that century, quite possibly the very greatest of them all. Last night a whole fistful of Chopin's greatest works were played in Carnegie Hall by one of our greatest living pianists, Artur Rubinstein.

Mr. Rubinstein is a delight to watch as well as to hear. Though he is as fastidious as one could wish in his musical execution, his platform manner is straightforward, well bred, businesslike. His delicacy is delicate, his fortes powerful, his melodic tone rich and deep. He can play loud and soft and fast and slow without interrupting the music's rhythmic progress. He is a master of his instrument and of the music he plays, and he finds no reason for attracting undue attention to anything else. He is authoritative, direct, and courteous, like the captain of a transatlantic liner.

His pianism is of the close-to-the-key school. Hence the good marksmanship. Hence, also, its lack of any bright, pearly brilliance. His arms and torso are of stocky build. Hence the power of his climaxes, the evenness of his pianissimo. He is Polish by birth, if I mistake not. Hence his complete at-homeness in Chopin's music, like a host in his father's house.

He is most at home in straightforward pieces, like the études, and in long, massive works like the sonatas, the ballades, the scherzos, works that call to action his mastery of dramatic line, of architectural sweep. He plays the tricky mazurkas and nocturnes with less ease. They don't give him enough room to move around in, and so he rather streamlines them than builds them.

His rubato is of the Paderewski tradition. I do not know how that tradition got started, but I do not think it comes from Chopin. It sounds Viennese to me.

Chopin's prescription for rubato-playing, which is almost word for word Mozart's prescription for playing an accompanied melody, is that the right hand should take liberties with the time values, while the left hand remains rhythmically unaltered. This is exactly the effect you get when a good blues singer is accompanied by a good swing band. It is known to the modern world as *le style hot*. The Paderewski tradition of Chopin-playing is more like the Viennese waltz style, in which the liberties in the melody line are followed exactly in the accompaniment, the two elements keeping always together and performing at the same time a flexible distortion of strict rhythm that manages by its very flexibility to keep the procedure from seeming arbitrary or the continuity from collapsing. Mr. Rubinstein is skillful with this kind of rubato. He keeps the music surging. But I don't believe for a moment it resembles anything Frédéric Chopin ever did or had in mind.

On more than this count does Rubinstein make one think of Paderewski. Among his encores (he played the C-sharp minor Waltz and the Étude for the Little Finger also) he did such a rendition of the A-flat Grande Polonaise as it has not been my pleasure to hear in many a day. Such speed, such power, such fury, such truly magnificent transcending both of the pianoforte's limitations and of his own customary accuracy were the very substance of Paderewski's greatness. They were Mr. Rubinstein's last night, a final jewel in his already laureate crown.

October 26, 1940

Master of Distortion and Exaggeration

VLADIMIR HOROWITZ, pianist, in recital.last night at Carnegie Hall.

CHORALES: "Now Comes the Heathen's Saviour"; "Rejoice, Beloved
    Christians"   BACH-BUSONI
TOCCATA IN C MAJOR   BACH-BUSONI
INTERMEZZI IN B-FLAT MINOR, OP. 117, AND C MAJOR, OP. 119   BRAHMS
SONATA IN B-FLAT MINOR   CHOPIN
ÉTUDES IN F MINOR, C-SHARP MINOR, AND G-FLAT MAJOR, OP. 25   CHOPIN
FUNERAILLES, VALSE OUBLIÉE   LISZT
DANSE MACABRE   SAINT-SAËNS-LISZT
                   (New revision by Mr. Horowitz)

IF one had never heard before the works Mr. Horowitz played last night in Carnegie Hall, or known others by the same authors, one might easily have been convinced that Sebastian Bach was a musician of the Leopold Stokowski type, that Brahms was a sort of flippant Gershwin who had worked in a high-class night club and that Chopin was a gypsy violinist. One might very well conclude also that Liszt's greatest musical pleasure was to write vehicles for just such pianists as Vladimir Horowitz. The last supposition would be correct. Liszt was that kind of pianist himself, and he turned off concert paraphrases of anything and everything from the *Faust* waltz to Palestrina motets. Whether he was quite the master of musical distortion that Horowitz is, history does not record; but I think there is little doubt possible that a kinship of spirit exists between the two pianists. One has only to hear Horowitz play Liszt's music to recognize that.

Do not think, please, that my use of the word *distortion* implies that Mr. Horowitz's interpretations are wholly false and reprehensible. Sometimes they are and sometimes they are not. His Bach is no worse and no better than Stokowski's, on which I take it to be modeled. His Brahms may be less light-minded on other occasions than it was last night. His Chopin varied a good deal during the evening. The sonata was violent, coarsely conceived, melodramatic. He made the Funeral March sound like a Russian boat song by accenting all the off-beats of the bass, and he turned

its serene middle section into the most affected of nocturnes. His
Études, however, were recognizable and, of course, quite brilliant, as they should be; and the A-flat Waltz (an encore) was as
normal as his Liszt.

Supernormal would be a better word for the way he renders
the works of the great Hungarian Romantic. He seems to have
a perfectly clear understanding of what they are about and a thorough respect for them. He exaggerates when exaggeration is of
the essence, but he never tampers with their linear continuity. He
makes all the right effects, and he makes them in the right places.
The only distortion is one of aggrandizement. He plays the Liszt
pieces faster and louder and more accurately than anybody else
ever plays them. Sometimes he plays the music of other composers
that way too, and the effect is more tremendous than pleasant. In
Liszt it is both tremendous and pleasant, because Liszt's music
was written for that kind of playing and because Mr. Horowitz
really loves and understands that kind of music. It is the only
kind that he approaches without fidgeting, and last night it was
the only kind the audience didn't cough through.

If I speak chiefly of interpretation, it is not that I am wanting
in admiration of Mr. Horowitz's justly acclaimed technical powers. But these powers are exploited by a violent and powerful
personality that is, after all, a part of his virtuoso equipment.
Paderewski had and Artur Rubinstein has a strength of crescendo
comparable. Schmitz has an equal cleanness of articulation and a
more even trill. Lhevinne's octaves and general marksmanship are
far from despicable by comparison. And almost any of the more
poetic virtuosos, Serkin or Casadesus, for example, has a lovelier
tone. But none of these pianists is so free from respect for the composer's intentions, as these are currently understood. Horowitz
pays no attention to such academic considerations. He is out to
wow the public, and wow it he does. He makes a false accent or
phrasing anywhere he thinks it will attract attention, and every
brilliant or rapid passage is executed with a huge crescendo or
with a die-away effect. It is all rather fun and interesting to students of what I like to call the wowing technique. It is a great deal
more than that, however, when he gets into his own arrangement
of Liszt's arrangement of Saint-Saën's arrangement for two pianos
of an orchestral version of a song called *Danse Macabre*. His rendition of that number is in every way the berries.

March 7, 1942

Pianism as a Sport

E. ROBERT SCHMITZ, pianist, in recital last night at Carnegie Hall.

Burlesca in G minor; Bourrée in B minor	Scarlatti
Chorale Prelude, "I Call on Thee, Creator"	Bach-Busoni
Prelude and Fugue in A minor	Bach-Liszt
Prelude, Chorale and Fugue	Franck
First Spanish Dance from La Vida Breve	de Falla-Schmitz
"El Puerto," from Iberia	Albeniz
Danza Iberica	Nin
Toccata and Rigaudon, from Le Tombeau de Couperin	Ravel
Préludes: "La Puerta del Vino"; "La Terrasse des audiences du clair de lune"; "Ce qu'a vu le vent d'ouest"; "La Cathédrale Engloutie"; "Feux d'Artifice"	Debussy
Dance in E major	Debussy

AFTER some years of absence from these parts E. Robert Schmitz returned last night to play in Carnegie Hall in a recital that can only properly be described as a triumph. It was a triumph from every point of view, musical and technical, as well as in terms of bravos shouted, of encores demanded and executed.

Mr. Schmitz's pianism is and always has been of a transcendant order. It was that twenty years ago when last I heard him play. Since that time it has been elaborated and perfected by practice and by pedagogical experience to such a degree that it resembles now more the work of Tilden or Budge on a tennis court than anything of a merely musico-poetic nature.

Not that his playing is lacking in either musicianship or poetry. On the contrary, his readings of the Bach A-minor organ fugue and of the Franck Prelude, Chorale, and Fugue were of a subtle and refined clarity, an apparent simplicity of architectonics that only the most comprehensive musicianship ever conceives and only the most commanding technique renders possible in execution. No slowing up for difficult changes of hand position, no pounding beyond the instrument's resources. When he wants to play fast octaves with the left hand he plays them. When he wants more volume he gets it. When he wants to let the music fall as lightly on the ear as summer rain, that is the way the music falls.

And what he wants is always a clear and sensible exposition, as well as a sensitive one, of the piece's shape and content.

As for poetry, he avoids at all times the personal and the pseudo-emotional. He expounds each piece through its own rhetoric, makes its instrumentation and continuity clear, lets it sing for itself. So that in addition to the intrinsic beauty of the melodic material and of its expressive ornament there is the abstract poetry of a physical act beautifully accomplished. That is what I mean by comparing his work to that of a good tennis-player. It isn't that his motions are merely agreeable to watch. So are those of many a third-rate athlete. It is that the constant accuracy of the result, under the most varied musical circumstances, makes it evident that there is a fine harmony between the muscular effort and what it accomplishes.

Last night's triumph with the audience, though the warmth and the applause grew from the beginning, was crowned by the playing of six Debussy Preludes, plus two more and some other Debussy as encores. Here was the occasion to exploit the gamut of varied timbre and touch that Schmitz is master of as is no other pianist. He did so exploit it, but withal so musically, so intelligently, with such sweet comprehension of the works themselves, that they were as if viewed under a magnifying glass in high illumination.

There is a poesy of dim lights and fog and faint suggestion, and there are many musicians who think that is what Debussy should sound like. I know no historical evidence to make me believe that such vagueness ever was anything but a trickery of the not very competent. Debussy was a fanatic for precision and for delicate adjustments of timbre and of volume. To make these adjustments more than ever precise and elaborate by slightly magnifying the dynamic proportions is in no way to diminish the poetry of the final effect. Rather the contrary.

It has been a long time since we have heard Debussy played like great music. That it may not be so long before we hear it so played again is the fervent wish of this reviewer. That the next time Mr. Schmitz deigns to visit these parts he may honor us with a complete rendition of the Debussy Études, all twelve of them, is my equally fervent hope. It is absurd that these master works should be so neglected by pianists and unbelievable that they should not be in the repertory of a pianist so completely in sympathy with their content as Mr. Schmitz and so magnificently equipped to treat their difficulties as no more terrifying than a good serve from a worthy opponent.

March 27, 1941

Equalized Expressivity

NEW FRIENDS OF MUSIC, Carnegie Hall. Piano recital by *Artur Schnabel.* All-Beethoven program. SONATAS IN A-FLAT MAJOR, OP. 110; IN F MAJOR, OP. 10, No. 2; IN D MINOR, OP. 31, No. 2; IN C, OP. 111.

ARTUR SCHNABEL, who played last night in Carnegie Hall the second of three recitals, presented by the New Friends of Music, devoted to the piano music of Beethoven, has for some thirty or forty years made this composer the object of his especial attention. He passes, indeed, and with reason, for an expert on the subject, by which is usually meant that his knowledge of it is extensive and that his judgments about it are respected. Any issue taken with him on details of tempo, of phraseology, of accent is risky and, at best, of minor import. Minor, too, are criticisms of his piano technique, which, though not first class, is quite adequate for the expression of his ideas. His ideas about Beethoven's piano music in general, whether or not one finds his readings convincing, are not to be dismissed lightly.

Neither need they, I think, be taken as the voice of authority. For all the consistency and logic of his musicianship, there is too large a modicum of late-nineteenth-century Romanticism in Mr. Schnabel's own personality to make his Beethoven — who was, after all, a child of the late eighteenth — wholly convincing to musicians of the mid-twentieth. No one wishes to deny the Romantic elements in Beethoven. But I do think that they are another kind of Romanticism from Schnabel's, which seems to be based on the Wagnerian theories of expressivity.

Mr. Schnabel does not admit, or plays as if he did not admit, any difference between the expressive functions of melody and of passage work. The neutral material of music — scales, arpeggiated basses, accompanying figures, ostinato chordal backgrounds, formal cadences — he plays as if they were an intense communication, as if they were saying something as important as the main thematic material. They are important to Beethoven's composition, of course; but they are not directly expressive musical elements. They serve as amplification, as underpinning, frequently as mere acoustical brilliance. To execute them all with climactic emphasis is to rob the melodic material, the expressive phrases, of their singing power.

This equalized expressivity ends by making Beethoven sound sometimes a little meretricious as a composer. His large-scale forms include, of necessity, a large amount of material that has a structural rather than a directly expressive function. Emphasizing all this as if it were phrase by phrase of the deepest emotional portent not only reduces the emotional portent of the expressive material; it blows up the commonplaces of musical rhetoric and communication into a form of bombast that makes Beethoven's early sonatas, which have many formal observances in them, sound empty of meaning and the later ones, which sometimes skip formal transitions, sound like the improvisations of a talented youth.

The work that suffered least last night from the disproportionate emphasizing of secondary material was the Sonata opus 111. Here Mr. Schnabel achieved in the first movement a more convincing relation than one currently hears between the declamatory and the lyrical subjects. And in the finale he produced for us that beatific tranquillity that was a characteristic part of Beethoven's mature expression and that had been noticeably wanting, though there were plenty of occasions for it, in the earlier part of the evening.

March 28, 1944

Personal and Viennese

RUDOLF SERKIN, pianist, in recital last night at Carnegie Hall, playing the following program.

FANTASIA AND FUGUE IN C MAJOR (K. 394)	MOZART
SONATA IN G MAJOR (K. 283)	MOZART
SONATA IN F MINOR, OP. 57, ("Appassionata")	BEETHOVEN
VARIATIONS AND FUGUE ON A THEME BY TELEMANN, OP. 134	REGER

RUDOLF SERKIN's pianism is Viennese by schooling, close to the key, unerring in text and weight. He exploits no Parisian gamut of bell and piccolo and trumpet evocation. His tone is the same in all the ranges of its power, rich, smooth, and mat, never tinkling, never forced. It resembles in a most surprising way Fritz Kreisler's diapason-like violin tone, still sounding in the ear from Thursday night.

One is reminded, too, of Josef Hofmann as I first heard him thirty-odd years ago. Like Hofmann, Mr. Serkin is not only a master pianist, firm and possessive with the loved instrument; he is a master of music as well. Without an iota of textual violation, with, on the contrary, a closer observance of Mozart's and Beethoven's indications than one practically ever hears from the concert stage, he transforms each piece into a song of his own, warms it in the palm of his youth and molds it to a living and personal expression of his own Sacred Flame.

Of the four works so lovingly presented last night, the Reger is the least interesting musically. It is skillful, superficial, not untuneful, and full of ingenious bravura figuration. The audience loved its finale, a *Grand Valse de Concert* in the form of a double fugue, a typical Reger idea and good fun.

Beethoven's "Appassionata" was built, like the drama of mystery and terror that it is, on an inexorable rhythm against which its dynamic and passional surprise-gamut was thrown into relief without seeming querulous or exasperated. The interpreter understood that Beethoven, as always, was putting into a concert piece a dramatic conception of life. Beethoven never succeeded in making his dramatic concepts dramatic on a stage. But those who have heard the *Leonora* Overture No. 3 played between two acts of *Fidelio,* as is the custom in some opera houses, usually sense that Beethoven's instrumental music is all of the theater and its drama conceived. The last movement was disappointing. Taken as a *presto possibile,* it lost weight and grandeur; and its coda sounded gay rather than victorious.

It is natural that I should love the Serkin Mozart, because it concords with my own pet theories, though I doubt if it is a product of the reason. Rather, it sounded to me like a creation of taste and instinct. In any case, it was broad without being brutal, refined with no trace of effeminacy.

The G major Sonata was played for what it most certainly is, a symphonic ensemble piece evoked at the pianoforte. The pianist used no rhythmic trickery here, either. He played it with the rhythmic regularity of ensemble music and observed Mozart's accents convincingly. The tempos were those appropriate to ensemble evocation, excepting, as in Beethoven, that of the last movement, which was fast and pianistic. The piece thereby lost body.

November 16, 1940

The Strange Case of Claudio Arrau

CLAUDIO ARRAU, pianist, in recital at Carnegie Hall.

RONDO IN A MINOR	MOZART
FIFTEEN VARIATIONS AND FUGUE, OP. 35 ("Eroica" Variations)	BEETHOVEN
BALLADE IN F MINOR	CHOPIN
JEUX D'EAU À LA VILLA D'ESTE; MEPHISTO WALTZ	LISZT
ESTAMPES: "PAGODES"; "LA SOIRÉE DANS GRENADE"; "JARDINS SOUS LA PLUIE"	DEBUSSY
SUBURBIO (first New York performance)	LECUNA
TOCCATA (first New York performance)	CASTRO
VIGNETA, No. 4 (first New York performance)	SANTA CRUZ
"EL PELELO" (from GOYESCAS)	GRANADOS

To find a musical parallel for the pianism of Claudio Arrau, one must look outside the circle of keyboard virtuosos. His particular combination of technical security and musical irresponsibility, which used to be found among singers, today is chiefly limited to violinists. He delights a vast audience (Carnegie Hall had even its stage full last night) and impresses the most serious musicians. (I could have touched five world-famous pianists from where I sat.) His physical mastery of the art of piano-playing is so satisfactory and the charm of his explosive temperament is so acute that one does not always realize right off how shallow is the musical thought behind all the brilliance (and solidity, even) of the execution. Perhaps at the last no one will care about the faults, in view of his overpowering appeal; but just for the present your reviewer is torn between his admiration for skillful hand work and his inveterate prejudice against faulty musical conceptions.

Mr. Arrau's musical conceptions seem scarcely to have been reflected at all. Phraseology, architecture, continuity, all the ob-

jective rhetorical devices for conveying the substance of a composition, are replaced by a subjective, instinctive rhetoric that is
in itself a mark of high musical gifts. One may even consider that
it doesn't make much difference how he reads a piece, since he
always makes it sound like music. Well, that is what I mean by
musical irresponsibility. Mr. Arrau is no traitor to his own musical
feelings. But those feelings seem chiefly to be concentrated on his
own act of playing the piano and to have very little to do with
his music's author beyond the use of that author's text as a vehicle
for improvisation. He doesn't improvise any notes in the music he
plays; these he renders with greater power and exactitude than
most. He merely improvises its sense.

This divergence from customary readings is chiefly a question
of rhythm. That is where all musical texts allow liberty and require discernment. In playing Debussy last night Mr. Arrau seemed
wholly unaware that neither Spanish nor Javanese rhythms admit the use of rubato. He played a fragile Mozart rondo in the
declamatory style. He read a Chopin ballade as if he were accompanying a film. His Beethoven began beautifully (as did the Liszt
Mephisto Waltz) and fell to pieces in the middle. Saving the
South American works, which I most regrettably was unable to
stay for, the only single piece that sounded to me as sensibly as
it did beautifully was Liszt's *Fountains at the Villa d'Este*. That
was unsurpassable pianism and a clear musical communication.

October 28, 1943

American Rhythm

JOHN KIRKPATRICK, pianist, in recital in Times Hall.

PRELUDE AND FUGUE IN D MAJOR; PRELUDE IN C MINOR (first performances);
  TOCCATA IN E-FLAT MAJOR   CHANLER
CONCORD, MASS., 1840–60   IVES
WOODLAND SKETCHES: "To a Wild Rose," "Will o' the Wisp," "From Uncle
  Remus," "To a Water Lily"; Fireside Tales: "Of Br'er Rabbit," "Of Sala-
  manders"; New England Idyls: "The Joy of Autumn"   MACDOWELL
SONATA, OP. 1   HARRIS

JOHN KIRKPATRICK, who gave a piano recital last night in Times
Hall, has a way of making one feel happy about American music.
He does this by loving it, understanding it, and playing it very

beautifully. He plays, in fact, everything very beautifully that I have ever heard him play. But people who play that beautifully so rarely play American music that Mr. Kirkpatrick's recitals are doubly welcome, once for their repertory and again for his unique understanding of it.

The loveliness of his playing comes from a combination of tonal delicacy with really firm rhythm. Exactitude with flexibility at all the levels of loudness is the characteristic of American pianism that transcends all our local schools of composition and lack of same. It is what makes us a major musical people, and it is exactly the rhythmic quality that escapes our European interpreters. European tonal beauty, of course, more often than not escapes American pianists. Mr. Kirkpatrick's combination of European tonal technique with full understanding of American rhythm makes his playing of American works a profoundly exciting thing and a new thing in music.

Charles Ives's *Concord* Sonata was esteemed by Lawrence Gilman the finest piece of music ever written by an American, and it very well may be just that. Certainly it is a massive hunk of creation; four massive hunks, in fact. Because it is really four symphonic poems, named respectively, "Emerson," "Hawthorne," "The Alcotts," and "Thoreau": four full-length portraits done with breadth, tenderness, and wit. "The Alcotts" is the best integrated formally of these and probably the most original, or indigenous, in its musical material and fancy. I suspect that concert audiences would take eventually to all these portraits if they were performed separately for a time, since the whole work is longer than the ones people are now used to listening to. In any case, here is music, real music; and Americans should have no serious difficulty accepting its subject-matter or understanding its ingenuous grandeurs.

Of the other works performed last night Theodore Chanler's Toccata seemed to me the most finely conceived and the most delicately indited. Roy Harris's early Piano Sonata, opus 1, is a coarse work and laborious. The MacDowell pieces seemed charming and poetic, as always, but a little soft in their melodic material.

The encores consisted of two works by Stephen Foster, *The Old Folks' Quadrille* and a flute piece called *Anadolia;* a Prelude by Robert Palmer; Arthur Farwell's *Navajo War Dance,* and a *Trumpet Aire* by James Bremner, a composer of Revolutionary times. All these were good to hear, especially Mr. Palmer's strongly

knit Prelude and Farwell's handsome evocation of Indian themes
and rhythms. The others were agreeably antiquarian. And everything Kirkpatrick played turned into a poem.

November 24, 1943

A Good Start

WILLIAM KAPELL, pianist, in recital in Town Hall last night.

SONATA, G MAJOR, OP. 31, NO. 1	BEETHOVEN
CAT'S FUGUE	SCARLATTI
FANTASY AND FUGUE, C MAJOR	MOZART
PRELUDE, CHORALE, AND FUGUE	FRANCK
POLONAISE-FANTASY	CHOPIN
PRELUDE, G-FLAT MAJOR; ÉTUDE TABLEAU	RACHMANINOFF
SONATA NO. 3	PROKOFIEV
THREE POEMS	PERSICHETTI
SYRTOS	FULEIHAN
SONETTO DEL PETRARCA NO. 104; RHAPSODY NO. 6	LISZT

OPERATING on the principle that one good recital deserves another,
the Town Hall chooses each year a debutant musician of noteworthy qualities and awards him an engagement the following
year in its endowment series of musical events. Last year's laureate was William Kapell, pianist, nineteen years old at the time
of his first Town Hall recital. Last night he gave his award recital;
and pretty fine it was, I must say.

It is a mistake to expect of youth any unusual concentration of
fire and poetry. This is more normally an attribute of middle
age. What youth has, at its best, is a small, hard, real musical gift
and a certain freshness of technical training. The latter is likely
to be tensely efficient rather than beautiful, the former clearly
visible through it rather than wholly expressed. In Mr. Kapell's
case the technical proficiency is most impressive. He plays clearly
and cleanly and powerfully, with good tone and with an ample
range of weights and colors. His natural musicality shows up in
the rhythm and in his tonal proportions and balances, which are
always interesting, occasionally quite novel. His temperament is
evident in the way different pieces come out sounding like different pieces in spite of the fact that they are all approached
with the same grandiose preoccupation.

Mr. Kapell was better in the modern works than in the classical ones. Scarlatti, Beethoven, and Mozart might have been three pseudonyms of one man, so little did he appear to feel any necessity for varying his stylistic approach to them. The Beethoven sonata, however, was notable for its final rondo, which was dry and precise, and high in coloristic relief. Everywhere, too, there was a sense of music's continuity, an over-all conception that is characteristic of musicians with more than average mental powers. It was this continuous progress, indeed, that saved Mr. Kapell from superficiality in the pieces of Chopin and Liszt.

Prokofiev, Persichetti, and Fuleihan, however, were the writers who drew from him the completest intellectual understanding. He made them all sound rather alike, I must say, as he had previously done with his classics and his Romantics. But they sounded as if he had chosen them for their resemblance to his own image of the modern world, not as if he were imposing an inappropriate similarity upon them. He gave, thus, a most unusual tone to his recital, namely, that of an unconscious but perfectly real modernism. And here his youth served him well. The middle-aged play old music as if they owned it; but they are mostly pretty inept, in spite of goodwill, at rendering the contemporary. Mr. Kapell walked through the ancients (if so we may refer to our predecessors) like an intelligent somnambulist, making no false steps, but seeming to be aware of nothing beyond the exactitude and grace of his locomotion. But when he played the music of his own time he woke up and made sense.

January 21, 1943

Very Loud and Very Soft

ROBERT CASADESUS, pianist, in recital in Carnegie Hall last night.

SONATA, OP. 111, IN C MINOR	BEETHOVEN
TWELVE ÉTUDES: OP. 10, NOS. 8, 9, 10, 6, 2, 12; OP. 25, NOS. 1, 5, 6, 11;	
A-FLAT MAJOR; OP. 25, No. 12	CHOPIN
THÈME ET VARIATIONS, OP. 75	FAURÉ
EL PUERTO; EL ALBAICÍN; TRIANA	ALBÉNIZ

ROBERT CASADESUS, who played a piano recital last night in Carnegie Hall, is an ace technician and a clear-headed man of music. He lays a piece before you without any confusion of its phraseology or any obscurity of its detail. And his pianistic and analytic powers are all the more dramatically exposed because of his constant differentiation between meter and accent. This gives a thrilling steadiness to runs, trills, and passage work and a grand onward sweep to the progress of a piece. It is regrettable that his extraordinary skill and musicianship are not complemented by an instinct for dynamic proportion.

No matter what he plays, the volume range is always extreme; he plays very loud or very soft most of the time. This lack of imagination about the middle sizes of loudness amounts, in the long run, to a lack of poetry in the musical renderings. In the Beethoven Sonata opus 111, for example, he dramatized handsomely the violence of the opening theme against the beatific pathos of the succeeding one, but the less broad expression of the variations escaped him. Similarly, twelve Chopin Études, though handsomely phrased and fingered, were chiefly a contrast of light and dark, of *ppp* and *fff*, which is tiresome.

The Fauré Theme and Variations, though not a great work, is an agreeably lyrical one. But Mr. Casadesus weakened it beyond any real carrying-power by trying to make a "strong" work out of it. The evening's worst example of ineffective proportion was in the three pieces of Albéniz with which the program ended. Here the guitar imitations lost all their color and flamboyance through being played too loud. They might as well have been the evocation of a calliope.

The folly of the "big" tone is one that affects many excellent musicians, especially in this country. Cellists are notably prone to it, though neither fiddlers nor pianists are immune. Mr. Casadesus is the most exaggerated case I have encountered among the last. It is not that there is anything wrong about playing majestically loud from time to time. The folly consists in distorting music's natural dynamic proportions, in leaning on passages that should be only medium loud with such persistence that the only possible contrast is to play the softer passages very, very soft. The vice starts by neglecting the most sensitive part of the dynamic range — that between *p* and *f* — and ends by obliterating all the shades of tone color that exist only in that range, which means nine tenths of them. The "big" tone is thought to be box-

office, though whether it can last long even there I doubt; but
certainly it is an unfortunate investment musically.

February 17, 1944

Rhythmic Grandeurs

WANDA LANDOWSKA, harpsichordist, playing BACH'S GOLDBERG
VARIATIONS in its complete and original form for the harpsichord with
two keyboards yesterday afternoon at Town Hall.

WANDA LANDOWSKA's return to us after a fourteen-year interval
was celebrated yesterday afternoon at the Town Hall in a ceremony both imposing and heart-warming. She played Bach's thirty
"Goldberg Variations" to a full house that was virtually a social
register of professional musicians; and she received a welcome and
a final ovation from the distinguished assembly that were tribute
equally to her penetrating musicianship and to her powers of virtuoso execution on that most exacting of all keyboard instruments,
the harpsichord.

I am not going to review the "Goldberg Variations," which
are one of the monuments of musical art, except to note that, as
Madame Landowska played them, there were no dull moments,
though the concert lasted little less than two hours. I should like
rather to cast an analytic eye on the work of this extraordinary
performer, whose execution, no matter what she plays, is one of
the richest and grandest experiences available to lovers of the
tonal art. That she should play for two hours without striking a
false note is admirable, of course; that she should play thirty pieces
varying greatly in volume without ever allowing us to hear any
thumping down of the keys proves a mastery of the harpsichord
that is, to my knowledge, unique. That she should phrase and
register the "Goldberg Variations" with such clarity and freedom
that they all sound like new pieces is evidence of some quality
at work besides mere musicianship, though the musicianship
does run high in this case.

A performance so complete, so wholly integrated, so prepared,
is rarely to be encountered. Most artists, by the time they have
worked out that much detail, are heartily sick of any piece and
either walk through it half asleep or ham it up. It is part of the
harpsichord's curious power that the more one is meticulous and

finicky about detail, the livelier the whole effect becomes.

All musicianly and expert qualities are observable at their highest in Madame Landowska's harpsichord-playing. But so are they in the work of many another virtuoso. Her especial and unique grandeur is her rhythm. It is modern quantitative scansion at its purest. Benny Goodman himself can do no better. And it is Bach's rhythm, as that must have been. Writing constantly for instruments of no tonic accent, like the harpsichord and the organ, all Bach's music is made up out of length values. If you want to realize how difficult it is to express a clear rhythm without the aid of tonic stresses, or down-beats, just try it on an electric buzzer. And if you want to realize what elaborate rhythmic complications the eighteenth-century performers did manage to make clear (else these would not have been written) on accentless instruments, just take a look at Bach's music for organ and that for harpsichord, particularly the "Goldberg Variations."

The introduction of the pianoforte and the invention of the orchestral crescendo at the end of the eighteenth century changed the nature of music radically by substituting pulse for measure and punch for complexity. Only in our day, through the dissemination of American and South American popular music, which differs from European in being more dependent on quantitative patterns than on strong pulsations, has a correct understanding of Bach's rhythm been possible and a technique reinvented for rendering it cleanly and forcibly. (Highly dramatic accents can be obtained with no added force, for instance, by delaying ever so slightly the attack on the note it is desired to accent. Also, expressive liberties of rhythm only take on their full expression as liberties when they are liberties taken upon some previously established rhythmic exactitude.)

Of all these matters Landowska is mistress. The pungency and high relief of her playing are the result of such a mastery's being placed at the service of a penetrating intelligence and a passionate Polish temperament. The final achievement is a musical experience that clarifies the past by revealing it to us through the present, through something we all take for granted nowadays, as Bach's century took it for granted, but that for a hundred and fifty years has been neglected, out of style, forgotten. That is the cultivation of rhythmic complexity by an elimination from musical thought of all dependence on rhythmic beat.

February 22, 1942

A Shower of Gold

WANDA LANDOWSKA, harpsichordist, in recital last night at Town Hall.

PRELUDE AND FUGUE IN E-FLAT MINOR, from THE WELL-TEMPERED
    CLAVIER, BOOK I   BACH
PARTITA IN B-FLAT MAJOR   BACH
SUITE IN E MINOR   RAMEAU
LAMENT COMPOSED IN LONDON TO DISPEL MELANCHOLY, TO BE PLAYED
    SLOWLY WITH DISCRETION   J. J. FROBERGER
CHROMATIC FANTASY AND FUGUE   BACH

WANDA LANDOWSKA's harpsichord recital of last evening at the Town Hall was as stimulating as a needle shower. Indeed, the sound of that princely instrument, when it is played with art and fury, makes one think of golden rain and of how Danaë's flesh must have tingled when she found herself caught out in just such a downpour.

Madame Landowska's program was all Bach and Rameau, with the exception of one short piece by Froberger. She played everything better than anybody else ever does. One might almost say, were not such a comparison foolish, that she plays the harpsichord better than anybody else ever plays anything. That is to say that the way she makes music is so deeply satisfactory that one has the feeling of a fruition, of a completeness at once intellectual and sensuously auditory beyond which it is difficult to imagine anything further.

On examination this amplitude reveals itself as the product of a highly perfected digital technique operating under the direction of a mind which not only knows music in detail and in historical perspective but has an unusual thoroughness about all its operations. There are also present a great gift of theatrical simplicity (she makes all her points clearly and broadly) and a fiery Slavic temperament. The latter is both concealed and revealed by a unique rhythmic virtuosity that is at the same time characteristic of our century and convincingly authentic when applied to the execution of another century's music.

It is when this rhythm is most relentless that I find Madame Landowska's work most absorbing. Free recitative and the affetuoso style she does with taste, and she spaces her fugal entries cleanly. But music becomes as grand and as impersonal as an element when she gets into a sustained rhythmic pattern. It makes no difference then whether the music is dainty, as in the Rameau suite, or dancy and vigorously expository, as in both the Rameau suite and the Bach Partita. It is full of a divine fury and irresistibly insistent.

There is no need of my reviewing the works played, which are all great music, save perhaps to pay tribute to Rameau, who got so much of the sweetness of France, as well as its grace and its grandeur, into his E-minor Suite. And to mention the romantic and rhapsodical beauty of the Froberger *Lament*. There is even less occasion to point out stylistic misconceptions and interpretative errors on the executant's part, because there weren't any. At least, it seemed to this listener that every work was fully possessed by her. If the audience was as fully possessed by these superbly convincing renditions of some of the grandest music in the world as this auditor was (and certainly it appeared to be), there really isn't much that any of us can do about it further, except to make sure of not missing this great artist's next performance. Last night's was as complete as that.

October 22, 1942

Complete Authority

JOSEF LHEVINNE, pianist, in recital last night at Carnegie Hall.

Toccata in C major	Schumann
Sonata in F minor, Op. 5	Brahms
Twelve Études, Op. 25	Chopin
The Lark	Glinka-Balakirev
Islamey (Oriental Fantasy)	Balakirev

Mr. Lhevinne seems to have replaced the late Leopold Godowsky as the acknowledged master of pianoforte-mastery. A full house paid him homage last night at Carnegie Hall, as he, in turn, paid his audience the honor of executing a distinguished program of the piano's masterworks with authority and no playing down to anybody.

A more satisfactory academicism could scarcely be imagined.

Mr. Lhevinne's performance, especially of the Schumann Toccata and the Chopin Études, was both a lesson and an inspiration. He made no effort to charm or to seduce or to preach or to impress. He played as if he were expounding to a graduate seminar: "This is the music, and this is the way to play it."

Any authoritative execution derives as much of its excellence from what the artist does not do as from what he does. If he doesn't do anything off color at all, he is correctly said to have taste. Mr. Lhevinne's taste is as authoritative as his technical method. Not one sectarian interpretation, not one personal fancy, not one stroke below the belt, not a sliver of ham, mars the universal acceptability of his readings. Everything he does is right and clear and complete. Everything he doesn't do is the whole list of all the things that mar the musical executions of lesser men.

This is not to say that tenderness and poetry and personal warmth and fire are faults of musical style, though they frequently do excuse a faulty technique. I am saying that Mr. Lhevinne does not need them. They would mar his style; hence he eschews them. He eschews them because his concept of piano music is an impersonal one. It is norm-centered; it is for all musical men. Any intrusion of the executant's private soul would limit its appeal, diminish its authority.

Thus it is that Mr. Lhevinne's performance is worthy of the honorable word *academic*. And if he seems to some a little distant, let us remind ourselves that remoteness is, after all, inevitable to those who inhabit Olympus.

November 18, 1940

Correct and Beautiful

KIRSTEN FLAGSTAD, soprano; recital last night at Carnegie Hall with *Edwin McArthur* as accompanist.

DIE MAINACHT; DIE LIEBENDE SCHREIBT; AN DIE NACHTIGALL;
    STÄNDCHEN; FRÜHLINGSTROST   BRAHMS
HAUGTUSSA CYCLE: DET SYNG ("It Sings"); VESLEMOY ("Young
    Maiden"); BLAABAERLI ("Blueberry Field"); MOTE ("Tryst");
    ELSK ("Ecstasy"); KILLINGDANS ("Dance of the Goatlings");
    VOND DAG ("Day of Ache"); VED GJAETLEBEKKEN ("The
    Brook")   GRIEG

CLOUDS   A. WALTER KRAMER
MUSIC I MADE WITH YOU   HAGEMAN
THE DREAMY LAKE   GRIFFES
DAYBREAK   McDONALD
GESANG WEYLAS; WENN DU ZU DEN BLUMEN GEHST; WER SICH
    DER EINSAMKEIT ERGIEBT; LIEBE MIR IM BUSEN; NEUE LIEBE
                                                              HUGO WOLF

STRAIGHTFORWARDNESS on the concert platform is something rarely
encountered except on the part of children and of the very greatest
artists. Straightforwardness in musical execution is met with practically only on the part of great artists. Madame Flagstad is
straightforward in her platform manner and in her musical interpretations.

She is not, for that, an unsubtle musician. Nor is her splendidly
majestic voice an unsubtle instrument. All the shading is there
that one might wish and all the refinement of expression that
lieder repertory requires, which is much. But such an assured
mistress is she of her voice, and so clear is her comprehension of
the songs she sings, that she is not constrained to seek to please
her listeners by any trick of willful charm or cuteness or feigned
emotion.

In consequence, she can afford the highest luxury of the concert stage, which is to sing the songs of Brahms and Grieg and
Hugo Wolf and of our American song-writers as simply and as
candidly as Miss Helen Hayes, say, might read Shakespeare's
sonnets in a drawing-room. No intonation is false, no word unclear, no sentiment either under- or overstated. By eschewing
exploitation of her personality, she warms all hearts to that personality. By not feeling obliged to give her operatic all to every tender
melody, she offers us each song as if it were a living and a fragile
thing in our hands, like a bird.

Our century has known great mistresses of vocalism and many
intelligent interpreters of songs. I doubt if there has existed within
the memory of living musicians another singer so gifted as to voice,
so satisfying as to taste, and withal such mistress of her vocal
instrument as Madame Flagstad. Some singers sing by nature,
others take lessons for years. It is scarcely more than once or twice
in a century that any vocalist ever masters his voice with the kind
of mastery that pianists have of the pianoforte, masters it seriously
and completely, while he is still in command of all his vocal resources. Mostly they sing by ear and learn to use the voice cor-

rectly only after its best notes are worn out and gone. Madame Flagstad has a great voice now which she handles as if it were a race-horse she had bred and trained.

She can sing loud and she can sing soft. She can sing fast and she can sing slow. She can sing high, low, in strict time, in free time, with clear words, on pitch, swelling or diminishing in volume. This, plus a clear comprehension of the human significance of the music one wishes to sing, is the whole art of singing.

Her voice must not have been an easy one to train, either. Her high, low, and middle registers are noticeably different in timbre. Her scale is as smooth as that of a flute or trumpet; but her ranges, heard separately, are as sharply differentiated as the ranges are of any wind instrument. One of the most satisfying qualities of her singing is the way her chest-voice sounds like chest-voice, her head-voice like head-voice, and her middle-voice like ordinary speech, while at the same time the transition from one range to another is so gentle and so even as to be virtually imperceptible excepting when there is a skip in the melodic line.

Mr. Edwin McArthur accompanied from memory. He gave support, allowed flexibility, was in general straightforward and highly pleasant to hear. He was more like a partner in an adequately rehearsed duet than like the more usual obsequious accompanist.

November 9, 1940

Glamour and Loyalty

MARIAN ANDERSON, contralto. Carnegie Hall, last night. Accompanist, *Franz Rupp.*

"E'ingrato lo reggio," from ADRIANA IN SIRIA	GALUPPI
"Dal sen del caro sposa," from VOLOGOSO	DA CAPUA
IL MIO BEL FOCO	MARCELLO
VIER ERNSTE GESÄNGE	BRAHMS
"Plus grand dans son obscurité," from THE QUEEN OF SHEBA	GOUNOD
LA CLOCHE	SAINT-SAËNS
NELL; DANS LES RUINES D'UNE ABBAYE; L'HIVER A CESSÉ	FAURÉ
VOCALISE	RAVEL
FOUR NEGRO SPIRITUALS	arr. BROWN; DETT; BURLEIGH

MARIAN ANDERSON's recitals (she gave one last night in Carnegie Hall) have more quality than most such events. The beauty of her person, the glamour of her personality, which has something of royalty in its simultaneous graciousness and reserve, the rigid sumptuousness of her costumes, the charm of her voice, the excellence of her vocal command, the high musical distinction of her programs, the careful musicianship of her executions — all these elements make for an occasion of no mean impressiveness. If your reviewer's enthusiasm is a little less intense than what a summation of such glories might normally have produced, that is perhaps because he thought he ought, in view of Miss Anderson's great loyalty to the art of music-making, to put his mind chiefly on the nature of that music-making.

He found it, under the physical appearance of simplicity, to be a little ornate for his taste, ornate and timid. Rarely does she attack a note frankly; she hums her way into them nearly all. Almost never does she end one, either, without tapering it off. This constant crescendo and decrescendo, though most tastefully encrusted upon every phrase, gives to the whole articulation of a song or aria, as well as to its phrases, a carved-in-mahogany quality that is more genteel than authentically stylish, more ladylike than wholly frank.

Miss Anderson's best quality, indeed, as an interpreter is a kind of inwardness that comes from that same timidity. It is lovely in German and French songs, hopelessly out of place in operatic arias. She sings all foreign languages, in fact — and that meant four fifths of last night's program — with her eyes closed. The effect is that of a very, very, very good student being careful not to do anything wrong. When she drops her timidity and inwardness, opens her eyes, and sings English, she is the most straightforward artist in the world and one of the most satisfying. Your reviewer considers it rather a pity that she feels obliged, out of her loyalty to recital conventions, to go through so much Classical and Romantic repertory — all of which others do better — before she gets down to singing in her own language the religious music of her own people. That is where she leaves off being a lovely icicle and becomes a flame.

November 4, 1943

God Bless Ireland

JOHN CHARLES THOMAS, baritone; recital last night in Carnegie Hall, with *Carroll Hollister* as accompanist.

TU LO SAI	TORELLI
ALMA DEL CORE	CALDARA
CHANSON À MANGER	LEMAIRE
RUHE MEINE SEELE	STRAUSS
LA PROCESSION	FRANCK
EN BARQUE	PIERNÉ
"Eri tu," from BALLO IN MASCHERA	VERDI
DER TON	MARX
New Songs:	
CHRISTMAS CANDLE	ELINOR WARREN
THE NOISE OF WATERS	RUTH VANDERLIP
DOWN BY THE SALLEY GARDENS	ALICE DE CEVEE
"STRICTLY GERM-PROOF"	JOHN SACCO
AMONG THE LIVING; O THE FIERCE DELIGHT	A. H. MALOTTE
American Folk-Songs:	
GENTLE ANNIE	STEPHEN FOSTER
THE DEAF WOMAN'S COURTSHIP	arr. JOHN POWELL
TAKE MY MOTHER HOME	arr. HALL JOHNSON
AT THE FOOT OF YONDERS MOUNTAIN	arr. JOHN POWELL
Low Bridge, or THE ERIE CANAL	ERNST BACON
ALL DAY ON THE PRAIRIE	arr. GUION

JOHN CHARLES THOMAS pleases all. Not necessarily everybody all the time. But at some point or other in each program, everybody. Last night he gave us old Italian songs of finest vintage, poured to perfection. He gave us works from French and German masters who bridged the nineteenth and twentieth centuries. There was a famous operatic aria, "Eri tu," from Verdi's *Ballo in Maschera*. There was a group of recital ballads in the American recital style. And there was a group of highly dramatized American folk-songs that included even a Negro spiritual. All were executed with consummate art, and all were enthusiastically received by some part of the large audience. Most were applauded heartily by the whole house.

Mr. Thomas has a different style of delivery for each kind of thing he does, and each style is appropriate to its kind. What permeates all the styles is his remarkable and instinctive musicality.

This is not to say that his voice and style are untrained. They are very well trained indeed, though I think his voice would gain in beauty if he placed its resonance more squarely in what Americans call, not very clearly, the head and what French vocalists refer to as the *masque*. High baritones sometimes fear to sound like heroic tenors, but the simple truth is that they are heroic tenors and have everything to gain by displaying to the full the beauties of the so-called head resonance. Aside from this reserve, I can find no fault in his schooling. He sings beautifully.

I call his musicality instinctive, because only those with melody in the soul ever sing so easily or pronounce so clearly. He does not pronounce words to a vocal line; he makes a vocal line out of words sung. Naturally they come out clear in any language. And naturally the music comes out as melody.

His is the Irish * gift at his best, which means thoroughly trained. He reminds one at the same time of Chauncey Olcott and of John McCormack. The first because of his combination of personal charm with dramatic power; the second because of his high perfection in the kind of easily floated melody-with-ornaments that used to be called, when singers still had enough nervous control to master it, *bel canto*.

If Mr. Thomas were not such a fine musician, it would be difficult to forgive him for making every number a wow. If he were not such a natural musician, his lighter numbers would be ham. Gifted so rarely and schooled so soundly, everything he touches becomes, in a different way and for a different public, beauty.

November 26, 1940

* Mr. Thomas's racial origins are actually Welsh.

Chestnuts, but Not Roasted

DUSOLINA GIANNINI, soprano, and JAN PEERCE, tenor; joint recital last night in Carnegie Hall, with *Edwin McArthur* and *Fritz Kitzinger* as accompanists.

WHERE'ER YOU WALK	HANDEL
TU LO SAI	TORELLI
DANZA DANZA FANCIULLA	DURANTE
"Cielo e mar," from LA GIOCONDA	PONCHIELLI

Mr. Peerce

VON EWIGER LIEBE; SCHWERMUT; O LIEBLICHE WANGEN; SCHÖN
WAR DES ICH WEIHT; BOTSCHAFT   BRAHMS
Miss Giannini
PSYCHÉ   PALADILHE
LE SOLEIL ET LA MER   FOURDRAIN
LIFE AND DEATH   COLERIDGE-TAYLOR
BLOW, BLOW, THOU WINTER WIND   QUILTER
Mr. Peerce
THE LAMENT OF IAN THE PROUD   GRIFFES
JOY   WINTTER WATTS
IT IS A SPRING NIGHT   VITTORIO GIANNINI
MANELLA MIA; MANECHE   arr. V. GIANNINI
Miss Giannini
Duet, "Ah, lo vedi," from CAVALLERIA RUSTICANA   MASCAGNI
Miss Giannini and Mr. Peerce

MISS DUSOLINA GIANNINI and Mr. Jan Peerce, who sang a joint
recital last night in Carnegie Hall, are two of America's finest
vocalists. Mr. Peerce (he pinch-hit for Pinza, who was ill) is a
tenor of excellent voice and unimpeachable vocalization, though
his work leans toward monotony. Miss Giannini has a dramatic
soprano voice that resembles no other among the living, though its
similarity to that of the late Emma Calvé has often been remarked.
She is, morever, a mistress of vocal art with a dramatic temperament of great power. The program was made up of chestnuts,
and all the encores were war-horses. I have rarely had so good a
time at a recital of vocalism. The audience was still applauding
when I left at eleven.

In a concert of that kind it is always the encores that are the
real substance. The printed program is made up chiefly of studio
material, songs that everybody has worked on or heard worked
on. The encores are the great vocal numbers that students are
rarely allowed to work on. Mr. Peerce sang the tenor aria from
Halévy's *La Juive* and the *Rigoletto* "La donna è mobile." Miss
Giannini did the "Pace, pace" from *La Forza del Destino* and
the *Carmen* Habanera. As I left for my office, they had just finished adding to the *Cavalleria Rusticana* duet the one from the
first act of *La Tosca*. There had been a half-dozen famous songs
added previously. You can see what a display of vocalism was
offered and why the whole thing, given by two such excellent
vocalists, was invigorating and fun.

Miss Giannini is my favorite of the two. She has more flexibility of style and a wider range of vocal color. Mr. Peerce is an
American from New York City who has made his singing into a

perfect replica of the Italian tenor style. His production is rather more even than that of most Italian tenors, I must say. But his imitation of their faults of style is complete and just a shade comic. His voice is not really so robust as his vocal manner, and his sliding and scooping à la Caruso is just permissible for the singing of modern Italian works. It is out of place with music more than seventy-five years old, and it is certainly no way to sing anything French. It will do for the English claptrap he rendered, merely because there is no sensible way of singing that kind of thing anyway. The genuine pleasure of Mr. Peerce's work lies in the unvarying placement of his middle and upper tones (though his low register is not sufficiently projected). The unvarying color of these is also the source of a certain monotony.

Miss Giannini's voice is the subject of much dispute in vocal circles. Its admirers are devoted, its detractors rather impatient. Again the Calvé parallel comes to mind. Myself, I love it. Of her vocal mastery there is no question. Her way of singing songs (she did Brahms last night) is intelligent and musical but not wholly satisfactory. They do not give sufficient scope for her dramatic temperament. The sound of them seems to come from no lower than the lungs, the expression from no farther down than the heart. When she sings opera airs she sings from the hips, projects character and feeling with her whole body. I have never at any time in my life heard a rendition of the *Carmen* Habanera that was even faintly comparable to hers for acuity of expression, for controlled variety of vocal color. The Italian folk-songs, arranged by her brother, Vittorio Giannini, were similarly dramatic and vocally masterful. I regret never having had occasion to hear this great vocal artist in opera, because it is obvious that the musical theater is her home.

Two accompanists were listed. I could have sworn they were the same man, because they looked alike and played alike. My guest assured me they were really two and that Mr. Kitzinger played fewer wrong notes than Mr. McArthur. Both played plenty. And neither seemed to have much care for piano tone or for any of the other musical amenities beyond playing fast and loud and keeping up a general hubbub under the singing. It didn't seem to make much difference, though.

February 4, 1942

Some Beautiful Songs and the Sad Story of Dorothy Maynor

DOROTHY MAYNOR, soprano; recital last night at Town Hall, with *Arpad Sandor* as accompanist.

"Now let every tongue adore Thee,"   Nicolai-Bach
"O sleep, why dost thou leave me," from Semele; "O had I
  Jubal's lyre," from Joshua   Handel
Im Spätboot; Ich schwebe; Wiegenlied; Wie sollten wir
  geheim sie halten   Strauss
Clair de lune; Après un rêve   Fauré
Adieu de l'hôtesse arabe   Bizet
Negro spirituals:
  Oh, what a beautiful city   arr. Boatner
  His name so sweet; Witness   arr. Hall Johnson
"Cake and Sack"; "Old Shellover"; "Tillie"; from de la Mare's cycle
  Five Rhymes from "Peacock Pie"   Theodore Chanler
  Composed for Miss Maynor in connection with the 1940 Award
  in Composition, sponsored by Town Hall and the League of
  Composers; first performance.
Cupid Captive   La Forge
Little Star; Parasha's Reverie and Dance   Mussorgsky

The chief purpose of my visit to Town Hall last night was to hear the *Five Rhymes from "Peacock Pie"* by Theodore Chanler. Three were sung, and very nicely indeed, by Miss Maynor. They were a pleasure in every possible way.

Mr. Chanler's music is French by schooling, though not imitative of any Frenchman's mannerisms. It hasn't any mannerisms of its own, even. It is the expression of a man so gently and so delicately bred that he would consider the conscious injection of his own personality into his music an affectation. He writes, therefore, with conscious sincerity and with unconscious distinction. The vulgar, the careless, the meretricious are as if unthinkable. There is precision in the melodies without any harshness, and amplitude in the musical structure without any boasting. His particular achievement, of abundance in musical expression without extravagance, I can only describe as Gallic. His songs have what is known in French manners as *tenue*.

Miss Dorothy Maynor's recital, which included the three Chanler songs, was on the whole a disappointment, though it did clear up one matter that has bothered all her admirers of late. There can be no further question, I think, that her vocal technique is woefully inadequate and that her voice itself is in danger.

Vocal gift she has in abundance, and good musical instincts, and a platform personality of great power. She has one of those characteristically negroid voices that seem to be three voices at the same time. Trained one way, she might become a female baritone. Trained another, she might sing coloratura. Without any training at all she might have sung as simply and as beautifully in the middle range as she does now. With exactly the amount of training that she has, she sings simply and beautifully in the middle range and nowhere else. Her lower tones are forced and breathy. Above D she is usually flat. She scoops, she spreads, she hoots; and she is not above screaming if she can't get her note any other way.

If she were not such a good comedienne, so assured in her ability to put over virtually any number she likes, her performance last night would have sounded amateurish. Vocally it was. She sang as if she were vocalizing first and pronouncing only incidentally. In consequence she was very difficult to understand. For two thirds of the evening she was tense and highly inaccurate, as if she had no confidence at all in what might be coming out of her throat, as if anything might happen vocally. With the spirituals she started singing words for the first time instead of vocalizing. Having no secure vocal method for doing this, she simply threw all vocal method aside and sang like any enthusiastic untrained colored girl. The human effect was agreeable, but only her youth and strong vocal chords prevented her from cracking. There was betting in my row as to whether she would be able to finish the recital.

Curiously enough, she went right into the Chanler songs without any trouble. Lying chiefly in the middle range, they probably rested her. After that she whooped it up and screamed some more.

How long Miss Maynor can continue to overwork her vocal resources without working them out I could not say. Not long, I imagine. Already her voice has lost its velvet. She has no real power; and there is a very small range, about an octave, where she can sing with ease. Also, a telltale tremolo is developing. It is all very much too bad, for she was gifted with voice, with musical talent, and with a rare personal projection.

January 9, 1941

High-Quality Singing

JENNIE TOUREL, mezzo-soprano; recital in Town Hall Saturday night. Accompanist, *Erich Itor Kahn.*

PER PIETÀ	STRADELLA
RECIT. ET AIR TENDRE from cantata L'IMPATIENCE	RAMEAU
AIR DE SEXTUS, from CLEMENZA DE TITO	MOZART
TROIS POÈMES DE BAUDELAIRE	DEBUSSY
RONDO from CENERENTOLA	ROSSINI
ON THE RIVER DON; THE MUSHROOMS	MUSSORGSKY
IT WAS IN THE EARLY SPRING	RIMSKY-KORSAKOV
THE LILACS	RACHMANINOFF
THE FLOWER; THE BELLS OF NOVGOROD	GRETCHANINOV
I HATE MUSIC ("Five Kid Songs")	BERNSTEIN
(First New York performance)	
MUSIC, WHEN SOFT VOICES DIE (first performance)	DIAMOND
SAI ARUE	GUARNIERI
TWO SONGS	NIN

ALL through Jennie Tourel's recital on Saturday night at Town Hall one had the impression of being present at the take-off of some new and powerful airplane for a round-the-world flight. One was aware that her previous vocal performances here, her test flights, so to speak, had inspired high confidence. Word had gone round the music world that her work was excellent in a way far beyond that of the average good singer; and a packed-in house-ful of that world was present to judge, to describe, and, hope-fully, to acclaim it. Miss Tourel's conquest of this well-disposed but critical audience was of a completeness without any local parallel since Kirsten Flagstad's debut at the Metropolitan Opera House some nine seasons ago.

Miss Tourel is of a wholly different musical temperament from Miss Flagstad, the only basis for comparison between the two artists being the degree of their vocal mastery, which places them together in the top category of living vocal musicians — together and virtually alone. Miss Tourel, who is a young woman (not far off thirty, I should guess), is not quite the mistress of her throat and face muscles in big climaxes that Miss Flagstad was (already over forty when she came here). Her fault in this respect comes, I fancy, from a way she has of opening her mouth very wide without compensating at the lips for this excessive relaxation. My explanation may not be physiologically correct, but I do think there is a slight fault in Miss Tourel's jaw position that shows up when she sings high notes loud. I also fancy that that fault is neither grave nor irremediable. With this single reserve, I found her vocal performance, generally speaking, impeccable.

The voice is a mezzo-soprano of wide range, warm in timbre and unbelievably flexible. Miss Tourel is mistress of a wider range of coloration in all ranges and at all volumes than any other singer I have ever heard. Her pitch is perfect in the most difficult modern music. Her legato skips are the kind of *bel canto* one dreams about. Her enunciation in all languages, even in so introspective a work as Debussy's songs to words by Baudelaire, is cleanly projected at all times. Her musicianship in every domain is so thorough that from the whole technical and intellectual aspect her work belongs clearly with that of the great virtuosos of music.

Her gift for languages is at the bottom of much of her stylistic virtuosity. On Saturday night she sang in Italian, French, Russian, English, Portuguese, and Spanish, making them all sound like themselves, coloring her vowels to the characteristic timbres of those languages, revealing their special music, and cherishing their particular ways of expressing feeling. She moved around in each tongue as if it were a whole landscape and climate, untranslated, untranslatable, and unique. In none of the European ones did I sense any accent. Certainly in her English there was none.

This extreme mental and emotional flexibility, commanding a vocal skill of transcendent nature and commanded by musicianship of the highest order, produced, in a program of diversified works, a variety of musical experiences that is rarely encountered in a soloist's recital. There are singers who have her stylistic knowledge, but they mostly have inferior vocal powers. There are other singers, though few, who sing that well; but they are mostly either inferior as musicians or limited in their expressive scope. Miss Tourel is, I believe, unequaled among living singers for the high concentration in one artist of vocal skill, sound musicianship, and stylistic flexibility.

Fine Fiddling

EFREM ZIMBALIST, violinist, in recital last night in Carnegie Hall, with *Vladimir Sokoloff* at the piano.

FANTASY	SCHUMANN-KREISLER
BALLADE (violin alone)	YSAYE
SONATA IN A MAJOR, OP. 47 ("Kreutzer")	BEETHOVEN
CONCERTO IN D MAJOR	TCHAIKOVSKY
SIEGFRIED PARAPHRASE	WAGNER-WILHELMJ
CALIFORNIA (on a tune by Paladilhe)	ARTHUR LOESSER
SEA-SHELL	CARL ENGEL
LA CLOCHETTE	PAGANINI-KREISLER

THE FULLEST house I have seen this season (chairs and standers on the stage, too) listened last night with rapt faces to Mr. Zimbalist in Carnegie Hall. I confess to a not great taste for violin recitals myself, because the Baroque instrument has somehow not managed to inspire our best composers to do their best work. At least, not since the invention of the oversensitive Tourte bow made, the playing of it a pure virtuoso job. Nevertheless, virtuoso workmanship has its interest for almost anybody; and last night's concert was a noble display of that.

Mr. Zimbalist, as a musician, is sound and straightforward, seldom strikingly original, never commonplace. He gives himself the trouble to play a long melodic phrase with steady tone, for instance. This means real trouble, because it requires complete control of the bow arm and of its weight. I do not know a more dependable right arm in the violin-playing world. Consequently his phrasing is musical and architectural. There are no inexplicable crescendos due to changes of direction in the bowing. He is not obliged to substitute for clear articulation a simulation of intense personal feeling in the form of heavy vibrato. His vibrato is most discreet, indeed. His right-arm control permits him to use a variety of tonal color that makes for auditory relief and produces a certain lightness in the whole texture of his work that keeps the violin sound from becoming oppressive.

Each of the great violinists has his characteristic fiddle tone. Kreisler, Heifetz, all of them one can recognize blindfolded, as one can a well-known singer's voice. Of all the fiddle tones, Mr.

Zimbalist's is the least strained, the most pure. It is also one of the most human. It is not so organlike as Kreisler's nor so suggestive of precious stuffs as that of Heifetz. It is not nearly so sharp and brilliant as Szigeti's nor so discreetly inexpressive as that of Busch. It is nevertheless a more truly musical sound than any of these, because it is round. It is round like the sound a good singer makes when he hums. Its vocal placement is perfect. Also, like a good singer, Mr. Zimbalist never forces.

The program was usual enough. Its reading might have passed for usual, too, if one didn't know from experience what liberties most violinists, even the best of them, are prone to permit themselves. The Beethoven last movement was lacking in rhythmic weight, perhaps; but the slow one profited by this same absence of dynamic insistence. The Tchaikovsky was a dream of graciousness and elegance. The arrangements and the violinistic stuff were exactly as you can imagine them. The only one that seemed to me worth especially noting is Mr. Carl Engel's *Sea-Shell,* a songlike piece in the MacDowell taste which, though not thematically very original, is musically sophisticated and instrumentally most gracious.

The evening's great success seemed to me to be due to fine technical work and genuine musicianship. It was pleasant to observe a large musical public being completely responsive to these qualities without the artist's having recourse to the sentimental, the violent, or the meretricious.

January 21, 1942

Silk-Underwear Music

JASCHA HEIFETZ, violinist; recital last night at Carnegie Hall, with *Emmanuel Bay* as accompanist.

SONATENSATZ	BRAHMS
SONATA No. 10 (K. 378)	MOZART
SONATA	STRAUSS
CONCERTO No. 8 (GESANGSCENE)	SPOHR
TWO PRELUDES	GERSHWIN
HEXAPODA (Five Studies in Jitteroptera)	BENNETT
1. "Gut-Bucket Gus"	

2. "Jane Shakes Her Hair"
3. "Betty and Harold Close Their Eyes"
4. "Jim Jives"
5. ". . . Till Dawn Sunday"

ROBERT RUSSELL BENNETT's musical sketches of the jitterbug world are pretty music. Also they are evocative of swing music without being themselves swing music or any imitation of swing music. They manage with skill and integrity to use swing formulas as a décor for the musical depiction of those nerve reflexes and soul states that swing-lovers commonly manifest when exposed to swing music. They are, in addition, expertly written for the violin. They come off, as the phrase has it, like a million dollars.

Mr. Heifetz's whole concert rather reminded one of large sums of money like that. If ever I heard luxury expressed in music it was there. His famous silken tone, his equally famous double-stops, his well-known way of hitting the true pitch squarely in the middle, his justly remunerated mastery of the musical marsh-mallow, were like so many cushions of damask and down to the musical ear.

He is like Sarah Bernhardt, with her famous "small voice of purest gold" and her mastery of the wow-technique. First-class plays got in her way; she seldom appeared in one after thirty. Heifetz is at his best in short encore pieces (the Bennetts are beautifully that) and in lengthy chestnuts like Spohr's *Gesang-scene* (an old-time war-horse for violinists), where every device of recitative style, of melodic phrase turning, and of brilliant passage work is laid out, like the best evening clothes and the best jewelry, for Monsieur to put his elegant person into. No destination, no musical or emotional significance, is implied.

The Strauss Sonata, a work of the author's early manhood, lacks none of that composer's characteristic style. The themes could only be his (albeit one was practically straight out of *Carmen*), bombastic, second-rate (I except the one that starts the last movement, which is bombastic and first-rate), inflated, expressing nothing but the composer's fantastic facility, his jubilant gusto at writing music. Mr. Heifetz's execution of this was almost embarrassingly refined.

Of his Mozart, the less said the better. It is of the school that makes a diminuendo on every feminine phrase-ending, that never plays any phrase through with the same weight, that thinks Mozart's whole aim was to charm, that tries so hard to make

out of the greatest musician the world has ever known (those are
Joseph Haydn's words) something between a sentimental Pierrot and a Dresden china clock that his music ends by sounding
affected, frivolous, and picayune. If that is Mozart, I'll buy a hat
and eat it.

I realize that my liking or not liking what Mr. Heifetz plays
and how he plays it is a matter of no import to the stellar spaces
in which he moves. But it happens that I did go to the concert last
night and that I did observe pretty carefully his virtuosity. It was
admirable and occasionally very, very beautiful. The fellow can
fiddle. But he sacrifices everything to polish. He does it knowingly.
He is justly admired and handsomely paid for it. To ask anything
else of him is like asking tenderness of the ocelot.

Four-starred super-luxury hotels are a legitimate commerce.
The fact remains, however, that there is about their machine-
tooled finish and empty elegance something more than just a trifle
vulgar.

October 31, 1940

In Tune, but Not with the Infinite

ISAAC STERN, violinist, in recital in Carnegie Hall last night. Accompanist, *Alexander Zakin.*

SONATA IN C MINOR, OP. 30, No. 2	BEETHOVEN
PARTITA IN D MINOR (for violin alone)	BACH
CONCERTO No. 5, IN A MINOR	VIEUXTEMPS
SONATA IN G MINOR	DEBUSSY
BERCEUSE AND SCHERZO, from THE FIREBIRD	STRAVINSKY
NOTTURNO E TARANTELLA	SZYMANOWSKI

ISAAC STERN, who played a violin recital last night in Carnegie
Hall, is one of the world's master fiddle-players. His tone is large
and deep and never forced; his finger and bow control are impeccable, and he plays in tune virtually all the time. His musicianship, moreover, is marked by an astonishing purity of taste; his
interpretations are quite without sentimental gimcrackery.

It is difficult to isolate the fault in his work; but there is one,
nevertheless. It lies, I think, in a certain absence of poetic con-

tinuity. His intellectual penetration is mature, and he has a way of sweeping through a long piece that leaves the whole shape and sonorous substance of it clear in the memory. This ability to build a wide and towering structure out of the most handsome auditory materials is no less a proof of genius for all the care and all the intellection that are involved. The trouble is that nobody seems to live in his houses. Their structure and their style are perfect, but they lack human warmth. Neither the executant of the music nor its designer seems to have any personal involvement with it.

The nearest to a personal rendering among last night's interpretations was that of the Beethoven Sonata opus 30, no. 2. This had, along with its sweeping architectonics, an improvisational fury that suggested a bit Beethoven the man, the young man, who loved nothing better than to improvise with fury grand architectural forms. The least personal but the most satisfactory sonorously was that of the Bach Suite in D minor for violin alone, where no piano was present to falsify the accuracy of Mr. Stern's amazingly correct pitch. True intervals and good tone filled great Carnegie Hall with resonance as only true intervals and a correct tone production can do.

The Vieuxtemps was breath-taking for its brilliance and surety. The Debussy was intoned with delicate understanding of its auditory line. The whole evening was full of competence and of lovely music. It is rare to encounter artistry of this excellence. Mr. Stern would have transported us all (or *sent* us, as the young people say) if he had not lacked a final commitment to passion and to poetry.

January 12, 1944

Extraordinary Cello-Playing

LUIGI SILVA, cellist, and LEOPOLD MANNES, pianist, in recital last night at the Mannes Music School, 157 East Seventy-fourth Street.

TOCCATA AND CANZONE	DELLA CIAJA
SONATA IN A MAJOR, OP. 69	BEETHOVEN
SONATA IN F MAJOR, OP. 99	BRAHMS
SONATA IN C MAJOR	BOCCHERINI

LUIGI SILVA is a unique and profoundly original cello-player. His originality lies in certain technical innovations about fingering and bowing. These are a carrying forward of the innovations of Pablo Casals, who revolutionized cello-playing by introducing violin fingerings and violin bowing style to that instrument. The musical advantages of these were many — lightness, speed, accuracy of intonation, greater melodic smoothness, greater facility in the upper positions of all four strings. Mr. Silva's carrying forward of these innovations sets him apart both technically and musically from the rest of the cello-playing world.

For a listener uninitiated to the characteristic difficulties of the instrument and unacquainted with the classical methods of overcoming these, Silva's unique musical performance might well seem to be merely a matter of musicianship. It is not entirely that. He is a musician of great gifts, of broad experience, and of unusual penetration. His knowledge, temperament, and scholarship are of the best. But it is his broadening of the cello's technical resources that has enabled his musicality to flower, that has permitted him to give a greater clarity and amplitude to his renditions of cello literature than one is likely to hear elsewhere these days, excepting perhaps in some of the Casals recordings. That is why I call his work both original and unique.

Last night's program included Mr. Silva's own transcription of a work for cembalo by Azzolino Bernardino della Ciaja, the Beethoven Sonata in A major, opus 69, the Brahms F major, op. 99, and a sonata by Boccherini, the figured-bass realization in this being Mr. Silva's work also. Each of these works was executed in a musical style appropriate to its epoch and authorship. The della Ciaja was neat, clean, and organlike. The Beethoven was broad, its soft passages incredibly poetic and flutelike. The Brahms was more passionately sung, its timbre richer and more reedlike, its bass accents more dramatic, its fingered tremolos mysterious and nearly inaudible. The Boccherini was played in an orchestral gamut of sharp and thin colorations that brought out all the delicacy and the brilliance of that composer's cello-writing. For good measure, and possibly for a bit of a joke, Mr. Silva added a transcription for cello of the Paganini Capriccio for Violin, No. 13, in B-flat major, commonly known as "La Risata," a virtuoso study in double-stops.

I have described so far the singular mastery and unusual breadth of Mr. Silva's work in terms of what he does. Further I cannot go except by saying what he does not do. He does not play off pitch, for example. This exactitude sets him apart from all cellists below the rank of the very great. Neither does he slide or scoop. His changes of hand position are made with such speed and such accuracy that they are virtually unheard. Neither does he attempt to avoid technical difficulties by making expression out of them. He makes crescendos and diminuendos to express the music's long-line phraseology, never to excuse a lack of control over the bow arm. Nor does he allow melodic passages that go from one string to another to sound as if they were being played on different instruments.

This skill at equalizing the tone color of his four strings is perhaps a positive skill rather than a negative virtue. It is, in fact, the complement to his extraordinary repertory of tone colorations. For just as he makes the cello sound at different times like many different instruments or voices, he sounds each of these at all times in an equalized scale from the bottom of the C-string to the top of the A. To hear the cello's finest literature expounded so orchestrally in tone, so pungently in rhythm, so penetratingly as to stylistic comprehension and so broadly as to sustained passion and rhetoric, the whole backed up by such musicianly accompaniments as Mr. Leopold Mannes provided last night, is a musical experience of the first water.

February 24, 1941

A Noble and Lovely Evening

RENÉ LE ROY, flutist, in concert last night at Town Hall with *Marjorie Call Salzedo* and *Carlos Salzedo*, harpists; *Janos Scholz*, cellist; *Bernard Wagenaar*, composer-pianist, and a chamber orchestra of twenty musicians.

CONCERTO IN D MAJOR FOR FLUTE AND ORCHESTRA   MOZART
Mr. Le Roy
CONCERTO IN C MAJOR FOR FLUTE, HARP, AND ORCHESTRA   MOZART
Mr. Le Roy and Mrs. Salzedo
TRIPLE CONCERTO FOR FLUTE, CELLO, HARP, AND ORCHESTRA   WAGENAAR
(First movement; new version for chamber orchestra by
Mr. Wagenaar; harp cadenza by *Mr. Salzedo*)
Messrs. *Le Roy, Scholz,* and *Salzedo*

CONCERTO IN C MAJOR FOR FLUTE AND ORCHESTRA WITH HARP-
SICHORD OBBLIGATO   JEAN-MARIE LE CLAIR
(First performance in America)
Mr. Le Roy; Mr. Salzedo at the harpsichord

THE ELEGANT informality of René Le Roy's concert of last night in Town Hall has not been equaled this season (in my experience) at any public gathering. Neither has the musical excellence of it been surpassed. A chamber orchestra of twenty playing impeccably, four distinguished soloists and two composers performing, not a conductor in sight. The program consisted of four concertos, one for flute, one for flute and harp, one for flute, harp, and cello, and a final one for flute again, this time with an imitation harpsichord in the orchestra. Two were by Mozart, one by the great Jean-Marie Le Clair, one by our own Bernard Wagenaar. At the beginning of three, and during an occasional tutti, the beat was given by the flute soloist, Monsieur Le Roy. In the other, the composer, Mr. Wagenaar, indicated basic tempos from the pianoforte. Other needed leadership was supplied unobtrusively and most satisfactorily indeed by the concertmaster, Mr. Bernard Ocko. Everything sounded shipshape and beautiful, lively, intelligent, civilized.

Le Roy is a great artist of the greatest of all schools of flute-playing, which is the French. He is master of an incredible pianissimo in both the high and low ranges of his instrument and of a steady, pale-colored tone that blends most graciously with that of strings and of the harp. During the first two pieces he had some pitch trouble in the lower register that was due, I imagine, to temperature conditions in the crowded hall. The harp did not sound quite exactly, either, in the Mozart; but these maladjustments were alleviated after the intermission. From certain parts of the house, production noises were audible, too, such as a slight breathiness in the lower flute tones and some clatter of the key-mechanism in the trills. There is little to be done about these *bruits parasites,* as the French call them. The best flute-playing in the world is never wholly free from them. I mention them merely because Monsieur Le Roy, who is one of the best flute-players in the world, is not able to eliminate them entirely from the hearing of those close by. Nevertheless, he plays the flute with a lovely silken sound; and his mastery of its style and technique is that of the great virtuosos.

Indeed, what carried the evening to a height of musical distinction far beyond that of ordinary first-class execution was Le Roy's — and Salzedo's, too — power of sustained musical discourse. He shades a musical line without leaning on it. He diminishes his volume on the eighteenth-century feminine phrase-endings without letting the musical sentence fall apart. He plays Mozart on the flute as Beecham conducts it in the orchestra or at the theater. The grand line never breaks, and yet no detail of inflection is sacrificed. The result is a performance at once manly and delicate, noble and gracious, emphatic, sweet, and wholly elegant.

Mr. Wagenaar's Triple Concerto is a handsome work and full of interesting sounds. I suspect the sounds of being a shade more interesting than the thematic substance. However, when Salzedo plays the harp, it is like Landowska playing the harpsichord. The instrument itself takes on such a fascination that I don't always care what the piece is like. I have heard this work before and I have always liked the sound of it. Last night it was a dream of trick sonorities and of graceful expression. I felt no need, any more than I have on previous occasions, of penetrating beneath its shimmering surface.

The Le Clair is a masterpiece of early eighteenth-century French style, vigorous, noble, and squarely gay. Monsieur Le Roy's pacing of it was something all musicians should be able to refer to when they get bothered about what Sebastian Bach meant by the *stile francese*. This was the real article, believe me. The whole evening, indeed, was the McCoy, including the excellent cello-playing of Janos Scholz, but not including the harp work of Marjorie Salzedo, which, though pretty enough to look at, sounded fuzzy and vague beside the rhythm and color of her husband's.

March 5, 1942

SACRED AND CHORAL

Styles in Sacred Music

LISTENING last week to a radio half-hour of flamboyant religious music has provoked your commentator to meditate on the world-wide decline of that kind of sacred art. The program, which is a weekly one, takes place on Monday evenings at 9.30, station WOR. Alfred Wallenstein conducts and there are an orchestra, a chorus, and excellent soloists. Last week Rose Dirman, soprano, and William Hain, tenor, were starred. The works rendered, which were all famous ones, might be called chestnuts except that, for all their currency, many accomplished consumers of music have never heard any of them.

There were the Gloria from Mozart's Twelfth Mass; Gounod's cantata (or anthem) *Gallia;* Handel's aria, "Sound an Alarm," from *Judas Maccabæus;* Mendelssohn's "If with All Your Hearts," from *Elijah; O bone Jesu,* a sixteenth-century motet incorrectly ascribed (or so the scholars tell me) to Palestrina; and the wonderfully theatrical "Inflammatus" from the *Stabat Mater* of Rossini. Excepting for the so-called Palestrina piece, every one of these works is written in a grandiloquent and ornate style. Any of them would do honor to an operatic score. All presuppose big, beautiful, well-trained voices and mobilize numerous instrumental effectives. All observe a liberty in the treatment of sacred text that the music world of our century considers to be of questionable taste.

The music world of our century does not feel quite at home with religious subjects, any more than the directors of our religious establishments feel confident about contemporary composition. The making of a joyful noise unto the Lord and the praising of Him upon a loud instrument are practiced in our time with more timidity than gusto. A lugubrious respectability overlays nearly all our religious music-making. And our best composers tend more and more to reserve their joyful noises, as well as their really terrifying ones, for secular circumstances.

The basis of this timidity is not so much, I fancy, a lack of religious faith on the part of musicians or any suspicion of music's efficacy on the part of religious administrators as it is an erroneous conception by both of what constitutes a proper sacred style. It is thought that profane associations invalidate stylistic elements for religious usage. And yet the history of religion, if it proves anything at all about music, proves the contrary. The exchange of material and of device between sacred and secular usage is the one constant pattern discernible in the musical history of the last twelve hundred years. And at no point in that time is it possible to distinguish save by sheer functional criteria, such as instruments or verbal texts employed, the music of worship from that of sheer entertainment.

Professionals of religion have constantly tried to censor the music used in their establishments. But whenever the censorship of tune or of technical device becomes strict, inspiration moves over to the market-place. The "purification" of church music that followed the pronouncements of the Council of Trent provoked in less than fifty years the invention of the opera. And the real originality of the seventeenth-century operatic style caused its adoption within twenty-five years by the religious establishments. The modernized plain-chant of the Benedictine monks made possible, too, the writing of Debussy's *Pelléas et Mélisande* and Satie's *Socrate*, although it has not yet produced one first-class piece of church composition.

Church music in our century, whether Catholic, Protestant, or Jewish, has been conservative and, compared to the music of theater and concert, inexpressive. It lacks self-confidence, liberty, assertion. The reforms of Pope Pius X have strangled it with the ideal of purity. These reforms, which have influenced the whole Western world, were no doubt useful as preparation for the reception of new influences. But in themselves they constitute no positive program. They are at best a housecleaning, a throwing out of operatic styles that had served well for three centuries but that had clearly lost, even in the theater, their expressive power. The recommendation of the Palestrina style to composers is even more backward-looking than the identical recommendation made by the Council of Trent nearly three hundred and fifty years before.

The next step, the only possible step forward today in music destined for church usage, is the full employment of the modern techniques. Musical advance is not now a specialty, as it has been during some epochs, of the religious establishments. Neither is it of the contemporary stage. The concert hall is where it flourishes. And it is our concert composers who have today the greatest mastery extant of all the composing techniques, ancient and modern, and the most expert acquaintance with their expressive possibilities. To any who may imagine that church music does not need to be expressive, let me point out that if it doesn't there is little besides habit, or some possible magic efficacy, to justify it. If our best modern church music seems, on the whole, less expressive, less moving than that of former centuries and of our own concert literature, that is because churchmen and musicians have been mutually suspicious ever since the encyclical *De Motu Proprio* of 1903 denounced the musical gang then in power.

That old gang is all dead now, and the generations now alive have been brought up with a healthy respect for religious decorum. It would be unfortunate if decorum itself became so stiff that it prevented living composers from writing live music for live worshippers. And if it did, it would just have to be reformed one day, like any other abuse.

Wherever religion is a wide enough house to have room in it for men of spirit, there is likely to be a lot of joyful noise-making, not only on psaltery and harp and timbrel but on quite loud instruments like the crashing cymbals, with high notes and trills and rapid arpeggios for voices and jostling counterpoints and terrifying harmonies. There never has been a Sacred Style; but sacred music, like any other, can have style, which is carrying-power. And it can have that today only on condition that, like all the memorable sacred music of past centuries, it be not afraid of its own time or timorous to employ the art's full resources.

July 23, 1944

Hymns of Tribulation and Rejoicing

BACH CHOIR, *Ifor Jones,* conductor, first day of 35th Bach Festival at the Packer Memorial Chapel of Lehigh University, Bethlehem, Pa., with members of the Philadelphia Orchestra. Organist, *T. Edgar Shields.* Accompanist to the choir, *Gretchen Newhard Iobst.* Vocal soloists: *Ruth Diehl,* soprano; *Saida Knox,* contralto; *Hardesty Johnson,* tenor; *Mack Harrell,* baritone. Two programs of music by JOHANN SEBASTIAN BACH.

Afternoon Program

CANTATA NO. 19, "Es erhub sich ein Streit" ("There uprose a great strife"); Motet, "Come, Jesu, Come"; CANTATA NO. 180, "Schmucke dich, O liebe Seele" ("Beautify Thyself, My Spirit").

Evening Program

CHRISTMAS ORATORIO, PART 4; CANTATA NO. 146, "Wir müssen durch viel Trübsal" ("We Must through Great Tribulation"); MAGNIFICAT.

Bach chorales played by the *Moravian Trombone Choir* before each program.

THE NOT so little town of Bethlehem, Pennsylvania, permanently the seat of a steel manufactory of the same name, as well as of Lehigh University, becomes temporarily in May the center of a musical pilgrimage. Friday the thirty-fifth Bach festival began, and Saturday it was over. The first Friday session consisted of two choral cantatas with soloists and orchestra and one unaccompanied motet for eight-part double chorus. The evening brought Part IV of the *Christmas Oratorio,* another cantata, and the famous *Magnificat.* The soloists were from New York and the orchestral musicians, forty or more, from Philadelphia; only the chorus was strictly local, Mr. Ifor Jones, the conductor, being a Philadelphian too, I believe.

Under these circumstances there was every reason for the performances to be excellent. They were. Orchestral balances and the beauty of the soloists' tone-production, excepting for some of Mr. Hardesty Johnson's work, were of rare distinction. The choral work had gusto and some precision. It was rough in timbre, but handsomely balanced and blended; and the soft work was beau-

tifully alive. All in all, saving certain inexactitudes in the rapid
passages, it was top-flight choral singing.

The size of the chorus and orchestra, though determined, no
doubt, by the space available for musicians in the Packer Memorial Chapel of Lehigh University, is a good one for Bach. Fewer
give a good result, too, provided the auditorium is not too large.
More make a messy effect in any size of auditorium. The chorus
at Bethlehem numbers about a hundred. The voices are mature
and resonant. An orchestra of forty provides ample support without crushing the soloists. Really, both as to the manner of execution, the dimensions, style, and professional integrity of it all, and
in the spirit that informed the renditions, Friday's Bach was something well out of the ordinary run of festival performances.

Of the works performed, two seemed to stand out as particularly rich and expressive, the lovely cantata No. 180, "Beautify
Thyself, My Spirit," and the cantata No. 146, "We Must Come
through Great Tribulation." The latter was notable not only for its
fine solos and its touching final hymn, but for its lengthy and fanciful instrumental overture. Beyond all these, of course, towered
the superb and impossible *Magnificat*. Superb, also, were the soloists in this, all of them; and equally so were the flutes and oboes
of the Philadelphia Orchestra. It was grand to hear so nobly rendered this noble and difficult work.

May 16, 1942

Sacred Swing

LAST Sunday I went to Newark to attend the evening services of
a Negro congregation known as The Church of God in Christ,
where Brother Utah Smith, a traveling evangelist of that denomination, was closing his engagement. Brother Smith is a stocky
gentleman in the mid-forties, neither old nor young, whose musical accomplishments had been signaled to me by swing experts.
He is known in religious circles as The One-Man Band, was so
introduced, in fact, by the local pastor, or rather by his *locum
tenens*, the pastor himself having been detained that evening by
religious work elsewhere. His whole musical equipment is an
electric guitar, his only vestment an ordinary sack suit of dark

blue, with a pair of white wings made of feathered paper and attached to his shoulders like a knapsack by crossed bands of white tape.

His religious message is delivered more by music and dancing than by preaching. Only after the preliminary prayers, solos and congregational hymns are over does he take charge of the meeting. Then an open space is cleared between the chancel rail and the first congregational seats. These last are allowed to be wholly occupied, no mourners' bench being reserved at all, since the nature of the service is one rather of general rejoicing than of personal penitence. The Brother makes a few remarks to the congregation and then, without any formal address or other preface, goes straight into his number, if I may so refer without irreverence to his music-making.

He plays the guitar with a high pick-up that fills the auditorium with a rich and booming sonority. He does not sing. He only plays and, like all swingsters, pats his foot. His musical fancy is of the highest order. I have rarely heard such intricate and interesting swing. From time to time he shouts: "I've got wings! Dust my feet!" Persons in the congregation reply with: "Dust my feet!" with "Praise the Lord!" and similar ceremonial phrases, as is customary among many colored religious groups. Practically everybody claps his hands in time to the music, claps on the off-beat, as is also customary in swing circles.

The music goes on for quite a long time, the Brother swinging chorus after chorus with ever increasing fantasy and insistence. Various persons of the congregation who feel so inclined first edge timidly toward the edge of the open space and then one by one start dancing. Each dances alone, some with raised and some with lowered head, all with eyes closed. Some jerk a little; others do rapid and complex footwork. The floor sways with their impact as if about to collapse. When the music stops, the dancers come out of their trancelike absorption and regain their seats as calmly as persons leaving any ballroom floor.

At no time during my stay did I observe any licentious behavior or other evidence that the ceremony was not a bona fide religious manifestation. Brother Smith himself, though full of humor and jollity, and not without a certain naïve showmanship, impressed me as a sincere and probably a consecrated character. And if I was not conscious during my one brief visit to his services of any extraordinary or commanding inspiration in them, neither was I aware of anything that might make me think them phony.

In any case, his musical gift is real and his musical imagination abundant. I am, consequently, taking occasion this Easter Sunday to make a seasonal reference to what struck me as an interesting musical manifestation and to point an example from contemporary life of the truism that in those societies or groups where religion is most vigorous there is no difference whatever between the sacred and the secular musical styles, the consideration of what is sacred and what is profane in music applying only to the moral prestige in society of the ceremonies that it accompanies. As a swing artist Brother Utah Smith is worthy to rank among the best. As a stimulator of choric transports he incites the faithful to movements and behavior not very different from those of any true jitterbug. Myself, I found it distinctly pleasant to hear good swing and to observe its effects in surroundings imbued with the white magic of Protestant Christianity, rather than among the somber diabolisms and the alcoholic stupidities of the nightclub world.

April 13, 1941

For Choral Music

NEW YORK has never been a major center of choral singing. Its musical ideals are instrumental, chiefly. Also, it is deeply suspicious of amateur effort. Explanations of all this are not hard to think up, the diversity of our language traditions being one that jumps to mind and the plethora of distracting activities that pre-empts our leisure being another. But the reasons are less certain than the fact. And the fact is that New York, though a first-class power in the orchestral world, is inferior to London and possibly to Berlin, even, as a producer of choral performance. It is only a little better off than Paris in this regard and far poorer, in the proportion of its choral activities, than secondary musical centers like Zurich and Geneva and Amsterdam and Boston and Barcelona.

For all the complaining that goes on in musical circles and in this column about the limitations of the orchestral repertory available to us here, our instrumental fare is richer and more catholic than our vocal. In the course of a season we get from concert and broadcast a pretty large selection of orchestral music, ancient, Romantic, and modern, most of it admirably rendered. We are lucky if we hear a half-dozen choral works properly presented in the same period. One or two of the Handel oratorios (usually one), a bit of Bach, a revival of something by Mozart or Berlioz, Beethoven's Ninth Symphony or *Missa Solemnis,* a concert or two of Renaissance polyphony and maybe a modern work — this would represent an average New York season's choral performances with stylistic pretensions.

Obviously, it is not enough. There are other oratorios of Handel than *Messiah* and *Judas Maccabæus.* There are other Masses by Mozart than the Requiem and the unfinished C minor. There are many Masses by Haydn and two lovely oratorios, *The Seasons* and *The Creation.* There are masterpieces on the *Stabat Mater* text by Dvořák and by Rossini. There are a dozen beautiful works by Purcell for orchestra and chorus with soloists. There are religious pieces of the highest skill and poetry by Heinrich Schütz and by other German predecessors of Bach. There is the whole seventeenth century of Italy and an abundance of French material from Lully to Couperin. Surprisingly enough, there is a large modern repertory, too, twentieth-century masterpieces by twentieth-century masters, that makes a fine effect when properly presented. And then there is the opera.

Operas based on a choral background are hardly appropriate for the Metropolitan in the present state of its choral forces. But many of these could be presented in concert form, or even, with a bit of staging, by the singing societies. Purcell's *King Arthur,* with text by Dryden, Mozart's *Idomeneo* (though the solo roles are difficult), the operas of Monteverdi, Lully, and Rameau, the proud dramatic works of Handel, the whole Russian repertory from Glinka to Shostakovich (though the latter's *Lady Macbeth of Mzensk* is no longer considered *in motu proprio* by the Soviet government), and a dozen modern stage pieces from Debussy's *Le Martyre de Saint Sébastien* to my own *Four Saints in Three Acts* offer musical interest even without stage presentation. All they need is trained vocal effectives and proper conducting.

The conducting is available. Paul Boepple, of the Dessoff Choirs, and Robert Shaw, of the Collegiate Chorale, are choral conductors of the very first quality. Finley J. Williamson, of the West-

minster Choir, and Hugh Ross, of the Schola Cantorum and Saint
Cecilia Club, are highly accomplished chorus masters, though
the latter is a little disappointing in public performance because
of his rhythmic indecisiveness. There are other leaders and choir
masters, too, of notable abilities and elaborate musical knowledge.
Leonard De Paur, of the Hall Johnson Choir, and Lehman Engel
(both at present in military service) have done distinguished
work. So has Arthur Mendel, of the Cantata Singers. And various
of the orchestral conductors are effective in vocal repertory, though
they usually require that somebody else prepare the chorus for
them. Toscanini, Beecham, Walter, Rodzinski, and Smallens —
opera men, all of them — have vocal understanding and lots of
experience with choral works. Koussevitzky and Stokowski communicate inspiration to singers less dependably than to instrumentalists. Ormandy's hand with vocalists is unknown to me: I
have never heard him conduct them. Alfred Wallenstein's is excellent.

I suspect that in the long run the finest renderings of choral
works are those that have been prepared entirely by the conductor of the performance. A choir never sings so beautifully as for
its own leader. The members will sing on pitch and in tune for
another; they will obey him with vigor and all promptitude. But
their work will not have the poetry, the personality, the expressive
variety that it has under the man they are used to, the man with
whom they have an accustomed spiritual intimacy. I think it is
probably this habit in our big orchestral foundations of having in
a choir just from time to time that gives to the best of their
choral performances a certain lumpiness, a thickness of choral
texture, and a lack of vibrancy in the expression that make these
occasions less stimulating musically than the purely instrumental
concerts of the same orchestral groups. Certainly the most sensitive renditions I have heard of works for chorus and orchestra
have been performances organized by choirs under their own
leader, the orchestra being had in for the occasion, or else performances given by orchestral or operatic organizations where a
well-trained choir was part of the permanent set-up.

In the former category the annual performances of the Bach
Mass at Bethlehem, Pennsylvania, and the recent performance of
Bach's St. John Passion under Mr. Paul Boepple in Carnegie Hall
are memorable. In the latter one belong the celebrated performances of similar works under Mengelberg by the chorus and or-

chestra of his own Concertgebouw in Amsterdam and an occasional performance of opera by some Russian troupe. Toscanini and Walter have given us massive renditions with the aid of the Westminster Choir, and the latter has recently given us a *St. Matthew Passion* of more than ordinary delicacy. But the best of these have shown a tendency toward the opaque and the monumental that makes for unfavorable comparisons between choral and purely orchestral music. Even the Verdi *Requiem,* which was certainly intended to be monumental, can lose by moments the acuity of its dramatic impact and become a bludgeon, while Bach and Handel and Mozart and Haydn and Beethoven, for all their grandeur, can easily sound (and not seldom do) more than a shade stuffy.

Now, choral music is not a stuffy literature, though the performances of many an oratorio society, including New York's own, may have pretty systematically given out that impression. Nor is the chorus an insensitive instrument. Indeed, it is almost too sensitive. It cannot be manhandled, like an orchestra; and guest conducting does it no good. But choral literature, ancient and modern, is as extensive and as beautiful as instrumental literature. Not to perform it more than we do is a mistake. To perform it the way we usually do is unfortunate. Our major orchestras should have permanent choral establishments. And it is preposterous that the Metropolitan Opera should maintain its own at so low a level of musical efficiency.

Lest anyone suppose the loss of male voices to the military services may have created an insoluble crisis in choral circles, I hasten to add that the recent season has been marked by better choral balances and better choral performance all round than either of the previous ones during which I have reviewed concerts.

May 9, 1943

Musical Matriarchate

TRAPP FAMILY SINGERS, in the first of two Christmas concerts in
Town Hall yesterday afternoon. The program.

Es ist ein' Ros' entsprungen	Praetorius
Alle Psallite Cum Luja	Anonymous
(Composed in England around 1300)	
Ave Maria	Tomas Luis de Victoria
Christus Hodie Natus Est	Sweelinck
In These Delightful Pleasant Groves	Henry Purcell
Sweet Honey-Sucking Bees	John Wilbye
Eriskey Love Lilt (from the Hebrides)	arr. by H. S. Robertson
Sonata for alto recorder, spinet, and viola da gamba	J. B. L'Oeillet
Jesus, Thine Be Praise (Air)	J. S. Bach
Terzetto for two soprano recorders and tenor recorder	Franz Wasner
As I Outrode This Endris Night	arr. by W. Douglas

Intermission

Carols:
Hirten, auf um Mitternacht (Tyrolean)
Away in a Manger (Austrian)
Es hat sich halt eröffnet (Tyrolean)
Bethlehem (Basque)
Deck the Halls (Welsh)
Deine Wangelen (Tyrolean)

Silent Night　　　　　　　　　　　　　　　　　　　Franz Gruber

THE TRAPPS are thirteen, if you count Dr. Wasner, their musical
(and presumably religious) director. Papa and the baby, however,
are merely exhibited; they do not sing. This leaves a musical
matriarchate of eleven. And pretty impressive it is, both artistically and humanly. If it did not perform so well as it does, the
charm of the *famille nombreuse* might cloy, as do eventually the
Baroness's little speeches. But the ensemble is so neat, the repertory and style so musically high class that one cannot really mind
the big play made for additional sympathy on grounds of family
solidarity. It is rare enough, after all, that we encounter such
excellent music-making in madrigal vein; it is even rarer to meet
a family of twelve in which everybody is good-looking, good mannered, cheerful, and, to all appearances, intelligent and well. The
spectacle of them would be heart-warming whether they sang
or not.

They perform motets, madrigals, and glees in English, in German, and in Tyrolerdialekt. Also Christmas carols of divers origins and instrumental music for spinet, viola da gamba (without gamba), and recorders in all sizes. Their execution is well bred, modest, and thoroughly clear. They sing on pitch and play in time, never very loud, but always with full projection of the words and the notes. They seem to be *at home* with music as well as *en famille*.

They represent the ideal conditions of amateur music-making as well as I have ever seen these displayed. And the fact that they are a professional touring organization (in the business sense) does not diminish, augments rather, the essentially amateur spirit of their performance. Their voices are sweet but not brilliant, and their vocalization competent (in the dynamic range suitable to persons of gentle breeding) without being stylized. Their diction is the speech of intelligent, educated people. And if their expression is never passionate or dramatically exciting, it is none the less animated by good spirits, goodwill and a real tenderness about family relationships.

Maternity and family life are, indeed, the subjects they render with deepest conviction. And since the hallowed nature of these is what Christmas carols are all about, one can scarcely imagine carol-singing more touching than that of the Trapps. They are harmonious, very quiet, straightforward and wholly united at such moments. They don't go in for theatrical pathos or vocal effect. They sing the music and the words as sincerely as they might recite the Lord's Prayer at a breakfast table or build a toy manger for Christmas Eve. And so, in the midst of a gentleness and a quiet that are dominated ever so lightly (but firmly) by mother and priest, arises a sort of vibrancy; and the family unit becomes a humming dynamo energized at once by the god of domesticity and by the Prince of Peace. At such moments anything might happen.

December 14, 1942

Harvard Fair but No Warmer

HARVARD GLEE CLUB and RADCLIFFE CHORAL SOCIETY,
G. *Wallace Woodworth,* conductor; concert last night at Town Hall.

ALLELUIA	RANDALL THOMPSON
GLORIA IN EXCELSIS DEO	KODALY
DIRGE FOR TWO VETERANS	HOLST
(With brass and drums)	
THE LAMENTATIONS OF JEREMIAH (Part I).	TALLIS
TWO ELEGIES	APOLLONIAN HARMONY (1790)
JUSTORUM ANIMÆ (GRADUALIA, Book 1, 1605)	BYRD
"Dona Nobis Pacem," from MASS IN B MINOR	BACH
(With the assistance of former members of these two choruses)	
THE RIO GRANDE	LAMBERT
Piano solo: *William W. Austin,* '39	
Opening Scene from OTELLO	VERDI
Choruses from LA REINE INDIGO (Paris version)	J. STRAUSS

THE CONCERT of Harvard's boys and girls, for Radcliffe College is, indeed, a part of Harvard University, left many questions in one's mind. Why did they sing six funeral pieces, for instance? These were set off in the printed program by black lines, as if to memorialize somebody; but no name was mentioned. Could it be that these young men, presumably about to be mobilized, were singing us their own requiescat, that those who imagine themselves about to die were saluting themselves before us in valedictory vein? One hesitates to believe Mr. Woodworth, their leader and program-maker, capable of such a breach in taste. Could it be that these works were intended to honor the recent European war dead? If so, why not say so? Or were they thought merely appropriate to the Lenten season? In that case, the operatic selection from Verdi and the utterly frivolous selections from Constant Lambert and from Johann Strauss that followed remain inexplicable.

Another question raised is perhaps more easily answered. From the straightforward and serious style with which the naughty French words of Strauss's *Reine Indigo* were rendered, I wondered for just a moment whether the boys and girls really knew about harems. Further reflection assured me that they were most likely pulling Strauss's (and the audience's) leg, rather in the way Eva Gauthier used to do when she sang *Alexander's Ragtime Band* and Gershwin's *Do It Again* in the best funereal concert style at Aeolian Hall, back in 1922, holding a little black book as if to remind herself of the words, as was the concert custom of the time.

A third question was brought to mind by a study of the program's word book and program notes. The printing of vocal texts and of ascertainable historical facts about the works to be performed and about their authors is normal procedure at serious musical occasions. The addition to these ascertainable facts of admiring phrases about the works, giving us cues on why we must approve them, is neither good concert manners nor good Harvard tradition. Can it be that since the retirement some years ago of Professor Walter Spalding, formerly head of the Music Division, who opposed them firmly, the Music Appreciation interests have gained entry to the oldest of our university music departments?

These and like matters furnished more material for reflection during the concert than the music itself did. It is difficult to analyze objectively the performance of an organization with which one has been so intimately and so actively associated in the past as I have been with the Harvard Glee Club. I tend to opine that the Radcliffe Choral Society sings better than it did twenty years ago and that the Harvard Glee Club sings less well. Certainly the programs, if last night's was typical, have slipped a little.

Claptraps like Holst's *Dirge for Two Veterans* and Lambert's *Rio Grande* are all right to do, either of them. Both on one program, plus the *Otello* storm scene, in excruciating English text, plus the charming but frivolous *Reine Indigo* choruses, gave to the evening's entertainment an air of eagerness to please at any price, of apology for the high seriousness of the works of Bach and Tallis and Byrd and Dr. Arne and Francis Hutchinson.

Great choral literature needs no such apology. And if young people's passion for musical experience is today like what it was in my day (as there is every reason to suppose it is), college men and women seriously disposed to show us what they are doing up in Cambridge do not need to kid us along with all the folksy "production" numbers in their repertory in order to make us take their better ones. It is possible that musically Harvard is not what she used to be. From last night's concert I couldn't tell. But the program did raise my suspicions.

March 31, 1941

The Collegiate Chorale

COLLEGIATE CHORALE, *Robert Shaw,* conductor; concert in Town
Hall last night.

MATER ORA FILIUM	BAX
Excerpts from HYMN TO ST. CECELIA	BRITTEN
THE FULL HEART; BALULALOW; CORPUS CHRISTI	WARLOCK
Excerpts from BELSHAZZAR'S FEAST	WALTON
MY SPIRIT SANG ALL DAY	FINZI
MISSA BREVIS	WILLAN
JIG FOR VOICES	ROWLEY
THE SHEPHERDS HAD AN ANGEL	BESLEY
QUID PETIS O FILI	COPE
THE MYSTERY	BENJAMIN
MIDSUMMER SONG	DELIUS
O BROTHER MAN	DARKE
THREE CHILDREN'S SONGS	VAUGHAN-WILLIAMS
WASSAIL SONG	VAUGHAN-WILLIAMS
GOD SAVE THE KING	

MODERN English music is at its best in choral form, and almost
any choral music is at its best when rendered by the Collegiate
Chorale under Robert Shaw's direction. We had a full evening
of both on Saturday night at Town Hall, and very fresh indeed
it all was.

Mr. Shaw's full chorus consists of about a hundred and twenty-
five singers, as nearly as I could estimate. A smaller group of about
forty sang certain pieces. The full ensemble sings as precisely as
the smaller one; but it has, of course, a fuzzier tone, as well as a
more powerful fortissimo. Music in madrigal vein and texts of
personal sentiment sound rather better from the smaller group
than from the large one, where the strength of crescendo is out
of proportion to such music's expression. In massive works, like
Walton's *Belshazzar's Feast,* the full effect is most impressive.

Impressive at all times in the work of this chorus is its impeccable pitch. This is maintained by mixing the singers homogene-
ously — instead of separating them into soprano, alto, tenor, and
bass sections — and by a discreet use of piano support. When the
instrument is concealed behind the singers, as it was last year in
the Museum of Modern Art Serenades, it is heard by them but

remains imperceptible to the audience. In last night's arrangement, which was determined by space limitations, the two pianos were frequently audible in *a capella* music. The effect was not ideal; but, even so, the advantages to intonation were so great that one cannot regret their use.

The music performed was of high quality, particularly agreeable to this reviewer being the pieces that followed the Walton *Belshazzar*, with the single exception of Darke's *O Brother Man*. The works of Bax, Britten, and Warlock seemed to me less clearly composed than those by men not so famous. Walton's cantata, though not without its dramatic accents, sounded to me shallow, flashy, laborious, and, on the whole, less barbaric and sumptuous than its text. Healy Willan's *Missa Brevis* in E flat (performed without the Credo) appeared to me as a skillful and gracious work in the Elizabethan taste that would do honor to any musical or religious occasion. The Vaughan Williams pieces in folk vein for children were of the highest melodic beauty.

One man's preferences among eighteen works, all heard by him for the first time, are, of course, tentative; and they are not here advanced as reflected opinions. What seems fairly clear, however, from Saturday night's concert and from former acquaintances with Mr. Shaw's work is that this conductor is a musician of taste, high temperament, and no mean skill. I do not know his equal in the choral field today, and I have not heard in some years choral renderings at once so musicianly and so vivid as those produced by the smaller group of the Collegiate Chorale.

November 8, 1943

Renaissance Musical Grandeurs

DESSOFF CHOIRS, Adesdi Chorus, and A Cappella Singers, *Paul Boepple*, conductor, singing the following program of music by ORLANDUS LASSUS last night in Town Hall.

PROVIDEBAM DOMINUM (Magnum Opus 705)
THREE GERMAN PSALMS (1588)
TIMOR ET TREMOR (Magnum Opus 673–4)
Motets for two voices: OCULUS NON VIDIT; QUI VULT VENIRE; SERVE BONE
  (Magnum Opus 3, 9, and 10; 1577)

LAMENTATIONS OF JEREMIAH (1585)
OCCHI, PIANGETE (1555); AMOR, CHE VED'OGNI PENSIER APERTO (1563);
     PASSAN VOSTRI TRIOMPHI (1584); texts by Petrarch
BONJOUR MON CŒUR (1565); LA TERRE LES EAUX VA BEUVANT (1564);
     O DOUX PARLER (1571); texts by Ronsard.
CÉLÉBRONS SANS CESSE (1576); MAIS QUI POURROIT ESTRE CELUY (1584);
     O LA, O CHE BON ECHO; texts anonymous.

ROLAND DELATTRE, of Mons, variously known as Roland de Lasse,
Orlando di Lasso, and Orlandus Lassus, was the most internationally famous and accomplished of all the Netherlands masters
who ruled European music in the sixteenth century. He worked
in Antwerp, traveled and conducted in England, France, Italy,
and Germany, Munich being the longest of his residences, where
he conducted and wrote for a choral and instrumental band of
great virtuosity, got together from all the musical centers. His
works, which number more than 2,500, are in both sacred and
secular vein. He wrote with perfection in all the known styles of
his time and set to music verses by all the most celebrated poets,
regardless of their native languages, all of which he prosodized
with ease and with freedom.

It is not every day that we hear his music performed. Last
night's concert of the Dessoff Choirs in Town Hall, which was
devoted entirely to his works, was consequently, by that mere
fact, an event of the highest musical interest. It was additionally
agreeable by the excellence of the chorus's work and by Paul
Boepple's completely intelligible conducting. The singers sang
on pitch and in rhythm and pronounced perfectly comprehensible
Latin, Italian, and French. The French was especially good; I
have not heard such correct vowel sounds sung, even by a soloist,
all season. The German, strangely enough, was less well articulated.

The weakness of the Dessoff Choirs is the inevitable one of
all amateur and semi-amateur groups. The sound of it lacks character. Its fortes are not brilliant, and its pianissimos lack vibrancy.
There is nothing to be done about that, however, in a choral society that does not consist of singers prepared by previous training to sing both brilliantly and vibrantly. Neither is there anything
to be done about the insoluble difficulty of rendering works written for male voices (men's and boys') with mixed voices. The
mixed chorus is a modern social formula; men and women like
to get together and sing. And they have to sing something. So

the more cultivated groups of them sing the great choral literature of Renaissance times.

This is musical education for them and for those who listen. But the sound it makes is a far cry from the kind of sound it made when men and boys sang it. There is no possibility of making a dead social custom function; men and boys do not work well together in the modern world. Adults and children, generally, are enemies. Consequently, if we are to have a singing acquaintance with the greatest singing music in the world, the mixed chorus of adults is the only formula we can employ.

Nevertheless, a great deal of fine harshness is lost and most of the syncopation. For women's voices are round and breathy, compared with boys'; and their rhythmic attack is fuzzy. Also, there is no even choral scale from bass to soprano, as there is with males. The sex of each part is always audible, and the sonorities invariably align themselves as two kinds of sonority in rather the same way as a violin and a pianoforte never really blend.

This dichotomy is most evident in the four- and five-part writing, least evident in the massive ten-part scores and in the ten-part double choruses with interlocking chord-distribution. The two most impressive performances of the evening were, consequently, the Biblical *Timor et Tremor* and Petrarch's *Passan vostri triomphi.*

The final echo-song was fun, as all such numbers are, but musically less interesting than the more complex polyphonic textures. The much admired (in script) *Lamentations of Jeremiah* were thin by comparison and less expressive than ritualistic in their content. The Ronsard madrigals, however, were of a tenderness and beauty incredible, solidly fragile and sincere, like all good things French.

A fine evening it was, though a shade on the cultural side, full of good music (the best) and good ensemble singing. A fault of style deserves correction, which is the holding on to final *m's, n's,* and *l's* by humming. This is one of those so-called "cathedral effects" dear to Anglican choir-masters, like the Stokowskian closing chordal diminuendos. It is unworthy of so straightforward a musician as Mr. Boepple.

January 28, 1942

Fa Sol La Fa Sol La Mi Fa

THESE are the syllables used by oldsters in rural regions of the South to intone the major scale, exactly as they were used in the British Isles long before Shakespeare. Indeed, the Elizabethan fa la la is no more than a conventional reference to the habit of singing any part-song first with the tonal syllables, so that melodies may be learned before words are attempted. So, still, is the custom in all those parts of America where *The Sacred Harp* and *Southern Harmony* are used as singing-books.

The former is common in Georgia, the Carolinas, Kentucky, Tennessee, Alabama, Arkansas, Louisiana, and Texas. It has been reissued four times since its first appearance in 1844 and has sold upward of five million copies.

Southern Harmony, published in 1835, sold a half-million copies before the Civil War, then was out of print till the Federal Writers' Project of Kentucky, under the sponsorship of the Young Men's Progress Club of Benton, Marshall County, reprinted it in facsimile in 1939.

By far the most celebrated in musicology circles of all the American song books, since Dr. George Pullen Jackson, of Vanderbilt University, revealed it to the learned world in *White Spirituals in the Southern Uplands,* its usage among the folk is confined today to a very small region in southwest Kentucky. William ("Singing Billy") Walker, its author, considered it so highly that he ever after signed himself, even on his tombstone, A. S. H., meaning "Author of *Southern Harmony.*" Today it is used by about forty old people, who meet every year at the County Court House of Benton and sing from nine till four.

I went to hear the *Southern Harmony* singing this year, lest it cease to exist before another, though most of the ancients looked healthy enough, I must say, and sang with a husky buzz; and a handful of youngsters of forty or more seemed active in perpetuating the style and repertory of it all.

The style is that of all back-country vocalism: a rather nasal intonation, a strict observance of rhythm and note (plus certain traditional ornaments and off tones), and no shadings of an ex-

pressive nature at all. Each song is sung first with the Fa Sol La
syllables and then with its words. Various persons take turns at
leading. The effect of the syllable singing is rather that of a
Mozart quintet for oboes; the effect of the verbal singing rather
that of a fourteenth- or fifteenth-century motet.

The repertory is all the grand and ancient melodies that our
Protestant ancestors brought to America in the seventeenth and
eighteenth centuries. Most are pentatonic and hexatonic, many of
them Dorian or Phrygian in mode. The part-writing is French
fifteenth-century. There are usually three parts: a bass, a tenor
(the melody) and a treble. Both of the latter are doubled at the
octave by women and men, making of the whole a five-part piece.
Since chords of the open fifth are the rule and parallel fifths common, the addition of these constant octaves gives to the whole
an effect at once of antiquity and of the most rigorous modernism.
Each part is a free melody, constantly crossing above or below
the others; no mere harmonic filling attenuates the contrapuntal
democracy. There is something of the bagpipe, too, in the sound
of it all, as well as in the configuration of many of the tunes.

Though the words are always sacred words (often of high
poetic quality), neither the *Southern Harmony* nor *Sacred Harp*
singings are, strictly speaking, religious manifestations. The proof
of that is the fact that they have never become involved in the
sectarian disputes that are the life of religion. Religion is rather
the protective dignity under which a purely musical rite is celebrated. That rite is the repetition year after year of a repertory
that is older than America itself, that is the musical basis of almost everything we make, of Negro spirituals, of cowboy songs,
of popular ballads, of blues, of hymns, of doggerel ditties, of all
our operas and symphonies. It contains our basic conceptions of
melody, of rhythm, and of poetic prosody. It contains in addition
the conception of freedom in part-writing that has made of our
jazz and swing the richest popular instrumental music in the
world.

To persons traveling southward I do not recommend the
Southern Harmony singing as the best introduction to this richness
of style and repertory. The ancients are too few in number and
too note-bound, and the singing is far too slow for nervous city
tastes. Easier to find on any summer Sunday and more lively in
tone and rhythm are the devotees of the *Sacred Harp*. The style

and repertory are similar, but the vigor of the rendition is greater.
If possible, buy a book and learn to sing yourself from the square
and triangular notes. It is more fun that way.

May 26, 1941

Wedding Music

WEDDING music is like children's books; it is usually most successful when it was written for some other purpose. The classic Mendelssohn and Wagner marches are no exceptions, since, though
their original subjects are nuptial, their composers' intention in
each case was theatrical rather than sacramental. It is probably
their lack of specific liturgical meaning that makes them so useful.
They express a happiness and a sweet tenderness that are appo-
priate to the occasion without engaging the participants of it to
any particular dogma or sectarian observance. They are used for
Jewish weddings and for Christian weddings, both Catholic and
Protestant, their direct religious significance being limited to the
establishment of a general atmosphere of love and legality. Indeed, their association with marital benediction is so firmly a part
of life among the bourgeoisie of Europe and America that the con-
vention of their usage in this connection may legitimately be said
to constitute a part of what Mr. Thurman Arnold terms "the
folklore of capitalism."

Note that that usage violates all the most sacred pretenses of
the musical world. It violates the pretense that one does not use
theater music in religious ceremonies, and it violates the equally
sacred pretense that one does not "arrange" and "adapt" the
musical classics indiscriminately. The Mendelssohn march, which
is a part of the incidental music written for Shakespeare's *Midsummer Night's Dream*, was scored by its author for full symphony orchestra. The Wagner Bridal Chorus from *Lohengrin* is
a choral piece for mixed voices with orchestral accompaniment.
Neither piece is ever heard at a wedding in anything like its original version. They are played on pipe organs and cottage pianos,
on Belgian chimes and marimbas, on fiddles, pantechnicons, harps,
and concertinas. All of which proves the pieces to be a sort of
folklore, since no single instrumental investiture is ever consid-

ered, for nuptial uses, to be the authentic one, least of all that which, for theatrical or concert purposes, bears the signature of the composer.

Every now and then, however, some bride revolts, says she's tired of the old things and wants a change. French composers have always found a market for the composition of Marches Nuptiales, but none of these works has ever achieved the world-wide usage that the Mendelssohn and Wagner pieces have. In the days when I was a church organist I used to recommend to customers desirous of varying the wedding routine the organ works of Sebastian Bach. Various of these are appropriate, but two in particular I always found admirably suited to both marital and funereal occasions. They are the Canzona in D minor and the E-minor Prelude and Fugue known as "The Judgment Day." These works are noble and churchly and serious. They lack the tearful note that is so unwelcome at funerals and the sentimental note that can so easily make a marriage sound silly, keeping present in the minds of all the sacramental nature of both occasions.

A few weeks ago I went to a church wedding where all the music used was by Mozart. Mark you that Mozart, though he played the organ all his life, never, to my knowledge, wrote a piece for the instrument.* The nearest thing to organ music I know of in his published works is a sort of Toccata for a mechanical clock. This can be played almost note for note on the organ and sounds extremely well. At the wedding I recently attended the organist had added some transcriptions of his own of other Mozart works. A part of one of the sonatas for violin and piano was played by a violin soloist with the organ. The famous *Ave Verum* communion motet was executed in the same manner, and divers Andantes and Larghettos from the instrumental concerted works were played on the organ alone. There was something from *Il Re Pastore*. The bridal procession entered to the March of the Priests from *Idomeneo* and went out to the triumphal Agnus Dei of the Coronation Mass.

I must say that in spite of the far from purist attitude shown by the organist and his clients in their employment of theater music for church usage and in their toleration of "arrangements," an attitude no different, after all, from that which tolerates the Mendelssohn and Wagner marches, the whole thing sounded ex-

---

* Grove's *Dictionary of Music and Musicians* lists, to my dismay, "17 sonatas for organ, usually with violin and bass, intended as graduales."

traordinarily well. There was a cheerfully festive note about it all that was most appropriate. There were joy and a refreshing loveliness in the music that no other music ever quite has. And if Mozart's ecclesiastical style may seem to some a little ornate for ordinary church services, its flowery grace is, on the other hand, exactly right for a June wedding.

Most curiously, also, the organ seemed to be as advantageous to Mozart's music as Mozart's music was to the occasion. One has long suffered from the nervousness and the general insecurity both of tonal balance and of rhythm that mark the usual renditions of this master's work. Even the greatest among our contemporary interpreters are prone to make it sound impossibly delicate and difficult. On the organ all that disappears. The instrument's steady tonal volumes give a welcome feeling of ease and of security against which the characteristic exuberance of the melodic lines and of their ornamentation stands out to great advantage. Nothing simpers; nothing flirts; nothing says: "See how cute I am!" The music is as sumptuously florid as that of old Sebastian Bach himself, and its harmony is every bit as noble. In addition it has its own kind of matchless grace and joy. I wish organists would play more Mozart. It might rid the public mind of the idea that there is something essentially fragile about this music, something nervously malequilibrated and ill at ease. On the organ it sounds as solid as Handel; and its animation, as well as its lyricism, is doubly delicious for the presence at all times of a mechanically sustained wind pressure.

June 28, 1942

PROCESSED MUSIC

Processed Music

THE GRAMOPHONE, the cinema, and the radio are what make the difference between today's musical life and that of preceding centuries. The concert, the theater, the opera, the social dance, church services, military parades, and musical practice in the home go on much as they have always done, subject to influences no more radical than those that determine fashions in the kinds of music employed. The music that we make up fresh and use on the spot has probably not changed much in amount, either, though there has been some shifting around of the proportions. We support more symphony orchestras, for instance, than our grandfathers did and fewer troupes performing light opera. If there has been any change in the total quantity of music executed each year, that change has probably been an increase. But I know no reason to suppose humanity has altered in any marked degree the musical habits it already had at the beginning of this century, habits that have remained, saving superficial changes, basically unaltered since the year 1600 and maybe since farther back than that. We have, however, added to our lives a new habit: that of consuming music not made on the spot.

This music is never wholly realistic. The electro-mechanical devices by which music is preserved or transmitted all give it a slight flavor as of canned food. The preserved stuff, however, is nourishing and incredibly abundant; and one could neither wish nor imagine its abolishment. Everybody, as a matter of fact, consumes it in some degree; many use it almost exclusively.

This does not mean that processed music is completely interchangeable with fresh. It will sustain life, of course, at least for brief periods; and some of it has a special charm of its own, like canned peaches, boxed sardines, and filets of anchovy. But for most people of high musical consumption it is a supplement to fresh musical fare rather than a substitute for it. Proof of this lies in the fact that in spite of there being a radio in every home and in nearly every drug store, there are just as many people as ever who earn their living by playing or singing in public. Nor has the sale of pianofortes diminished; it has increased, rather, since 1927.

The easily noticeable differences between fresh and processed music are several. Deformation of instrumental timbres is not the gravest of these, there being very little of it in what comes out of a really good instrument. Diminution of the original dynamic range is a far greater musical distortion. The limits between loud and soft at any given tuning are so much narrower than the dynamic range of a full orchestra, or even of a singer or of a pianoforte, that music which exploits a wide range of dynamic difference — Beethoven's, for instance — loses under any processing most of its build and emphasis. Music of a quiet lyrical character stands up better. Both these matters and their implications for culture are discussed in the published reports of Columbia University's Institute for Social Research. It is no derogation of recording, of radio, or of musical film-strip to repeat them. It is rather to the advantage of these media that their natures should be publicly defined.

It is desirable, I think, to remember that although the cinema is an art, a new narrative form, operating not at all essentially through an auditory medium but very essentially through the visual medium of animated photography, the gramophone and the radio are not art forms. They are merely means of conserving and distributing auditory art. The only device either of them possesses that is new to expression is that close-up of the human voice that makes crooning and soap operas so poignant. The cinema possesses two powerful and novel devices, the realistic depiction of natural scenery and the gigantic enlargement of the human face. No wonder it has become a fully conscious art in so brief a time. The mechanical means for conserving sound have not so far uncovered any comparable expressive possibilities.

Gramophone recording is like printing. Its function is the reproduction and preservation of something. Radio might develop into a new musical form, but so far it has not done so. And I see no new device of musical expression save the crooning technique which could serve as the basis for any musical form that would be specifically a radio thing. Consequently, for the present, we are obliged to consider these two media of communication as exactly that, as an enlargement of music's distribution, not of its expressive powers. Sociologically considered, they are new; but æsthetically they are just more of same.

Nevertheless, they are not quite the same as fresh music; and all the misunderstandings that arise from private or public criticism of them are due to a failure to consider what is different about them. Processed music may occasionally be preferable to fresh; but it does not sound like fresh music, and one's relation to it is not that of a listener to a live executant. It is like a photograph of somebody — that is to say, more or less resembling. But there is no communication between the observer and the subject of the picture. Distance is part of the set-up. And though many concerts are broadcast from places where there are a live audience as well as live performers, the private listener is no part of that audience. For him it is just another element in a far-away show. He cannot applaud with it and whistle with it and talk back to it and ask for an encore. He can only listen to the whole thing or else turn it off, take it or leave it as he would a book.

Now, since most families (and lunch counters and drug stores) leave the radio turned on all the time, another novel situation has come about. Never before has civilized humanity lived in an auditory décor, surrounded from morn till night, from cradle to coffin, by planned sound. It is harder today in the United States to avoid music than to hear it. Commercial music, folk music, art music, all day long they bathe us. Mozart and Schubert and Beethoven and Wagner are known to as many people as *God Bless America*. As cultural opportunity for all, this is a fine thing. As forced consumption of everything by everybody, it is a horrid thing. One used to have to work hard to keep in touch with the cultural tradition. Today educated people are obliged to immure themselves in order to avoid suffocation from constant contact with it.

This means that though a fresh performance of a classical or modern work is still a luxury product costing at least the price of a ticket, a processed performance of the same work is cheap as dirt and costs nothing at the time. There is, hence, a difference in the way we all feel about a processed performance. We may enjoy it either more or less than a fresh one, but we never enjoy it in just the same way as a fresh one. It is the same music, new or old, though it does taste somewhat of the preservative. What is not the same for us about it is its place in our day and in our budget. This is a new one altogether, not a replacement of anything but, for good or ill, an addition to our musical life.

May 16, 1943

Processing for Fidelity

PROCESSED music, as everybody knows, does not sound exactly like fresh music, though with good engineering at the source and with careful handling of a good receiving instrument, its final reception can be pretty convincing. Fidelity is the word used in radio and gramophone circles to express this convincingness. The highest fidelity in the rendering of processed music is not, however, a literal fidelity like print. It is a fidelity to sense, like that of a good translation. The actual sound that a symphony orchestra makes in Carnegie Hall or in NBC's Studio 8-H, even if it were transmissible intact to the hall bedroom of John Doe, Esq., would not be as convincing a rendition of symphonic sound as what comes out of the most modest radio instrument. Admitting, then, as I think we must, that the processing of music involves as much of translation as it does of literal rendering, let us consider for a moment the nature of the departures from exactitude involved in processing and what they do or do not do to music's sense.

A piece of music makes whatever sense it makes, holds the attention of any hearer, by the way its material, sound, is varied in pitch, volume, timbre, rhythm, and contrapuntal complexity. Processing methods deal imperfectly with every one of these elements. Low pitches, loud volumes, "dark," or non-brilliant, timbres, and ultra-complex rhythmic or tonal textures do not transmit as faithfully as high pitches, medium intensities of volume, bright timbres, and simple tonal textures. The reasons for this need not be expounded here, being largely of a technical nature. Technical progress in diminishing the acoustic limitations of processing has already gone far, however, and will certainly go farther in coming decades. Also, it is not only processed music that knows these limitations. Direct performance has its acoustic problems, too, as every musician knows who has performed the same piece in the same way in enclosures of varying size and different wall materials, not to speak of what happens when he tries it out of doors.

A good orchestra in a good hall produces the maximum today available of variation in all the elments of music named above, with the exception, possibly, of effective contrapuntal complexity. That seems to come off better on instruments of bright color with narrow limits of variation in both timbre and volume, like harpsichords, string quartets, and jazz ensembles not larger than ten. All such instruments and ensembles, incidentally, record and transmit beautifully. Processing reaches its highest fidelity, in fact, both acoustical and artistic, in dealing with them. And the transmission of their sound from studio to home involves no alteration of any æsthetic nature. Their music, recorded or broadcast, remains chamber music, which it does not always do when transported to the concert hall.

Orchestral music requires more translation. Volume variations must be reduced without destroying basic expression. The faithful rendering of high or bright sounds needs often be modified, too, in order to assure a credible rendering of lower or darker ones. And many complexities in the musical texture — of rhythm, of counterpoint, and of chord structure — have to be simplified. This necessity is due to an acoustic phenomenon known as "resultant tones."

Whenever any two tones are sounded at once the resultant, a third tone, lower than either, is heard at the same time. Resultants are less troublesome in direct performances than in processed ones, though their presence in large numbers is what limits always the effective contrapuntal complexity of orchestral writing. In processed renderings of complex music they make a sort of low-lying fog that will obscure the whole passage unless one alters the indicated balance of parts by picking out for emphasis one tune at a time and keeping the rest subdued. Leopold Stokowski, who is both learned and experienced in matters of processing, has told me that he is obliged to use orchestral balances far less delicate, for instance, when conducting Debussy for recording than he customarily employs in concert performances of the same music.

Since the acoustic limitations of radio transmission and of gramophone recording (by whatever process) are very similar, it turns out, therefore, that the most convincing broadcasts of orchestral music are those made from records. Real concerts, when broadcast, have a human quality, a warmth that is appealing and that often makes up to the listener for acoustical inefficiencies. Concerts broadcast from studios where no public is present are second in fidelity only to those broadcast from records, because the adjustments necessary to good transmission can be made without the music's having to sound well in both its processed and its unprocessed state. The least efficient kind of radio concert is the one with an invited audience. This has the acoustical disadvantages of the public concert without any of the warmth of the audience that has paid for the right to manifest its feelings.

This kind of broadcast is known by radio executives to be unsatisfactory. It is a compromise between the acoustical excellence of the pure studio execution and the comfort some conductors and soloists feel at having listeners around them. The invitational formula has been adopted in order to avoid taxes and circumvent municipal regulations governing places of public entertainment where admission is charged. For business reasons it may survive. But from the listener's point of view, orchestral music broadcast under studio conditions, or, better still, from records made at leisure under those conditions, will always be superior. The transmission of real public occasions is the only proper alternative.

October 31, 1943

Fantasia

MR. STOKOWSKI'S musical taste has always been questionable, his technical competence never. This is as true of his work in films as it was in flesh-and-blood concert work.

What he does to dead composers' music is nobody's business. Bach's organ music is anybody's to orchestrate, though why not just play it on the organ is a question I find hard to answer. Beethoven's "Pastoral" Symphony will no doubt survive its Walt Disney accompaniment, scenes from life among the centaurs that include the mating of these with young and attractive "centaurettes" in flowered brassières. It will certainly survive Mr. Stokowski's interpretative cuts and tempos. Tchaikovsky's *Nutcracker Suite* and Ponchielli's *Dance of the Hours* have already been through worse. And Schubert's *Ave Maria* has long ere now served church organists as a pretext to exploit echo effects from the back of the balcony.

The only live composer represented in *Fantasia* is Igor Stravinsky. Being on the job himself (and with his musical rights well protected in law and equity), he got the best musical deal of the evening. His *Rite of Spring* sounded, in consequence, more like "legitimate" music and less like vaudeville than the other pieces did. Dukas's *Sorcerer's Apprentice* ran it a close second. Both had appropriate pictorial accompaniments, the first a sort of geology lesson, the second a Mickey Mouse on the story the composer wrote his piece to illustrate.

As a spectacle with music, *Fantasia* is no high art job, though certain moments have charm and others humor. Only the geology lesson to Stravinsky's fine score is in any way superior to the famous *Silly Symphony* of several years back in which Donald Duck conducted the *William Tell* Overture.

The novelty of the film, as presented here, is a system of musical photography and its auditive projection called by the Disney promotion department "thrilling Fantasound." (The adjective is apparently inseparable from its noun as in "Holy Church.") The science of reproducing sound through photography will no doubt survive this, we hope, not copyrighted baptism. Stokowskisound, if one must have a trade name, might better honor its godfather. For Leopold Stokowski, whatever one may think of his musical taste, is unquestionably the man who has best watched over the upbringing of Hollywood's stepchild, musical recording and reproduction.

Alone among successful symphonic conductors he has given himself the trouble to find out something about musical reproduction techniques and to adapt these to the problems of orchestral execution. Alone among the famous musicians who have worked in films he has forced the spending of money and serious thought by film-producers and their engineers toward the achievement of a result in auditive photography comparable in excellence to the results that the expenditure of money and thought have produced in visual photography.

Musicians will thank him and bless his name. Producers may have a few headaches ahead. Because once the public has heard a good transmission of music, I doubt if it will ever again be satisfied with poor. On the other hand, a whole new field is opened for musical commentary in films that may very well pay receipts in the future.

Artistic receipts it will certainly pay. And here is where the careful art of Walt Disney begins to show up in *Fantasia*. Not that it is any different essentially from his previous work. It is simply that a whole evening of it, combined with music that really sounds like first-class music, makes it perfectly clear that the integration of music with pantomime produces a far more powerful effect on the beholder than the accompaniment of pantomime by "neutral," or unnoticed, music can do.

The integration, phrase by phrase, of music with naturalistic acting and speech is going to produce lots of directorial headaches; but sooner or later it will have to be done. Thanks to Disney and Stokowski, it will probably have to be done rather sooner than later.

The system of multiple loudspeakers that has been installed in the Broadway Theater, though advantageous to good sound-reproduction and essential to the best, does not oblige composers and conductors to make the same musical uses or abuses of its advantages that Mr. Stokowski makes. On the whole, he was discreet.

It was interesting to note, also, that he has taken some trouble to secure a good fortissimo. This fortissimo does not sound much like the fortissimo of the best symphony orchestras. But the fortissimo of the best symphony orchestras rarely sounds very good, anyway. Its effect is nearly always one of strain rather than of power. Power is not lacking in the Stokowski filmed fortissimos. And if they sound more like an organ than like a real live orchestra, the answer to that is that an organ is exactly what a real live orchestra should spend more time and money trying to sound like.

November 14, 1940

Chaplin Scores

As we know, Charlie Chaplin, though no musician, plans his own musical scores, working through a trained composer. In the case of *The Great Dictator*, the musical direction is credited to Meredith Willson. It is to be presumed that the opening fanfares and such occasional bits as occur throughout the film that are not recognizably quotations are of this musician's composition. They are not very good; they are musically uninteresting.

What is good and extremely interesting is Mr. Chaplin's way of using music in films. His concept of its function has been clear ever since his first sound-film, *City Lights*. He integrates auditive elements with animated photography by admitting them to the rank of co-star with the poetic and visual elements.

He does not try to use music as mere accompaniment, as neutral background. He knows that a well-cut film can get along without that. Nor does he try to drag in lyric appeal by making one of his characters a music student who can go into a song if necessary. Unless he can co-ordinate music with the action in such a way that the two play a duet, each commenting upon and heightening the other, he leaves it out altogether. For the same reason he has hitherto omitted the speaking voice from his own characterizations. He has not needed it. It would have introduced a jarring naturalistic element into his far from naturalistic acting-style.

The Mayor's wordless speech, sounded on a trombone, in *City Lights*, shows one of Chaplin's best procedures. The dictator's speeches in semi-nonsense German are the same trick done with his own voice. His bubble dance (to the *Lohengrin* Prelude) and the shaving scene (to a Brahms *Hungarian Dance*) are a different form of musical integration. The first procedure is a substitution of stylized sound for naturalistic speech. (Note that when he is acting naturalistically he speaks naturalistically.) The second procedure is not a substitution; it is an adding of stylized sound to stylized movement, to pantomime. He has here introduced the straight music-hall turn he was brought up to, as artificial a thing as the classical ballet, into movies, the most naturalistic form of theatre that has ever existed. The result is artistically successful.

Mr. Chaplin has not made a complete musical film. He has made a silent film with interpolated musical numbers. But he has obviously reflected about the auditive problem; and so far as he uses music at all, his use of it is unfailingly advantageous. He uses all the auditive effects correctly. He employs very little naturalistic noise, for instance. He takes as a basic æsthetic principle the fact that movies are pantomime. Anything expressible by pantomime is not expressed otherwise. He introduces speech, music, and sound-effects only when they are needed to do something pantomime can't do. There is a little bombing in the war scenes, a strict minimum. When he belches after having swallowed three coins, he lets the coins jingle. But nowhere does he overlay the film with speech that says nothing, with music that just accompanies, with noises that merely express hubbub.

This is the proper way to integrate auditive elements into any visual spectacle, not to use them at all unless you can use them to heighten the visual effect directly. The Hollywood idea of using background music for its emotional value without anybody ever noticing it is there is nonsense. Because music has to be either neutral or expressive. If it is neutral, it has no expressive value. If it is expressive (in the same way and at the same time as the incidents of the photographic narrative; that is to say, accurately expressive), then it is not neutral. It is very noticeable indeed and must be well written and correctly integrated with the action. Nobody knows how to write neutral music nowadays anyway, as I have explained elsewhere.* Bromides are all that ever result from that effort. And bromides solve no æsthetic difficulty. They merely obfuscate expression.

There are others in the world besides Chaplin who have sound instincts about musical usage with films. The wailing Russian locomotive at the end of *The Road to Life* was a case of what music and sound-effects can do together. René Clair, too, has often used music and sound to advantage as substitutes for complete visual depiction. Chaplin has not included in *The Great Dictator* every device known to film art of incorporated auditive effect. That was not his aim. But in no other film that I have seen are speech and music and sound incorporated into a photographed pantomimic narrative with such unvarying and deadly accuracy, nor omitted from the spectacle so rigorously when no way seems to have presented itself for using them to advantage.

* *The State of Music* (New York: William Morrow & Co.; 1939), pp. 173–90.

Beethoven in the Home

PHILHARMONIC–SYMPHONY ORCHESTRA, *Bruno Walter,* conductor; concert broadcast from Carnegie Hall yesterday afternoon. All-Beethoven program comprising LEONORE OVERTURE No. 3; SYMPHONY No. 8, F MAJOR; SYMPHONY No. 5, C MINOR.

THE PHILHARMONIC broadcast of yesterday afternoon, as listened to in the home, was a pleasantly domestic ceremony. Two Beethoven symphonies, a light one and a heavier one, preceded by a familiar overture and accompanied by those intermittent frying noises that my instrument likes to add to everything, gave the whole a flavor of church-going and of Sunday dinner with the preacher present that was in no wise contradicted by the edifying story about Abraham Lincoln that Mr. Carl Van Doren recounted so lugubriously between courses.

There is nothing banal about Bruno Walter's Beethoven. It is plain, sensible, eloquent, clear. And the tempos are all reasonable ones. I presume it was as a statement of faith and a proof of orthodoxy that he chose to begin the summer broadcasts with a full program of this music, which has been for over a century now the Credo and Gloria of the symphony-orchestra business. It must have been some theoretical consideration, at any rate, that determined his choice, since there is no other symphonic music that broadcasts so badly.

If one did not know the pieces and could not evoke from the radio performance memories of what they really sound like, one would have strange ideas indeed about them. In spite of Mr. Walter's lucid exposition and the charming way he has of making solo instruments sing, Beethoven, heard over the radio, sounds disjointed and picayune.

The limited dynamic range that a microphone will carry has something to do with this distortion; and so, I imagine, has the placing of the microphones. Yesterday, for instance, the fortes all lacked background, as if the violins were too close; and so the essential majesty of Beethoven, which comes from his constant contrasts of loud and soft, was reduced both by the radio's inability, at best, to transmit a really loud ensemble of musical sounds

and by the fact that the bottom was out of these, even in their
toned-down state. There was continuity in the rhythmic layout
but no real strength in the dynamic pattern or any massiveness in
individual chords. The lyrical passages came off prettily, as they
always do in broadcast music; but the dramatic eloquence that
constitutes such a large part of Beethoven's thought sounded
puny.

Mr. Fredric March, who read for Mr. Van Doren Lincoln's
farewell speech to his friends and neighbors of Springfield, Illi-
nois, was funereal in the extreme; and his voice lacked resonance.
I do not know on what authority he represents that great President, certainly no inexperienced public speaker, as pronouncing
the *u's* in *duty* and *endure* like double *o's*. I do know that the
gentleman who introduced the Beethoven symphonies, when he
endeavored to depict that composer as a jolly little man just like
you and me, sometimes gay and sometimes sad, did so on no historical authority whatsoever. And, of course, he had to repeat the
wheeze about how the first theme of the Fifth Symphony is rhythmically identical with the letter V in Morse code, three dots and
a dash. If that long E flat is a dash I'll eat a telegraph instrument
in public.

May 24, 1943

Music-Announcing

FAVORABLE comments received on a recent discussion here of the
state of program-note writing have encouraged me to continue
the subject. Particularly do the presentation speeches that accompany radio broadcasts of cultural music seem to me, for the most
part, unsatisfactory. Printed notes for house programs present no
novel literary problem. All they need is real scholarship and some
care in the writing — in other words, a return to the way they have
always been done whenever they have been done properly. But
a proper formula for radio introductions of music has never been
established; it still needs to be built from the ground up. And
though such a building up involves, of necessity, a large part of
proceeding by trial and error, it appears to me that there is already
a tendency in radio circles to accept as standard practice far more
error than is necessary.

By error I do not mean merely misstatements of fact, though these are numerous. I mean also every detail of material, style, and attitude that makes the framework in which music is presented appear unworthy beside the music itself and that tends, therefore, to trivialize the music. When an announcer tells us, as I heard one do recently, that François Couperin's *Tic-Toc Choc, ou Les Maillotins,* is a picture of bloodthirsty women knitting as they watch heads roll from the guillotine, that is merely a factual mistake. (It is really two mistakes. One is that the word *maillotin* does not refer to knitting but to the hammering of metal; and the other is that the author of the piece died about fifty years before the good Dr. Guillotin had even invented his famous machine for making decapitation efficient.) But when historical matter, even if true, is presented in an irrelevant context by men of uncouth speech and patronizing tone, it tends, I am sure, rather to offend the cultivated listener (for whom the broadcasts of classical music are, after all, intended) than to instruct him.

It is not desirable, I should think, that American radio speakers attempt BBC pronunciation, though I see no objection to the Boston Symphony Orchestra's being introduced in good Bostonian or to the Philharmonic's being associated in the nation's mind with cultivated New York speech. But certainly such informative matter as is provided with cultural broadcasts should be addressed to persons of the same intellectual attainments as the programs themselves postulate. Cultivated speech need not sound affected. Indeed, the use of anything else in association with distinguished musical executions can easily appear to a cultivated listener as both affected and patronizing.

How much talk really is needed with musical broadcasts is still uncertain. Obviously, the listener needs to be told what is being performed. Sometimes a further identification of work or author is valuable. Also, when the program originates at a public concert the intermission has to be filled up with something. I do not think lengthy explanations heard *before* a rendition are ever very enlightening, except when they recount a plot, as at the opera. Comment and analysis that take place *after* a piece has been played are, on the other hand, capable of being used by the listener as aids both to memory and to the formation of taste. I have always thought it would be valuable to hear the first part of a concert discussed by competent musicians while it was still fresh in everybody's mind. Instead of quiz programs that are nothing more than a game or of historical and patriotic diversions that are mere time-fillers, I should like to hear a real argument about the work just played, with fair statement of opposing points of view. I think some such discussion as goes on in a real intermission among real musicians and music-lovers would help any listener to form his own opinion and remove from the broadcasts of serious art music their present unfortunate air of being handouts from on high. In any case, by whatever formula this is to be operated, radio needs more of free discussion with its music and less of both tomfoolery and pompous exposition. The latter, especially when it precedes the hearing of the music, has a way of turning itself into blurb that is unbecoming to a serious musical presentation.

There is no bad will involved, I think, in the neglect by radio companies to observe the intellectual amenities. There just hasn't been time so far to bother about the framing of art in business establishments where the presence of art at all is still something of a surprise to everybody. But the time has come for framing to be considered. Virtually every first-class musical organization in the United States is now available on the air; and there are special ensembles, in addition, playing rare music ancient and modern all the time. Radio has long since surpassed the concert-giving agencies in the quantity of high-class music furnished weekly to the public. Real concerts, though a fine thing, are no longer what we musically live by. Processed music is nine tenths, at least, of every music-lover's diet; and the radio furnishes a big part of this. It is a matter of universal regret that the verbal presentation of it is almost invariably unworthy and as often as not ignoble. I have never encountered a habitual listener to serious radio music who did not deplore the way it is currently commented on and announced.

If my observation has been correct, if nobody at all likes the way music is being presented on the air, then some change in this may no doubt be anticipated. The purpose of this article is not, however, to encourage my readers in overhopefulness about quick results, but rather to remind the radio people of what we should like, of what most of the radio world itself, in fact, knows to be the next step in radio's amazing musical advance. Experiment all you like, gentlemen, with the dramatic form of your presentations. That is the way to find out a good one. But please couldn't you

maybe right now establish some minimum intellectual require-
ments among the boys that introduce Beethoven and Stravinsky?

October 24, 1943

The Cultural Obligation

It is a curious fact that the chief purveyors of processed music —
the broadcasting and recording companies — though far from in-
nocent of monopolistic tendencies in business, are less limited in
their æsthetic outlook than the purveyors of fresh performance
and in effect more public-spirited. Many of these latter are not
profit-making institutions at all. The Metropolitan Opera Company, the Philharmonic and other symphonic foundations, the
Stadium and similar summer establishments in other cities are, in
theory at least, devoted to performing only such music as will raise
the cultural standards of their communities and limited in that
effort only by the cultural resistance of those communities. And
yet the repertory performed by all these organizations over any
five-year period, for all the good intentions of their backers and
all the struggling of their conductors to enlarge it, is more notable
for its standardization than for its comprehensiveness.

The processors, on the other hand, perform everything. They
not only have a broader range of musical interest, covering, as they
do, popular, folk, and art music. But within the field of art music
itself their repertory is larger. They play everything the purveyors
of fresh music habitually play and a great deal that these do not.
Their musical habits are less institutionalized, less bound down to
the Classical and Romantic concepts of greatness. Their orchestral
musicians are better paid, their conductors (at least in radio) are
younger, more expansive, more alert. Compared to the opera-and-
symphony world, which is weighted down by all the conservatism
of a great tradition and all the stuffiness of its ancient but still
very real power, the radio people who deal with art music are a
lively crew. They are like an air force to the others' navy. And it is
far from certain yet which should command their joint operations.

No box-office neurasthenia of a philanthropic trustee class nor
any stylistic conservatism of elderly subscribers acts as a reper-

tory check in recording and broadcasting. The public for these is
not a unified group, nor has it any obligation to like everything.
Its members are isolated and free. And the processors have themselves no musical prejudices. They give the public everything
they can think of; and if any kind of music finds thus a response,
they have found a new way of pleasing the clientele. Radio, for instance, doesn't aim to please all its clientele all the time — a nar-
rowing purpose. It aims to interest all the tastes of all the popula-
tion at some time or other during the week — a broad purpose
and a progressive one.

The amount of excellent music excellently performed that is
available to radio listeners in the New York region is vast. It is less
vast in the middle regions of our country, where the local stations
are less elaborately cultural than ours, the musical fare in those
parts being chiefly what is available on two of the chain programs.
In the western European cities, however, it is enormous. In Paris,
with a quite modest instrument, I used to get thirty stations with
no trouble at all. A circumference described by London, Athlone,
Helsinki, Moscow, Ankara, Cairo, Rabat, and Lisbon, including
stations both governmental and commercial, comprises every na-
tionality in Europe and North Africa. Every kind of music — folk,
popular, and art — is available in peace times (or used to be)
from every tradition within this region, plus lots of American
swing.

In the New York region we have the chief American chain
programs — Columbia, NBC Red and Blue, and Mutual — plus five
local stations of medium wave-length and seven operating on fre-
quency modulation. Two of the local stations, QXR and NYC, are
devoted in large part to broadcasting art music of the highest
quality from everywhere, using gramophone records as well as
performers for this purpose. Alfred Wallenstein's Sinfonietta and
Symphonic Strings play year in and year out more music from
the eighteenth and twentieth centuries than do any two other
organizations in the world that I am acquainted with. Frank
Black, of NBC, Howard Barlow and Bernard Herrmann, of Columbia, do a broad repertory and are friendly toward contemporary composition. All winter our Philharmonic, the Boston, Philadelphia, Cleveland, and NBC symphony orchestras are available
weekly. So is the Metropolitan Opera.

I am not pretending that all this is equal to fresh performance.
Very little processed performance is. Or that all the abundance

of musical indulgence in the modern world is going to make better citizens of us. Because I don't think it will. Or that passively listening to music is a proper substitute for actively making it. I do not consider Radio City a nobler institution than Carnegie Hall, though I doubt equally that the contrary is tenable. I yield to no man in my contempt for radio announcers and in my private resistance to cultural paternalism in all its forms. The thesis I hold about processed music is very simply this: That the music available for consumption in any place at any time is the whole amount of music available for consumption in that place at that time. That at present the purveyors of processed music are supplying a larger repertory of art music to the lovers of same than any single concert-giving foundation is or than all of them together are. That for all their ineluctable ugliness as mere sound and for all the frank commercialism of their purveyors' motives, radio and the gramophone have a musical edge on the symphony orchestras.

Maybe these last are going to turn into just house organs of the radio companies and a pretext to rehearse for recording without paying the full fee. I hope not. For the present their repertory, their ambitions, and their outlook are smaller than those of the processors. Their chief advantage lies in the fact that they sound better. This is not enough. If they are to survive not as vassals of business but as instruments of culture, they will have to have a better program for culture than any of them is offering today. The Philharmonic long ago ceased to be a part of New York's intellectual life. The Chicago and Philadelphia orchestras do not represent to their intellectual communities what they did twenty years ago. Only the Boston Symphony still holds its rightful place between Harvard University and the Museum of Fine Arts.

What the Philharmonic will become between Artur Rodzinski and the United States Rubber Company nobody knows. The former can be counted on to clean up the execution, at least, and probably to make the repertory make more sense. I fancy the commercial sponsorship won't hurt. It may even act as a reminder of the orchestra's national obligation to be something more than a museum piece. Certainly a similar sponsorship has not hurt the Metropolitan Opera. The nation-wide audience of music-lovers is, after all, both more receptive and more demanding than any merely New York one has ever been in my lifetime.

May 23, 1943

GENERAL IDEAS

Season's Impressions

IN the course of attending musical events this season as a reviewer, it has been a source of considerable enlightenment to me to observe the state of the musical tradition in the metropolis, in so far as that is capable of being observed through its public manifestations. I have in mind a more detailed account of all this than could be exposed convincingly in one Sunday article, one which could be perhaps the thread of several during the vacation season. Today I should like merely to state some general impressions derived from my attendance at musical events and from some scrutinizing of the programs and announcements of those I have not been able to attend.

First of all, the soloists. By far the most interesting musically to me are the pianists. These have, we know, the largest repertory available to any soloists of great music that is still comprehensible to a twentieth-century audience. They have also the largest variety of technical styles. In violin technique there is only good, less good, and bad. There are at least three and maybe five ways of playing the pianoforte, all perfectly legitimate and musical. This richness both of repertory and of executional form gives to the piano-playing world a musical breadth unknown today among any other group of solo musicians. Also, that world is less hermetically sealed against knowledge of other music than it has been in the past. The acquaintance with the conceptions of ensemble music, that of the large orchestra in particular, that is universal in our day has tended to encourage a more penetrating comprehension of the piano works of the great symphonic composers and to eliminate among pianists the merely facile virtuosity that still gets by among the violinists.

Among string-players the cellists seem to me the most vigorous. I think this is due to the fact that the technique of cello-playing is at present in a state of lively expansion. There are not enough solo artists playing the viola or the double bass to give their situation any general significance. The concert halls can be said almost literally, however, to be lousy with violinists. Many of these are superb technicians. Few present an interest as interpreters that is at all comparable in either depth or originality with their technical abilities. As a group they are conservative about stylistic novelty and mostly preoccupied with slickness of execution. They are an unhappy group, in spite of their prosperity, and without much confidence in what the century may hold for them. They seem to have no clear orientation regarding their instrument's function in it.

Singers vary. The legend that they are mostly musical illiterates is, of course, utterly false. It comes from the fact that success in singing is still possible to musical illiterates. It goes on being repeated, simply because the irony of it is amusing, although everybody knows a vocalist or two who is a first-class musician as well. Their public work varies, like their talents and their education, between the sublime and the ridiculous.

Their recitals are among the most rigidly conventionalized ceremonies of the modern world. The public is accomplice in the maintenance of this rigidity. It has opposed itself firmly to the execution of any vocal music with pianoforte accompaniment excepting short songs. Operatic arias, which used to grace recital programs, are rarely heard nowadays in Town Hall, saving a few from Handel operas that might pass for oratorio music. All attempts to introduce long works containing a great variety of vocal effect have produced only momentary successes. For some reason, the repertory of voice recitalists is as limited and as conventional as is that of our major symphony orchestras.

These last are troubling indeed to the sincere musical conscience. The WPA orchestras, the second- and third-class professional groups, the student bands, the amateur symphony societies, present their musical results to the public without false pretense and with a minimum of publicitary chichi. Some play well, some badly; but on the whole the picture of their efforts all over the United States is one of healthiness and vigor. Their contribution to musical culture and its tradition is a real one and far more important, I suspect, than is currently imagined. The WPA groups, in particular, are indefatigable at playing and replaying the music of our own time, especially that composed in the United States. The major orchestras play comparatively little of this and a still smaller proportion of the classical and Romantic repertory that is the main storehouse from which all their programs are drawn. Like the virtuoso violinists, they seem to be consecrated chiefly to the resurfacing of a few standard numbers. About fifty pieces form the basis of international symphonic repertory among the high-hat organizations. Even the much advertised resurfacing that these pieces are constantly being put through is not always first-class work. The great provincial orchestras are more dependable at this than our local Philharmonic is, which varies from marvelous to awful in a way that can only be explained by its lack during the last thirty years of a constant musical discipline and of a personified responsibility before the public for all of its concerts.

Conductors are a special subject in themselves and not as fascinating a one to this reviewer as to some. Their profound musical knowledge and their ability to bluff have both been overemphasized in print. They are for the most part well-educated musicians. Their job is to discipline and train an orchestra and to lead it in public concerts. Many try to achieve success in the second job without going to the trouble of fulfilling their duties in the first. They fail. Few fail who accomplish the first duty adequately. Because nobody can give good concerts regularly with an orchestra he has not trained (though a certain effect can be made guest-conducting familiar works). Whereas anybody, literally anybody who is capable of training a first-class symphonic band, can give successful concerts with the band he has trained, because public execution is child's play compared to the technical preparation of a hundred musicians to read together both accurately and spontaneously music in all the known styles according to the trainer's understanding of those styles.

The only difference between the operatic picture and the symphonic is that there is no WPA opera, no amateur opera, and very little second- and third-class opera comparable in vitality and excellence to the similar range of symphonic playing in the United States. There is some, but not nearly enough. First-class opera is virtually a monopoly of the Metropolitan at present. This organization is as troublesome to the sincere musician as the luxury orchestras are. Like the Philharmonic, it is sometimes excellent, sometimes perfectly terrible. Considering that the house is usually sold out anyway, amelioration or radical change of any kind seems quite improbable for the present.

Between the oversized Metropolitan opera and the undersized and mostly amateurish chamber opera troupes, there isn't much opera available, in spite of the success in the last ten years of Gershwin's *Porgy and Bess*, of Blitzstein's *The Cradle Will Rock*, and of my own *Four Saints in Three Acts* at medium-sized theaters. Producers are not averse to the formula, and composers abound capable of doing any musical job successfully. It is libretti that are lacking, sensible dramatic works capable of being heightened by music and worth somebody's taking the trouble about them that such heightening involves. Neither the musical nor the literary world has yet faced squarely in our century the stylistic problems raised by the possibility of their collaboration. So that for the present we must admit that in spite of the existence of three American operas of outstanding originality (four if you count Hall Johnson's dramatic oratorio, *Green Pastures*), there is no local group of serious theater composers in any way comparable to the several groups of symphonic writers that produce annually reams of music that could only have been made in America.

As for composers in the local musical picture, they peer out from every nook and cranny. Neither France nor Italy nor Germany, not to speak of England, could show to the world anything like the number the United States can muster of first-quality composers resident on her soil. The number of these who are native-born citizens is about two fifths of the group, I should say. That is a larger proportion of native-born among the quality workmen than France or Austria or Germany has ever been able to show at the periods when the metropolis and capital of each of these countries has been a center of creative activity in music. The American composer is doing very well, thank you; and much pleasant music of domestic origin has been heard in our concert halls this winter.

May 11, 1941

Singing vs. Crooning

EVERYBODY knows that singing is not what it was thirty and forty years ago. The beautiful memories people have of Caruso and Melba and Muratore and Garden might be considered as romanticized if gramophone records were not there to prove them right. It isn't that nobody sings that well any more; it is simply that there aren't so many as there used to be who do. Only recently Kirsten Flagstad was among us, and Elisabeth Rethberg did perfect work well into the 1930's. There is some pretty grand vocalism available on the operatic boards today in Paris, in the Italian cities, in Buenos Aires, and in New York. The art of singing is not lost. Good examples of it have grown scarce, that's all.

Everybody knows, too, that fine vocal organs are not scarce, that musical talent has not ceased to flourish, and that instruction in all the musical branches is more easily available throughout the land than formerly. The mystery about the singing business is the fact that with all the talent there is around and all the studying that goes on so few singers nowadays ever arrive at mastery of their art.

It is the opinion of not a few experienced pedagogues that radio is responsible for our vocal decline. The dissemination by this means of symphonic and chamber music has certainly not lowered our standards of instrumental execution; and with equal certainty it has raised our level of musical taste, amplified our experience of skills and repertories hitherto difficult of access. But the microphone has toned our singing down for the simple reason that its own ceiling of dynamic power is a low one. And singing well depends on being able to sing out.

The human voice is a musical instrument (a wind instrument, to be exact); and, like all other instruments, it requires to be played both loud and soft. The pianoforte, the violin, the oboe, the flute, the trombone, the clarinet, and all the rest of them are mastered by constant practice at the extremes of their force ranges. Playing or singing mezzo-forte gets nobody anywhere, because progress in muscular control comes from working close to the limits, without overstepping them, of muscular strength. If one can execute a musical passage very softly with perfect evenness and very strongly with the same evenness, the moderate levels of power will give no trouble.

Formerly singers practiced this way, and when they sang in public they were always eager to show off their ability to sing both loud and soft. Opera singing was the crown of vocalism because it was at the opera that people sang the highest and the lowest, the loudest and (with a special technique of distance projection) the softest. Below this came, in descending order of technical mastery required, the oratorio, light opera, recital, and church. Everybody who sang anywhere sang both loud and soft every day.

Nowadays singers are constantly getting engagements on the radio. Even when they don't have such engagements they dream about them, because these often pay well. But radio singing encourages a different technique. It is of no value to sing loud, because the microphone can't take that. So the singers who work in radio during their formative years and those who practice with the radio in mind use their full power less and less. And since control in soft singing is largely a product of control in loud singing, both ends of the dynamic gamut tend to wither away, leaving only the mezzo-forte intact, since that is what is chiefly used. This is supplemented with a special form of soft singing that carries well over a microphone but that is not a part of classic vocal technique. On the lower levels of musical repertory this device, which is a sort of humming with the mouth open, is called crooning. When employed at the opera, as it often is nowadays, it shows up as faulty placement.

It is faulty placement because it works only at a low breath level. It cannot take much crescendo without getting ugly. It is a special effect, extremely limited in musical applicability. It is also an insidious habit that grows on singers before they know it, and it often ends by injuring the voice. The reason why so few singers today can sing out their high notes good and loud without screaming or wobbling is that the crooning technique has crept into all their lives and falsified their production a little bit. This shows up first at the extremes of range and of power. There are various ways of singing prettily in the middle of one's voice mezzo-forte. But there is only one way of singing high or low at a maximum of resonance, and that is the correct way. All other ways sound ineffectual, just as all singing that is not based on the constant testing of one's placement through singing every day high and low and really loud and soft (making all the transitions smoothly) ends by sounding timid, ineffectual, and amateurish.

I do not propose that opera singers should refuse radio engagements, though it is a curious fact that many of our best ones do not perform much on the air and that most of our great radio vocalists are disappointing in the theater. I merely wish to point out that radio, in this case, is not so much the disseminator of an already existing vocal art as it is the creator of a new vocal manner. It is also the destroyer of an old one exactly in so far as the workers in the new medium think the two singing styles are identical. The only way singing can be preserved as a great art that exploits to the full all the range and power of the human voice is to give to radio singing a place apart in the vocal tradition. It is not only a more limited medium of expression than public singing is; it also tends to exploit a low-breath production that is outside the great tradition of singing and that must be kept outside it.

It is all right to croon to the heart's content, so long as that amuses anybody and so long as there is money in it. But any singer who mistakes crooning for singing and starts mixing up the two techniques does so at the expense of his singing style. The future of classical vocalism depends on the recognition by pedagogues and by practitioners of the fact that microphone singing is another accomplishment. The two may not be mutually exclusive, but it is pretty certain that they are not mutually contributory.

January 9, 1944

Tempos

No element of musical execution is more variable from one interpreter to another than tempo. No problem, indeed, is more bothering to any musician, even to the composer, than that of determining the exact metronomic speed at which he wishes or advises that a piece be made to proceed in performance unless it is that of sticking to his tempo once he has decided on it. Many musical authors, beginning with Beethoven, have indicated in time units per minute their desires in this matter. And yet interpreters do not hesitate to alter these indications when conviction, based on reasoning or on feeling or on executional circumstances, impels them to do so.

The truth of the matter is that very few pieces require to be played at a given speed in order to make sense. Serge Koussevitzky last season gave an excellent performance of the Berlioz *Symphonie Fantastique* that took a good ten minutes more of actual playing time than Monteux or Beecham or Toscanini ever needs for this piece. Toscanini himself once angered Ravel considerably by sweeping brilliantly through his *Bolero*, which is not a long piece, in four minutes less time than the composer consid-

ered legitimate. I have heard the fugues and toccatas of Sebastian
Bach played by organists at the cathedral of Notre Dame in Paris,
which has some of the most complex echoes and reverberations of
any building in the world, at tempos twice, thrice, and even four
times as slow as those the same organists employ in churches of
drier acoustic properties. They sounded perfectly well, too.

The reason why such variations shock us as little as they do is
that speed itself is not nearly so expressive an element in musical
communication as clear phraseology and exact rhythmic articulation are. These matters require, in the course of studying a work
and preparing its execution, a great deal of thought on the interpreter's part and no small amount of adjustment to instrumental
limitations — to practicability, in short. But once set in the artist's
understanding, they are not likely to change for many years. They
constitute the whole shape and substance of what is correctly
called his "interpretation" of any score.

Within this pretty rigid framework he can alter speeds of execution, adapt them to unfavorable acoustic conditions, profit by
exceptional abilities, play up or down to audience psychology,
follow, even, his own fancy or inspiration about emphasizing certain aspects of a piece's expressive content. The more fixed and
firm, in fact, his convictions are about a work's correct rhythmic
articulation and phraseology, the greater his facility will be in
adapting this interpretation to varying executional circumstances
and the greater freedom his own temperament will have for producing an inspired performance.

It is of little value for young singers, soloists, or conductors to
try to imitate the exact tempos of Pinza or Lehmann; Rubinstein,
Horowitz, or Schmitz; Beecham, Stokowski, Toscanini, Koussevitzky, or Walter. These are not fixed quantities, anyway. What
counts is their phraseology and their articulation of each phrase's
exact rhythmic content. If one knows or has a conviction about
the musical meaning of a rhythm — whether its reference is to a
waltz, a minuet or a lullaby, a march, a tango or a jig — and about
the specific characteristics of a musical phrase — whether it imi-
tates the inflections of a voice, of a trumpet, or of a music-box,
whether it follows the cadence of rhymed poetry or the free accents of prose declamation — tempo will take care of itself; and
so will the pacing of the piece as a whole.

The greatness of the great interpreters is only in small part
due to any peculiar intensity of their musical feelings. It is far

more a product of intellectual thoroughness, of an insatiable curiosity to know what any given group of notes means, should mean, or can mean in terms of sheer sound. The composer himself is often less curious, because he works by more subconscious methods. He hears something in the mind and writes it down; too great an awareness of what he is doing will impede the flow. But the great interpreters are those who, whether they are capable or not of penetrating a work's whole musical substance, are impelled by inner necessity to give sharpness, precision, definition to the shape of each separate phrase.

The composer does not think much about exact speeds or exact volumes while writing down his thought. Whatever indications he may add about these matters — and some are fanatically detailed about them — are the result of later reflection. At this later point he is merely another interpreter. And like any interpreter who is fairly familiar with a work, he is capable of giving invaluable advice about its phraseology and its basic rhythms. Unless, however, he is an experienced conductor or executant, he is likely to imagine his adagios as taking place in an eternalized slow-motion that it is quite without the power of human breath or muscles to sustain and his prestos as being executed at a speed just within the ability of the human ear to follow.

It is not the purpose of this article to encourage interpreters in those violations of an author's clear wish or in those lapses from taste and discretion in general that the best of them are all too prone to commit. Neither is it to encourage composers toward any lazy dumping into the harassed performer's lap of interpretative problems that it is his duty to solve so far as he is able. It is rather my wish to recall to the attention of all musicians and music lovers the fact we all know but sometimes forget, that speeds (and volumes, too) do not offer half the expressive value to performance that a right and reasonable phraseology, a complete rhythmic articulation do. Force is relative; speeds are variable and contingent. But above that mere production of a reasonably good tone on pitch that is the foundation of all music-making, rhythm and breath constitute the fixed and indispensable framework for any inspired performance.

June 11, 1944

Transcriptions

WHETHER the transcribing and arranging of classical pieces for executional conditions different from those conceived by their authors is a legitimate practice or not is a question that frequently bothers music-lovers. Persons of refined taste are likely to disapprove it in principle but to tolerate it when it is carried out with brilliance or with some authoritative reference to the past. Stravinsky's modernization of music by Pergolesi in his ballet *Pulcinella* and the restorations by d'Indy and by Malipiero of the orchestral accompaniments to Monteverdi's operas, though anyone may question a detail or two, are nowhere considered to be improper musical efforts. To evoke the past in contemporary language or to reconstitute it in the closest resemblance we can achieve to what we believe was its original speech is, indeed, a triumph of musicianship.

What chiefly bothers people of taste is ignorance and the indiscriminate exploitation of the past for commercial purposes. Stokowski's enlargements for Wagnerian orchestra of organ pieces by Sebastian Bach and Liszt's reductions to pianoforte proportions of polyphonic church music and even of whole scenes from popular operas have never been considered quite loyal. Schönberg's orchestrations of Bach's organ music, on the other hand, and Mozart's reorchestration of Handel's oratorios, as well as Debussy's orchestral version of Satie's *Gymnopédies,* though they may well involve misconceptions about the character of the original works, are respected in musical circles for the purity of the arrangers' intentions. Each represents a serious homage from one man of genius to another.

Nevertheless, we cannot demand genius as a condition of music's legitimacy. If Beethoven was entitled to write symphonies, so is everybody else. And if Sebastian Bach can make orchestral or pipe-organ arrangements of Vivaldi's violin pieces, altering anything he feels like in the process, there is no reason why the Boston Pops Orchestra should be restrained from blowing up *Tiger Rag* to eighty musicians and tarantella speed. It is just a little comic; that's all. And it is more than a little absurd of Leopold Stokowski to have orchestrated a choral piece called *Ado-*

ramus Te, ascribing it to Palestrina and using a faulty text. He obviously accepted the Harvard Glee Club's published version without question, when a telephone call to the New York Public Library would have informed him that the piece has been known for years to be a fake. (Though inspired from a work by, I believe, Agnielli, it is in that edition largely the work of Dr. Archibald T. Davison.)

Musicians mostly don't hold, either, with the popular practice of swinging the classics, though they constantly do it to amuse one another at social gatherings. And yet every age has forced the music of previous ages to obey the rhythmic customs of its own. I have never been especially amused by Miss Hazel Scott's so-called swinging of Bach Inventions, because it has always seemed to me that these came out less "hot," even by modern standards, in her versions than in the originals; but I have never minded the attempt. And I have found charming entertainment in an evening radio hour during which Miss Sylvia Marlowe at the harpsichord and some excellent jazz musicians improvise in the American rhythmic style on melodies from Haydn and Rameau.

There is so much that is merely habitual about the way we long-hairs treat the classics, anyway, that a skillful violation of all we hold most familiar not only refreshes the old repertory but forces us to renovate a bit our treatment of it. The quotation from a Tchaikovsky piano concerto in a familar juke-box disk has not injured the popularity of the original work at all, though many young people who have first picked up this melody in a pub are surprised, when they meet it later at the pop concerts, to find that it is in three-four time. Beethoven's "Farewell" Sonata, Schubert's *Serenade,* and Rossini's *William Tell* Overture have, indeed, been transcribed, arranged, and misquoted so often that the correct execution of their original versions has come to have a certain novelty value in the concert hall.

Old music is everybody's property, and one is entitled to do what one likes with it. If anybody wants to play on the mouthorgan a violin transcription of Debussy's *Afternoon of a Faun,* as I once heard done in Town Hall, who is to pretend that this procedure is any different from the adoption in the twentieth century as our national anthem of a song about the War of 1812 that had previously been a drinking glee? Or from the adaptation by Handel and by Beethoven of their own works to different instrumental techniques and to wholly different expressive purposes? Or from the performance by Horowitz of his own version of Liszt's piano transcription of Saint-Saëns's orchestral tone-poem based on a song of the latter called *Danse Macabre*. Or, for that matter, from the playing on a pianoforte of any harpsichord piece by J. S. Bach.

All musical execution entails transformation, and it is not necessarily the part of taste to keep this minimal. Knowledge and skill and authority are valuable. But so is a common-sense approach. The two things most discreditable to any musician in dealing with the past of his own art are a degradation from commercial or ambitious motives of standards to which he has had access by education and the observance of scholastic taste canons at the wrong time and place. It has never accomplished much to have symphony orchestras play Beethoven's string quartets on sixty instruments. But the execution in the home of classical overtures and symphonies transcribed as piano duets is the very fundament of our musical culture.

June 4, 1944

Masterpieces

THE ENJOYMENT and understanding of music are dominated in a most curious way by the prestige of the masterpiece. Neither the theater nor the cinema nor poetry nor narrative fiction pays allegiance to its ideal of excellence in the tyrannical way that music does. They recognize no unbridgeable chasm between "great work" and the rest of production. Even the world of art painting, though it is no less a victim than that of music to Appreciation rackets based on the concept of gilt-edged quality, is more penetrable to reason in this regard, since such values, or the pretenses about them advanced by investing collectors and museums, are more easily unmasked as efforts to influence market prices. But music in our time (and in our country) seems to be committed to the idea that first-class work in composition is separable from the rest of music-writing by a distinction as radical as that recognized in theology between the elect and the damned. Or at the very least by as rigorous an exclusion from glory as that which formerly marked the difference between Mrs. Astor's Four Hundred and the rest of the human race.

This snobbish definition of excellence is opposed to the classical concept of a Republic of Letters. It reposes, rather, on the theocratic idea that inspiration is less a privilege of the private citizen that of the ordained prophet. Its weakness lies in the fact that music, though it serves most becomingly as religion's handmaiden, is not a religion. Music does not deal in general ideas or morality or salvation. It is an art. It expresses private sentiments through skill and sincerity, both of which last are a privilege, a duty, indeed, of the private citizen, and no monopoly of the prophetically inclined.

In the centuries when artistic skills were watched over by guilds of workmen, a masterpiece was nothing more than a graduation piece, a work that marked the student's advance from apprenticeship to master status. Later the word was used to mean any artist's most accomplished work, the high point of his production. It came thus to represent no corporate judgment, but any consumer's private one. Nowadays most people understand by it a piece differing from the run of repertory by a degree of concentration in its expressivity that establishes a difference of kind. And certain composers (Beethoven was the first of them) are considered to have worked consciously in that vein. The idea that any composer, however gifted and skillful, is merely a masterpiece factory would have been repellent to Bach or Haydn or Handel or Mozart, though Gluck was prone to advertise himself as just that. But all the successors of Beethoven who aspired to his position of authority — Brahms and Bruckner and Wagner and Mahler and Tchaikovsky — quite consciously imbued their music with the "masterpiece" tone.

This tone is lugubrious, portentous, world-shaking; and length, as well as heavy instrumentation, is essential to it. Its reduction to absurdity is manifest today through the later symphonies of Shostakovich. Advertised frankly and cynically as owing their particular character to a political directive imposed on their author by state disciplinary action, they have been broadcast throughout the United Nations as models of patriotic expression. And yet rarely in the history of music has any composer ever spread his substance so thin. Attention is not even required for their absorption. Only Anton Rubinstein's once popular symphony, "The Ocean," ever went in for so much water. They may have some value as national advertising, though I am not convinced they do; but their passive acceptance by musicians and music-lovers can certainly not be due to their melodic content (inoffensive as this is) or to their workmanship (roughly competent as this is, too).

What imposes about them is their obvious masterpiece-style one-trackness, their implacable concentration on what they are doing. That this quality, which includes also a certain never-knowing-when-to-stop persistence, should be admired by laymen as resembling superficially the Soviet war effort is natural enough. But that what these pieces are up to in any musical sense, chiefly rehashing bits of Borodin and Mahler, is of much intrinsic musical interest I have yet to hear averred by a musician. And that is the whole trouble with the masterpiece cult. It tends to substitute an impressive manner for specific expression, just as oratory does. That music should stoop to the procedures of contemporary political harangue is deplorable indeed.

There are occasions (funerals, for instance) where the tone of a discourse is more important than its content, but the concert is not one of them. The concert is a habitual thing like a meal; ceremonial is only incidental to it. And restricting its menu to what observes the fictitious "masterpiece" tone is like limiting one's nourishment to the heavier party foods. If the idea can be got rid of that a proper concert should consist only of historic "master-pieces" and of contemporary works written in the "masterpiece" tone, our programs will cease to be repetitive and monotonous. Arthur Judson, the manager of the Philharmonic, remarked recently that the orchestral repertory in concert use today is smaller than it was when he went into the business of concert management twenty-five years ago, and this in spite of the fact that orchestras and orchestral concerts are many times more numerous. I am sure that this shrinkage is due to a popular misconception about what constitutes quality in music.

If the Appreciation Racket were worth its salt, if the persons who explain music to laymen would teach it as a language and not as a guessing game, the fallacy of the masterpiece could be exposed in short order. Unfortunately, most of them know only about twenty pieces anyway, and they are merely bluffing when they pretend that these (and certain contemporary works that sort of sound like them) make up all the music in the world worth bothering about.

June 25, 1944

Understanding Modern Music

COMMON belief has it that new music is difficult to understand, while older and more familiar music presents comparatively few problems of comprehension. I do not think this is true. It is certain that in the epochs of rapid æsthetic advance there is always some time lag between the understanding of new work on the part of persons connected with the movement that produces it and the understanding or acceptance of that same work by the general public of music-lovers. Professional musicians and pedagogues, if they happen not to be part of the inner circle where such work is being produced, are sometimes more uncomprehending than the general public, even.

But this age is not one of rapid advance in music. It is one rather of recession. The great frontal attack on musical conservatism that is still known as Modern Music took place between 1885 and 1914. Its salient victories include the works of Richard Strauss, of Debussy, of Ravel, of Schönberg, Stravinsky, and Erik Satie. No composer has made since 1914, if we except the works that some of these same men wrote after that date, any impression on his time comparable to that made by these composers during the great revolutionary years before the other World War.

We have since witnessed the triumphal progress of careers laid down before that war, and we have assisted at the test flights of two minor musical movements. The first of these, characteristic of the 1920's, was known to its adepts as Contemporary Music and included two branches, the Twelve-tone School (seated in Vienna with an outpost in Berlin) and the Neo-Classicists, or School of Paris. A second movement (also seated in Paris) was the characteristic musical movement of the 1930's and is called Neo-Romanticism. It is exactly contemporaneous with the painting movement of the same name.

I call the last two decades and their characteristic movements minor, because they were occupied chiefly with the exploitation of technical devices invented by a previous generation. I may be underestimating the Neo-Romantics. Indeed, I hope I am, because I am one of their founding fathers. But the possibility that the progress of the movement may have been only interrupted by the

present war rather than terminated by it cannot obscure the fact
that the Neo-Romantics, like the Neo-Classicists before them, represent for the most part a novel usage of syntactical devices perfected long before rather than any notable discoveries in musical
technique.

The gamut of musical device that was correctly called Modern, or Revolutionary, before 1914 is now taught in most of our
schools and colleges. In any case, it is available to educated composers; and the whole musical public has been exposed to it for
twenty-five or more years. Many of the works that exemplify it
have enjoyed, indeed, a world-wide success. There is no reason
why anybody in the music world, professional or layman, should
find himself in the position of not understanding a piece of twentieth-century music, if he is willing to give himself a little trouble.

It is probably the fact that today's music is at least partially
comprehensible to all that makes it so amazing to some. The habit
of merely enjoying music without attempting to understand it
literally is a comfortable one. And it is far easier to indulge that
habit in listening to the music of another age and century than it
is when music made in our own time is being played. Because, in
spite of the worst will in the world, no listener can fail to penetrate, at least partially, a contemporary work.

The art music of the past, most of all that eighteenth- and nineteenth-century repertory known as "classical" music, is, on the
other hand, about as incomprehensible as anything could be. Its
idiom is comprehensible, because it is familiar. But its significant
content is as impenetrable as that of the art work of the Middle
Ages. It was made by men whose modes of thought and attitudes of passion were as different from ours as those of Voltaire
and Goethe and Rousseau and Casanova and Heine and Lamar-
tine and Victor Hugo were different from those of Bernard Shaw
and Marcel Proust and Ronald Firbank and E. E. Cummings and
Gertrude Stein and Mickey Mouse and William (if any) Saroyan.
Not that these writers are always of the utmost limpidity. On the
contrary, they are mostly either deceptively lucid or deceptively
obscure, as is the custom of our century. But it is difficult not to
find in ourselves, as twentieth-century men and women, some
spontaneous identification with the world that they depict.
Whereas the travels of Lord Byron, the private lives of John Keats
and of Emily Dickinson, are as far from anything we have ever
known as is the demise of Richard Wagner's Isolde, who, with

nothing wrong organically about her, stands in the middle of a stage and falls dead merely because her lover has just died, who had got himself some real wounds in a fight.

These reflections occurred to me one evening apropos of a gathering that I had attended to hear some musical compositions by Stefan Volpe. Mr. Volpe is a skilled and highly original composer whose works have so far been little performed here, on account of what passes in professional circles for their extreme difficulty both of execution and of interpretation. In one corner four musicians were gathered together to glance at the scores of the music played and to discuss its nature and merits. That they all understood it both as to technique and as to substance is proved by the fact that they found themselves in perfect agreement about these. Four musicians who agree on practically nothing else in music not only thought that Mr. Volpe's work was interesting and excellent (that would have been easy) but thought so for the same reasons.

Those same four musicians are irreconcilably divided about Mozart and about Sibelius. None of them would be capable of explaining in any reasonable manner at all a sonata by Haydn, much less of convincing the others that his explanation was correct. Their divers comprehensions of Schumann's piano music, of the Beethoven quartets, of Schubert, and of Chopin, though they might agree on the excellence of all these, have nothing in common. On controversial figures like Brahms and Berlioz and Wagner they could almost come to blows.

And so I got to thinking about what is called "difficult new music," and I concluded that there is no such thing any more. There used to be, I presume. It certainly must have taken more than goodwill and a mild effort of the mind for persons hitherto unacquainted with Debussy's work to accept and understand *Pélléas et Mélisande* in 1902. In 1941 there is no longer any really novel music. There is only live music and dead music, the music of our time and the music of other times.

Dead music is very beautiful sometimes and always pretty noble, even when it has been painted up and preened by the undertakers who play or conduct it with such funereal solemnity at our concerts. Live music is never quite that beautiful. Neither that beautiful nor that dumb. Because live music speaks to us all. We may not like what it says, but it does speak. Dead music, that whole Baroque, Rococo, and Romantic repertory we call "classical," is as comfortable and as solacing to mental inactivity as a lullaby heard on a pillow made from the down of a defunct swan.

I am not proposing its abolishment from our lives or from our concerts. No sensible person would wish to be without access to the history of culture. I am merely saying to those persons who think the music of today is accessible to the comprehension of only a limited group that it is, on the contrary, much easier to understand than the music of the past. Very few people have any real comprehension at all of the art of preceding generations, of what it is all about and of how the men felt who made it. Those who do have an inkling or two about it, who have made up for their own use a certain way of envisaging the relics of times past by applying to their interpretation facts and principles they have learned from modern life, are, of course, always persons who have a pretty comprehensive acquaintance with the music of the modern world. All modernists are not necessarily musicologists. I have known people who understood Stravinsky or Schönberg pretty thoroughly but whose knowledge of Bach and Beethoven was conventional and unreflected. I have never, however, known a person with any original or penetrating knowledge about the musical past who had not arrived at that understanding by first mastering the elements of the divers musical procedures that lay about him.

There are difficulties about presenting large quantities of new music in our orchestral concerts, but these are chiefly monetary. Live music requires the payment, for one thing, of a performing-rights fee to its author, which most dead music does not. More costly than this modest outlay is the rehearsal time (at the Philharmonic this comes to something like ten dollars a minute) necessary for getting a new piece into shape. These are not, however, unsurmountable difficulties, as has been proved during Mr. Mitropoulos's present visit. This skilled orchestral foreman has managed to prepare novelties for all his programs and to prepare them all, whether one approves or not of each interpretation, with complete thoroughness.

I do not pretend that the new works this conductor has been giving us are all of equal and certifiable excellence. If one wants guaranteed literature one has to stick pretty close to Shakespeare and the Bible. I am merely saying that the interpretation and the understanding reception of new music are not today rare or recondite accomplishments. Naturally, the separation of repertory into works we want to keep and works we want to throw away is a choice we are not obliged to face in dealing with the "classics." But that separation is a very exciting occupation both for producers and for audiences. It is what brings real life and occasionally real profits to the theater, to the movies, to the jazz world. Continuous opportunity for its practice at Carnegie Hall is the only means I have to suggest (and we have all worried about this) for restoring our major orchestra to its rightful place in our intellectual life.

January 4, 1942

Reviewing Modern Music

A MONTH or so ago, having been invited to address a group of students at the High School of Music and Art, and thinking that instead of giving them a speech on some set subject it might be livelier if I simply let these bright young people ask me questions, I found myself having to improvise on all the most fundamental themes of musical philosophy. One little girl asked if composers felt any obligation to "correct" the harmony in their free compositions. Another wanted to know how legitimate it was to arrange or orchestrate pieces by classic authors. The most breath-taking question of all was: "What criteria of judgment do you employ in reviewing modern music?"

I seem to remember making quite a speech on that subject. Also being reminded on my way home that I had omitted some important considerations. Having reflected a little further about the matter, I decided the best thing to do was to go on with the subject in this column, since, no matter how many of my readers may disagree with my conclusions, the theme itself, which is that of the relation of criticism to creation, is of interest to almost everybody.

One demands of any work, new or old, that it hold the attention. In order for it to do this it must bear some resemblance to something one has heard before. The obligation in this regard is upon the listener, not the author. A person who has never heard any Chinese music or any medieval polyphony or anything like either cannot easily find a point of reference for following their progress. Consequently the listener must ask himself what such

General Ideas   285

music most resembles among familiar music of the past and among what he knows of contemporary work, if he is to follow it at all. Such a resemblance may be one of contradiction. Music that sounds consistently discordant, for example, sounds so only when compared with music that is consistently harmonious, of which it is the reverse image. The avoidance of conventional "melody" implies, likewise, a stricter observance of the melodic conventions than plain melodiousness itself ever achieves.

This kind of contrariety, or of "contrariness," as some would consider it, is one of the classical procedures in Western art. Music, the most traditional of all the Western arts, is by that very fact the most frequently revolutionized, a constant violation of tradition being its most traditional requirement. Now, nobody can violate a tradition that doesn't exist or swear off a habit he hasn't acquired. Therefore the listener may rest assured that however direct or simple, pleasant or unpleasant, any piece may sound, its technique invariably constitutes some form of attack on the kind of thing it most resembles.

The technical comprehension of modern music consists, therefore, in the unmasking of its technical tradition. One must find what it most resembles, both by positive and by negative image, among the music of the past and of the present, before one can have a very good idea about whether its traditional observances and violations are major or trivial.

I speak first of the technical understanding of modern music because that is the first aspect of it the mind encounters. We know whether the mere sound of a piece, the kind of noise it makes, is attractive or boring long before we perceive its emotional significance, its message. An interesting texture is one of the most easily recognizable signs of interesting content. There can be no valid meaning in any art work that is expressed in bromides, because bromides have no meaning. That's why they are bromides. When a Tin Pan Alley hit-tune or an academic symphony sounds like all the other Tin Pan Alley hit-tunes or all the other academic symphonies, when they go in one ear and out the other leaving no sediment at all in memory's stream, we can be pretty sure that further acquaintance would bring little nourishment to the soul. The soul doesn't get much nourishment out of first hearings, anyway. But one can get a quite fair indication of music's inner nature from examining with the mind its surface of sound.

I put small faith in the "moving" effect of music as an indication of its quality, because our visceral responses are seldom significant and always capricious. The only rule I observe about my own is to respect their intensity. The force of any spontaneous reaction to music is more interesting than its nature or direction. That force is a product of traditional culture and of sensitivity to its violation. Violent manifestations of disapproval, as observed within oneself or in one's neighbors, are therefore another clinical sign that there is probably good stuff in the work that provoked them. An ovation may be only an expression of factitious excitement. A scandal is almost invariably evidence of quality. In any case, one has to be wary about what one merely likes and very wary indeed about disapproving of what one merely thinks one dislikes. Just as the emotions, being all alike, are only interesting by their intensity, music is, on the contrary, only interesting by its particular nature, its individuality, the differences between one piece of it and another.

The fact of the emotions being brought into play at all is of some importance, though not much. Love at first sight is rather the exception than the rule in music, as it is in human relations. What really counts in music is not attractiveness but style. Style is character, original variations on customary patterns. There is no style without tradition, but style is not tradition. It is a personal comment on tradition. It may be a rude comment, or it may be the gentlest of hints; but it must be corrective in its effect. From the composer's point of view, style is best achieved by forgetting all about it and concentrating on meaning, by saying only what one really means and by being perfectly certain one really means everything one has said. This makes for a functional, a note-by-note integrity of sense with sound that produces automatically a maximum of carrying-power in the whole work.

But though style, like happiness or success, is a by-product of efficiency and hence not a proper objective for a sincere workman, its presence in any completed work is a touchstone of that work's authenticity. Thus it is that the application of style criteria to the judgment of music is a legitimate way of estimating, or of beginning to estimate, the nature and worth of that music. Thus, also, since all real style inevitably contains a good deal that is novel, personal, individual to its author, it is perfectly correct to esteem in an unfamiliar work everything in it that is novel, fresh, original, personal, particular.

Let us not confuse reception with creation. Nothing is more

tiresome and stale than work animated by a desire to be original
or to play up what the author imagines to be his personality. An
author should strive not to be personal; objectivity is the nobler
aim. But a music-consumer, during the early stages of his acquaintance with any new work, has every reason to seize upon and
to cherish exactly those aspects of it that reveal its indissoluble
uniqueness. That a piece should please millions is a social and an
economic datum, but it proves nothing either way about artistic
worth. That a piece should please or displease any given critic, or
all the critics, proves no more. That a piece should be, in even
the tiniest way, different from anything one has ever heard before
is evidence that it will probably bear further acquaintance. But
before one can put one's finger on the elements of that originality,
it is necessary to explore a little the range of traditional observances in the same work.

And so I suppose my answer to the question, and my advice to
music-lovers bothered by the problem, is that the best procedure
I know for sizing up new music in a preliminary way is first to
identify it with all the music and all the kinds of music it resembles, and then to note the number and nature of the passages
where the writing most radically deviates from its models. All
such passages may thereupon be checked up confidently, I think,
in the piece's credit column. Nothing goes in the debit column,
because there is no such thing as sin or evil in music; there is only
a lack of virtue, art being entirely a positive conception.

A procedure like this should enable one to describe a piece to
somebody else with a fair degree of objectivity and to communicate something about its quality. In reviewing for print, it is only
fair to add some indication of one's own prejudices with regard to
the kind of tradition the piece represents. This enables the reader
to take account of the critic's personal equation and to have, therefore, a clearer idea of his own possible relation to the work than
he might have had if the critic had kept up a pretense of complete
neutrality.

January 11, 1942

Getting Used to Modern Music

On recent Sundays I have exposed in this column my conviction that modern music, by which I mean all the music written in our time, is easier to understand spontaneously than the music of another century. By "understand" I mean whatever is meant by that word in anybody's English. I mean recognition, acceptance, and retention. I have also counseled persons wishing to make a preliminary size-up of new work, provided they have a fair knowledge of historical repertory and some experience at musical analysis, not to bother too much trying to understand its meaning but to seek out rather the exterior signs of its originality, as these are manifest in the actual style of the work's writing. It is obvious, I hope, that nobody ever listens to music entirely for its inner substance or entirely for its surface texture. These two aspects of any art work are interpenetrative, the technical and stylistic elements of composition being really explicable only in terms of their animating inspiration and that spirit being only finally visible through, and in terms of, the body specially built for its habitation.

Nevertheless, complete understanding is rarely accomplished all at once. The various elements of anything are usually best encompassed by temporarily abstracting them from their context. Which of these one takes up first depends on which one is best prepared to take up. We prefer to leave the more difficult things for the last. Hence it is that persons not skilled in musical analysis often go more directly to the heart of modern music than musicians themselves. The musician's road, on the other hand, to a piece's central thought is always by way of its expressive means. Not till these have been encompassed and, as it were, understood does a musician even imagine he has an understanding of the whole work. The painters, the poets, the men of science and the men of prose letters, the philosophers, the political revolutionists, and the world of fashion have long been the bulwark of comprehension for musical advance. Even the general public of low musical literacy has shown less resistance to progressive tendencies in music than musicians have. A little knowledge makes anyone conservative.

Let us take for granted, as I think we may, that art is sometimes progressive and sometimes apparently retrogressive. I think
we can agree, too, that there is plenty of pseudo-progressive art
work around that is merely reaction *camouflé*. Also that history cites numerous examples of work animated by a strongly
conservative spirit that has turned out to be at once a pinnacle
added to its own or to some previous age's achievement and a
cornerstone of technical objectivity for succeeding epochs. The
Parthenon at Athens, the dramatic poetry of Racine, and the fugal
style of Sebastian Bach are cases in point. Consequently, when I
refer to modern music, I do not mean necessarily "modernistic"
music, much of which is a pale afterglow of the great and original
modernism of yesteryear, especially in this conservative decade;
I mean literally all the music that is being written today or that
has been written in our lifetime.

I also think we may assume that the vigor of any musical life
is dependent on the constant winnowing out, among the work that
is conservative and the work that is revolutionary, all the work
that represents retrogressive tendencies, in order that progressive
work be encouraged, understood, and accepted into that body of
reputable music literature we call our tradition. Also that this
process be speeded up by the employment of every natural sensitivity and every intellectual technique. For persons who are
acquainted with artistic or intellectual advance in some other domain but who lack familiarity with the technique of music, I recommend non-analytical listening, which is what they mostly do
anyway, whether I recommend it or not. And for persons capable
of following music in detail, I recommend listening analytically
to a piece they haven't heard before. Even though their analytical
technique may bog down, I think a failure to attack along that
line is intellectually retrogressive.

Now, the first group of persons operates more successfully
with regard to modern music than the second group does, for the
simple reason that the emotional acceptance of modern art work
is much easier than its technical comprehension. Persons quite
uneducated musically have accepted Stravinsky's *Rite of Spring*,
as that is rendered in Disney's film *Fantasia*, merely because it
seemed to them expressive of prehistoric life and landscape (as
was, indeed, the composer's intention). And audiences composed
of experts in modern musical analysis have been held in rapt
attention by the works of Berg, Schönberg and others of the

twelve-tone school without being in the least bothered by their essential meaning, simply because the mere following of that music was occupation enough to absorb the mind, and the discrimination of originality from cliché within the frame of that stylization a quite sufficient guide in judging the work's integrity.

From the foregoing it can be deduced that I advocate an attitude of goodwill toward contemporary music on everybody's part and a sincere attempt to digest it by whatever means are available to one's mental powers. I do not pretend, however, that such goodwill is universal. Roughly, its dissemination is something like this:

The ignorant are, on the whole, well disposed in advance toward all music. When they can't follow it, their attention merely wanders. They reproach the composer with nothing, the conductor or performing artist merely with failing to give a pleasing concert.

Persons who are highly educated but not very musical usually prefer modern music to old music. They buy tickets more often to modern than to "classical" concerts.

Managements have a slight prejudice against any novelty, ancient or modern, because they are not sure about its money-making power. Also because modern music requires payment of a performing-rights fee. This last, however, is no deterrant if there is confidence in the work's pleasing. Mostly they don't expect a modern work to please. They count its performance a goodwill gesture. Given a choice among new pieces, they almost invariably prefer the harmless and the insignificant to the incendiary or the in any way memorable. Managements, on the whole, may be said to be ill-disposed toward new music, though only for commercial reasons. If it's good business, they're for it.

Conductors, on the contrary, nearly always adore it. They have constantly been the arrowhead of its flight into the world, the missionaries of its propagation among the heathen. Rare are the leaders of international renown who have refused that responsibility and missed that cue to historical fame.

Pianists, violinists, and singers are well disposed but resistant. They can't afford to have much truck with it if they want to make big money. It is not as profitable to them as it is to a conductor.

Symphony and opera subscribers are very resistant. Their ability to analyze music is not, on the average, sufficient to enable them to get hold of it. They feel incompetent and hence inferior in front of it, hating, naturally enough, the cause of their inferiority feeling.

Critics, like subscribers, vary in their instinctive attitude about it in exact proportion to their ability to analyze its procedures. This does not apply to modern music work by work. One does not love a piece inevitably just because one knows how it is made. No, nor dislike it because its texture escapes one's analysis. I am speaking of a certain attitude of eagerness or of hesitation observable in any critic's approach to a new piece and verifiable by the average of his judgments. By and large, your critic, who is, after all, a form of musician and hence not wholly instinctive about music, if he depends on his instincts and his emotions for sizing up a new piece, is obliged to do so because his knowledge of modern musical procedures is inadequate. He can, therefore, be depended on, unless he hedges, to review unfavorably any new work that employs technical devices he is unable to follow. Your critic who is better equipped in this regard loves to practice his skill. You will find him regularly taking a more active part in the contemporary movement than his more instinctive colleague, who really feels most at home among the certified masterpieces of repertory and the sure-fire virtuosos of execution.

The moral of this piece is that although almost anybody (excepting, maybe, a musician) can get some communication out of modern music without half trying, merely because its author is alive in the world we all live in, any further penetration of its meaning or estimate of its value to the living musical tradition is dependent on one's acquaintance with the whole tradition, including the living part of it. Nevertheless, even without taking too much conscious thought about it, one can learn to swim by swimming; and that is why I advocate for all some regular immersion in the living stream. We can't all be pioneers, but there is profit to be derived from staking out a claim, however small, in those so-called new regions that have been opened up to musical habitation and investment for a good quarter of a century now.

January 18, 1942

Conducting Modern Music

THE PRIME consideration in interpreting new musical works is to avoid doing anything that might possibly make these appear to be emulating the music of the past. Such emulation may or may not have been a part of the composer's intention, but playing it up in presentation produces a false relation between a work and its own time that is fatal to the comprehension of the work by its own time. Dressing and directing *Hamlet* as if it were a modern play is a piquant procedure. Treating a modern play as if it were Shakespeare's *Hamlet* can only make for pretentiousness and obscurity.

There is a prestige attached to any art work that has survived the death of its author that no work by a living hand can enjoy. This fact of survival is correctly called immortality, and that immortality surrounds the surviving work with a white light. In that radiance all becomes beautiful. Obscurities disappear, too; or at least they cease to bother. When I refer, as not infrequently I do, to live music and dead music, I mean that there is the same difference between the two that there is between live persons and dead ones. The spirit and influence of the dead are often far more powerful than those of the living. But they are not the same thing, because you can only argue *about* them, never *with*. The dead have glory and a magnificent weight. The living have nothing but life.

The glorification of the dead is a perfectly good thing. Indeed, the greater civilizations have always done it more than the lesser. But a clear separation of the dead from the living is also a mark of the higher cultures. That is the fecundating drama between tradition and spontaneity that keeps peoples and empires alive. Consequently no good is accomplished by pretending, or seeming to pretend, that a work by Igor Stravinsky or Aaron Copland or myself is a museum piece, because it isn't and won't be till we're dead, if then. And framing such a work among museum pieces in such a way that it appears to be subsidiary to them invariably makes the living work seem deader than a doornail. Its lack of white-light immortality makes it appear gravely inferior to the works on the same program that have such an aura and glamour.

The moral of this explanation is that new works must be played alone, in company with other new works, or surrounded by old ones carefully chosen, if one wishes to bring out their resemblances to the traditional past as well as their essential differences from that past. A new work may not be the most important piece on the program; but unless it is the determining item in the choice of the whole program, it will always sound like second-rate music, because it is pretty certain to be placed in unfair glamour competition with the classics of repertory. Modern music indiscriminately programmed, no matter what kind of music it is, is framed to flop.

Neither can it be interpreted in the same style as older music. Insufficient rehearsal often works to a new piece's advantage. When there isn't time to do much but read the notes and observe the author's tempos, it gets a neutral reading that is at least better than a false interpretation. If the conductor has time to work it up into an imitation of all his favorite war-horses or to streamline it into a faint reminder of Beethoven and Tchaikovsky, it is very difficult for the listener to hear anything in it but a memory of these authors, or at most a feeble attempt to dethrone them by being arbitrarily different.

The best international style for playing the classics is one that reduces them to a common denominator of clarity and elegance. That was always Toscanini's force as a conductor of standard repertory. He was never very effective as a conductor of modern music (and he avoided it whenever possible, for that reason, I imagine), because he knew no other way of conducting anything. Characteristic national differences, which are of minor importance in standard repertory but which are the very essence of modern stylistic comprehension, seem to have escaped him. And being a musician of too high temperament to be satisfied with a mere neutral reading of anything, he wisely refrained from taking on a job in which neither he nor the living composer was likely to do much shining.

The conductors who do best by the music of our century are seldom equally good at interpreting all the kinds of it. Koussevitzky does well by anything Russian and fair by the English and the Americans, provided these last are not too local in flavor. He is not bad with German music, adds to it a Slavic elegance that is sometimes advantageous. French music escapes him utterly, in spite of his many years' residence in Paris. Mitropoulos is at his best with the central-European styles. Beecham is fine for English music, for all Slavic, for some German, for anything that has lyric afflatus or rhythmic punch. The Germans are rather messy when they play German music — always were, as Richard Wagner pointed out. Some are excellent with French music, however, Furtwängler, for instance, and Stock, of Chicago. Italians do not always do their best by Italian works, especially those of strong French influence, though they do beautifully by anything Germanic, even Brahms. Only the French (and a few Germans) make sense with French music. Nobody, literally nobody, who has not passed his formative adolescent years in this country ever conducts American music with complete intelligibility.

The basis of American musical thought is a special approach to rhythm. Underneath everything is a continuity of short quantities all equal in length and in percussive articulation. These are not always articulated, but they must always be understood. If for any expressive reason one alters the flow of them temporarily, they must start up again exactly as before, once the expressive alteration is terminated. In order to make the whole thing clear, all instruments, string and wind, must play with a clean, slightly percussive attack. This attack must never be sacrificed for the sake of a beautiful tone or even for pitch accuracy, because it is more important than either. Besides, once a steady rhythm is established, the music plays itself; pitch and sonorities adjust themselves automatically; as in a good jazz band the whole takes on an air of completeness.

French music is the nearest thing in Europe to our music, because French rhythm, like ours, is less accentual than quantitative. Keeping down-beats out of a Debussy rendition, for instance, is virtually impossible to anybody but a Frenchman. Steady quantities, a little longer than ours and requiring no percussive definition at all, are its rhythmic foundation. Definition is achieved by a leisurely breathing between phrases and an almost imperceptible waiting before attacking, with no added force, what in any other music would be played as a down-beat. As with American music, a proper rhythm is cardinal and must be achieved before the pitch and the tone-production can be polished up.

Modern German music is not very interesting rhythmically. It needs no exact quantities, only a thwacking down-beat. Even that can be advanced or held back, as is the Viennese custom, to express sentiment. What is most important is to get the harmony right, for pitch is all-important to the German mind. Get the harmony right and don't go *too* sentimental. Nothing else counts, provided care for the harmony includes a clear plotting out of the key-relations in the whole piece. This means being sure there is always plenty of bass at the piece's joints.

Russian music is an alternation of very free rhythms with rigid and insistent ones. The latter are easy to render. But few conductors ever take enough liberties with the sentimental passages. English formulas are always closely related to the Russian (*vide* the English novel and the English Church). In music, both peoples conceive of rhythm as either non-existent or quite inflexible. Both observe beat-rhythms, too, not quantities. And both alternate speech inflections with footwork, as in a song-and-dance. The chief difference between them is that the Russian mind dramatizes itself with a grandiloquent simplicity, whereas the English tradition values a more intimate and personal kind of forthrightness in the expression of tender thought. The grander passages of both repertories may be rendered with the utmost of pomp and of panache.

Matters like these seem to me more important to restate than international æsthetic principles. All conductors know nowadays what the Neo-Classic style is all about. Also the Neo-Romantic style and the twelve-tone syntax. And certainly the survivals of late Romanticism are not difficult to decipher. But these are the stylistic elements that underlie all modern music; they have been written about *ad infinitum* and *ad nauseam*. What I am pointing out is that underneath these international tendencies and observances there are ethnic differences that must be taken account of. Also to remind my readers that these ethnic differences preclude the possibility that conductors of foreign upbringing now resident among us will play a leading role in our present musical expansion. They render great service by their constant acts of goodwill toward home-made music. But they have only the vaguest idea of what it's all about. And so has that part of our musical public that hears it only through their well-intentioned but unconvincing renditions.

January 25, 1942

Music's Renewal

THE IDEA that theater music — the opera and the ballet — is inferior to the concert forms is a nineteenth-century German heresy that seems to be dying out as the whole German tradition breaks up. It is an idea that never spread far in France or in Russia and that never even penetrated at all into Italy. Indeed, the opposite has always been Italian belief. Verdi referred to Mozart, we are told, with some disdain as a "quartet-writer." Even in Germanic regions the theatrical forms bore a major prestige till well into the last century. It is probably the clear absence of theatrical gift in Beethoven and Schubert and Schumann and Mendelssohn and Brahms that led the central Europeans and their Anglo-Saxon pupils to build up a certain prejudice against music written for dramatic collaboration.

The career of Richard Wagner, instead of contradicting this prejudice, seems to have encouraged its spread. Gifted with as marked a genius for personal propaganda as for music itself, this remarkable man wrote many articles and several books to prove that all theater music since Gluck was inferior to his. He explained his own works away by refusing to admit they were operas. He invented the word *Musikdrama* for them; and he maintained to his dying day that they had nothing to do with anything we know as opera, that, on the contrary, they were a development of the Beethoven symphony. In my own youth there were still serious German musicians around who believed all opera except the Wagnerian to be a sort of light-hearted musical diversion suitable enough for the Latin mind but lacking both in musical interest and in profundity of expression.

This attitude toward the theater has brought German musicians to an impasse. By failing to center their attention on lyrical declamation and bodily gesture they have cut themselves off from the generative sources of melody and of rhythm. By counting on harmonic complexity as a chief means of expression they have sacrificed emphasis and coherence (which it is harmony's first function to support) to a secondary harmonic function and one incapable of sustaining complete interest. As a result the best German music of today — that of Hindemith, of Berg, and of Schönberg — is complex in manner out of all proportion to the meaning expressed.

It is to be hoped that America's present interest in the musical theater will serve to eradicate from our thinking once and for all whatever traces of the Germanic heresy may remain. Composers must write lots of operas and lots of ballets, and these must be performed. Musical authors must learn by lots of practice to express feeling through song alone and bodily motion through rhythm. Complexities for their own sake of harmony and of instrumentation are the bunk; anybody can learn to do them. They chiefly serve nowadays to conceal a lack of precise expression. Let the writers of music give us correct English declamation in cadences that can really be sung and the clear expression of unequivocal sentiments in melodies that mean what the play means; let them give us harmony that makes some kind of acoustical emphasis, and rhythms that can really be danced, or at least moved around to; and the whole art of music will take on new life.

At present the music world is clinging to an immediate past that becomes every year more recondite. There are a thousand refinements in the late Romantic and early modern styles that make no sense at all any more. The writing of music has become everywhere a foolishly complicated business. Among the Germans it has reached a point of Byzantine elaboration from which it can only fall, as their sonorities fall upon the ear, with a thud. Music's renewal will probably take place on this continent, where the ancient skills are less ingrown than they are in Europe. We listen to lots of elaborate symphonic music, I must say; it has become popular entertainment second only to the cinema in appeal and far more generally enjoyed than the spoken theater. But it is its very popularity that may prevent us eventually from taking symphonic music too seriously. What we need, anyway, is not less of that but more of opera and ballet; and that is what we are apparently going to have after the war. That, too, is what will cure us, if anything will, of our unhealthy attachment to a dying tradition.

Opera and ballet deal with prime elements in human expression — namely, the human voice and the human body. They deal also with precise meaning. Not only are these the broad stream of musical art; they are its fountain head as well. Because way back in the mind, where music gets born, it has a closer concord-

ance with language and with gesture than it can ever possibly
have with the obscure movements of the viscera or with states of
the soul.

January 16, 1944

The French Style

THE FRENCH style of musical execution, like the French school
of composition, is a little bit different from all the others. Central-
European artists have been for a century now such a standard
article of exportation — the Italian, the Slavic, and the British virtuosos being merely colorful variants of the model — that it is
something of a shock to encounter first-class French artistry in
phalanx and to realize how far removed it is in basic musical concepts from the rest of Europe. This does not mean that France is
in divergence from the main stem of our musical thought. On the
contrary, France in our century is closer to the great tradition
than the rest of Europe is. The pianism of Robert Casadesus, the
flute-playing of René Le Roy, the keyboard execution on both the
harpsichord and the pianoforte of Wanda Landowska, the vocal
interpretations of Jennie Tourel are not accidental phenomena.
They are the products of a musical tradition more ancient, more
sophisticated, and more continuous than anything available elsewhere in the Western world.

The life of French music has always been its rhythm, just as
that of Italian has always been its cantilena and that of German
its harmonic architecture. This rhythm is of two kinds, verbal and
muscular. The first is derived from declamation and represents
a pattern of varied tonal lengths. Accents, or stresses, may be composed with this; but the quantitative pattern can exist, and often
does, without any pulsation at all, any down-beat, being present.
The second is a pattern of varied stresses within an unvarying
pulsation. Both kinds of rhythm are likely to be present simultaneously in classical music.

The jerky rhythm that Sebastian Bach cultivated under the
name of the *"stile francese,"* a steady alternation of dotted quar-
ter-notes with sixteenths, is derived from French tragic declamation and its musical counterpart, the French opera, the short

notes representing a quick movement of the actor's arm or wrist as he adds a visual accent to the phrasing of his poetic syllables. To render this jerk as a measured sixteenth-note is incorrect, because it represents a gesture, not a verbal quantity. It must be short, like an ornamental drum tap. So rendered, many of the movements from the Brandenburg concertos and from Bach's keyboard works lose the unfortunate resemblance to the chugging of a model-T Ford that we have so long associated with them and take on that grandeur at once statuesque and animated that was beloved of the Baroque age.

Similarly, the playing of a dotted quarter-note rhythm against one in triplets, which one finds so frequently in the music of that time, becomes intelligible to the ear only when the jerky rhythm is exaggerated and made to stand thus in relief against the rigidity of the other. Madame Landowska's and Mr. Le Roy's correct renderings of these formulas are not mere refinements of style. They are simply musical sense. So is Miss Tourel's happy integration of real words with vowel vocalism. These artists do not evoke the past through a haze of romantic poesy; they give us the real article, or as much as it is possible to have, authentically backed up by modern scholarship and by a tradition of rhythmic discrimination that in France has never died.

It was Beethoven who first among the great masters of music made a serious effort to introduce rhythmic and dynamic exactitude into musical notation. And it was Berlioz who elaborated these efforts into the modern French practice of putting everything down in black and white just as one wishes it to be heard. An orchestral score of Chabrier or of Debussy or Ravel or Stravinsky is as accurate a project as any architect's blueprint. If it is still incomplete in certain respects, that is because musical notation is still incompetent to distinguish completely between quantitative and pulsating rhythmic patterns. Nevertheless, French musicians, just as they take greater liberties with old music than persons do who are not acquainted with the real meanings behind old notational inexactitudes, are more scrupulous than others about reading modern scores literally.

The French conservatory training in *solfège* is the most rigorous in the world. It teaches meter as a basic pattern of quantities and analyzes any passage into the smallest time units present in that passage. If there is a conflict among small units, a still smaller one is adopted, until the lowest common multiple is reached. The measure (or bar) is considered to be nothing more than a practical grouping of these values for convenience in ensemble playing. No down-beat is given stress unless the metrical formation of the whole passage seems to suggest a clear reference to one of the pulsating dance rhythms. No dynamic, coloristic, or sentimental expression is added that is not requested by the author or, in the opinion of the executant, logically implied by his indications. A reasonable breath between phrases is considered legitimate and, in most cases, desirable.

This is the sort of impersonal procedure that gives to French solo execution on the lower levels of mastery an air of childish incompetence and on the higher levels a breadth as of the classical humanities. The central-European style, for all its grand afflatus, is elementary in comparison and really only works with music of the Romantic period. It is excellent for revealing the dramas of the lonely soul, but delicate sensuality and high intellectual content are beyond the scope of its rhythmic understanding. Those who have heard the recent performances of old music by Le Roy and by Landowska have recognized in these artists something deeper than a preoccupation with prettiness or with the memory of passion, something broader and cleaner and more humane. And those who heard the playing lately at one of the Modern Museum Serenades of Debussy's Sonata for flute, harp, and viola by Messrs. Le Roy, Salzedo and Brieff witnessed a comparable achievement in modern music. Indeed, the elaboration of that work itself and the equally elaborate perfection of its performance represent not only a triumph of French music-writing and executional technique but a rare manifestation of the higher human faculties.

It is a principle of French thought that analysis and reflection are not inimical to spontaneity, that art, indeed, represents all these collaborating toward a single action. It has long been the practice of American music schools to neglect the training of students in rhythmic analysis, in the exact reading of musical notation, and in the quantities of the English language. As a result our instrumentalists, our vocalists, and our composers are lacking in the basic ability to read music correctly or to write it down as they want it to sound. In former times this defect was remedied (badly and late) by post-graduate European study. For the present there is no European study. I wonder if it would be hoping too much to wish that the directors of our music schools might reflect on the rigorous training in *solfège* and its allied subjects that makes the work of the great French artists now among us so solid an achievement. It is time our students stopped fooling around with beautiful tone and velocity execution and learned some basic musical literacy, without which beautiful tone and velocity execution are incapable of saying anything serious to anybody.

March 14, 1943

Index

A NOTE ON THE TYPE

The text of this book is set in Caledonia, a Linotype face which belongs to the family of printing types called "modern face" by printers — a term used to mark the change in style of type-letters that occurred about 1800. Caledonia borders on the general design of Scotch Modern, but is more freely drawn than that letter.

The book was composed, printed, and bound by The Plimpton Press, Norwood, Massachusetts. The typography and binding design are by W. A. Dwiggins.

THIS BOOK HAS BEEN PRODUCED
IN FULL COMPLIANCE
WITH ALL GOVERNMENT REGULATIONS
FOR THE CONSERVATION OF PAPER, METAL,
AND OTHER ESSENTIAL MATERIALS